Commission of the European Communities

Nineteenth Report
on Competition Policy

(Published in conjunction with the
'XXIIIrd General Report on the
Activities of the European Communities 1989')

Brussels ● Luxembourg ● 1990

This publication is also available in the following languages:

ES ISBN 92-826-1625-8
DA ISBN 92-826-1626-6
DE ISBN 92-826-1627-4
GR ISBN 92-826-1628-2
FR ISBN 92-826-1630-4
IT ISBN 92-826-1631-2
NL ISBN 92-826-1632-0
PT ISBN 92-826-1633-9

Cataloguing data can be found at the end of this publication

Luxembourg: Office for Official Publications of the European Communities, 1990

ISBN 92-826-1629-0

Catalogue number: CB-58-90-546-EN-C

Contents

Introduction

At the threshold of the new decade, the European economy faces major challenges. While the Community has re-established a sound economic base it must further underpin the internal factors underlying its growth and ensure that growth does not fade under the build-up of inflationary pressures and external or budgetary disequilibria that could undermine its cohesion.

The Commission has on numerous occasions drawn attention to the essential contribution which competition policy can make to the completion of the single market and to strengthening the competitiveness of the Community's economy. Such contribution, which is more necessary than ever against the background of the recovery in the Community economy, is a long-term process. However, continuity does not rule out change and 1989 saw substantial developments in areas in which there had previously been gaps or deficiencies in competition policy.

The year saw several fundamental developments in Community competition policy in the fields of merger control, greater competition in certain service activities and the strengthening of the Commission's monitoring of State aids.

The progress made towards completing the internal market and the new political environment provided the crucial impetus for the Council's adoption of the Commission's merger control proposal. The new Council Regulation provides the Community with a specific instrument for merger control, thus filling a gap in existing Community competition law. The new Regulation is fully justified by the need to ensure that moves towards the restructuring of Community industry and the mergers resulting from the process do not jeopardize competition. For the undertakings concerned, the Regulation also has the benefit of establishing single Community control in place of a multiplicity of national controls, thus avoiding any risk of differences in assessment.

The basic concept underlying the Regulation is to establish a clear distinction between mergers having a Community dimension, for which the Commission will be responsible and those whose main impact is at national level, which will come under the responsibility of the national authorities.

Its field of application is defined on the basis of quantitative criteria reflecting the overall economic and financial power of the undertakings concerned, their level of activity within the Community and the transnational nature of the operation. The current thresholds for intervention by the Commission have been set at a fairly high level for the initial phase of implementation of the Regulation. However, the thresholds are to be reviewed, on the basis of a qualified majority, within four years. The Commission intends to propose that the thresholds be revised downwards.

The criteria for assessing mergers falling within the field of application of the Regulation are linked to the basic concept of 'dominant position', which has to be assessed within the framework of an overall appraisal of competition.

There are only two limited derogations to the principle of exclusive Community responsibility within the field of application of the Regulation. Firstly, the Regulation provides for possible referral to the national authorities of a Member State where a problem involving a dominant position arises in a 'distinct market'. Secondly, the Regulation does not affect the right which the Treaty already gives Member States to ensure the protection of 'legitimate interests' other than those protected by the Regulation.

Conversely, with regard to merger operations not having a Community dimension, which in principle are the responsibility of the Member States, the Regulation gives the Commission the power to intervene at the request of one of the Member States concerned.

The new Regulation, which is to enter into force on 21 September 1990, will probably lead to the Commission receiving around 50 notifications a year if the trend of the last two years continues. It thus represents an important initial step in establishing Community merger control.

1989 marked another turning point in Community competition policy, in that very substantial progress was made in opening up certain service activities to greater competition. Examination of this question by the Commission and the Council highlighted the need to underpin the completion of the internal market by establishing the necessary structures. The achievement of the internal market would be incomplete if key activities such as energy distribution, the dissemination of information and the transport of passengers and goods were not pursued within a competitive framework applying throughout the Community.

This new objective will involve firstly the linking up of existing infrastructures, often designed to meet national requirements alone. It will also mean ensuring greater competition in the sectors concerned including transport, telecommunications, broadcasting and energy.

In the transport sector, the most striking changes have occurred in air transport, an area on which Community consumers' attention has rightly been focused. During the year, the Commission put forward proposals for a second package of measures following on from those introduced in 1987 with the aim of pursuing the liberalization process in this sector. The judgment given by the Court of Justice in the *Ahmed Saeed* Case confirmed the *Nouvelles Frontières* judgment with regard to Article 85 of the EEC Treaty and clarified the conditions governing direct applicability of Article 85 by national courts. In the light of this very important judgment and in order to give operators greater legal certainty, the Commission asked the Council to give it the necessary powers to clarify how Articles 85 and 86 of the Treaty can be applied to domestic and extra-Community air services.

In the telecommunications sector, the year was marked by the Commission's adoption of a new Directive, based on Article 90 of the EEC Treaty on competition in the markets for telecommunications services. The Directive will be notified to the Member States concurrently with the entry into force of the Council Directive on an open network provision, which is designed to harmonize the conditions governing access to telecommunications networks. In 1989, the Commission also examined the measures taken by the Member States to comply with its earlier Directive on competition in the markets in telecommunications terminal equipment.

With regard to audiovisual services, the Commission's main concern was to maintain the openness of markets and to dismantle barriers to entry, notably through decisions on the production or distribution of films and television products. It also took note of the recommendations put forward at the 'Assises européennes de l'Audio-visuel' on the application of the competition rules to the media and reiterated the principles which it applies in assessing agreements on the granting of exclusive television broadcasting rights.

In the energy sector, the Commission began to apply the competition rules more strictly than in the past, witness the investigation launched into vertical agreements between electricity producers and coal producers, and the examination begun into the desirability of applying the common carrier principle generally at Community level. The Commission staff carried out an examination of the laws and rules in force in the Member States in the electricity sector.

The stricter monitoring of State aids was another priority brought to the fore in 1989. The first survey on State aids in the Community, which the Commission has now drawn up, is a valuable source of reference for focusing action on those aids which pose the greatest risk of distorting competition and thwarting the achievement of the single market.

The time has come for the Commission to use more systematically the provisions of Article 93(1) in order to review the legitimacy of existing aids which, by their nature and volume, may threaten the proper functioning of intra-Community trade.

Some such aid, even if tolerated or accepted in the past, must be viewed in the light of increased integration of the Community market and its compatibility with the common market must be re-examined accordingly. Such is the case with aid to certain industries, sometimes granted to national champions under the guise of general investment aid or capital injections. Such is also the case with aid for extra-Community exports whose effects may be felt within the common market. The Commission's well-established view is that it is first and foremost for the market, and not subsidies, to ensure that the Community has a rational and competitive industrial structure that is both open to the outside world and forward looking.

The entry into force of the framework for aid to the motor-vehicle industry, the extension of the framework for aid to the man-made fibres industry, the reduction in authorized aid for shipbuilding and the efforts to ensure transparency in R&D aid are all measures which reflect the Commission's determination in this area. The extension of the code on aid to the steel industry, moreover, facilitated the recent renewal of the voluntary restraint agreement on European steel exports to the United States of America.

At a meeting held in December 1989, the Commission outlined to the Member States the new policy stance it had adopted on aid as part of the review process begun in this area. Other meetings of this type should in future allow such joint discussions to be continued.

The Commission also adopted a number of decisions during the year.

In the field of anti-trust policy, 15 substantive decisions were adopted under Articles 85 and 86 of the EEC Treaty, 15 implementing decisions under Articles 65 and 66 of the ECSC Treaty and 46 procedures were terminated through the sending of an administrative letter.

The heaviest penalty imposed in 1989 related to a series of restrictive agreements and concerted practices involving welded mesh, which is widely used in the building industry, public works and other industrial activities. The 14 undertakings concerned, which had engaged in price-fixing and market-sharing practices, were fined a total of ECU 9.5 million.

The Commission also persuaded a number of undertakings to desist from conduct that was liable to be penalized under the competition rules. Thus, in the car refinish products sector, AKZO Coatings undertook not to hinder parallel trade and agreed to provide 'essential services' to body shops free of charge irrespective of the Member States in which the product was purchased. Volkswagen adjusted its order and production procedures to allow United Kingdom purchasers of right-hand-drive vehicles a normal delivery period on the Continent. Coca-Cola Export Corporation agreed to give a unilateral undertaking to end certain unlawful rebates granted to its distributors in Italy that had impeded competition on the market for soft drinks. Several associations of Dutch banks ended a series of agreements on commissions for customer services. In the field of industrial property rights, the pharmaceutical manufacturers, Syntex and Sythelabo amended an anti-competitive agreement on the validity of their trade marks in several Community countries.

Following the initiation of Article 86 proceedings, the major European and world producers of industrial gas amended their sales contracts, particularly as regards exclusivity clauses and the duration of undertakings to supply and purchase.

However, as in previous years, the Commission did not, after detailed examination, raise any objections to a good many cases notified to it. Thus, Rhône-Poulenc's acquisition of several of Monsanto's production units and the mergers between Carnaud and Metal Box and Pechiney and American Can were authorized. Similarly, the agreements concluded between Eurotunnel and the British and French railways on the use of the Channel Tunnel was granted a three-year exemption, the Commission having decided not to raise any objection to it.

On the State aids front, 296 notifications were registered in 1989, which is roughly in line with the figures for the two previous years, bearing in mind the fact that the number of notifications in 1988 included 90 from Portugal. The strictness with which State aids are controlled may be seen from the fact that 22 of the proposed schemes were prohibited by the Commission or withdrawn by the Member States themselves, the highest level reached since the end of the steel crisis. The Commission adopted eight decisions requiring the recovery of aid paid unlawfully.

Aid for research and development, which is now governed by well-established transparency requirements, continued to account for a substantial percentage of the cases notified and decisions adopted. Two-thirds of the decisions on R&D aid related to the Eureka programme. The proceedings initiated by the Commission and the unfavourable decisions, however, related mainly to proposed aid for sectors facing structural problems or overcapacity: examples include proposed aid in the shipbuilding and textile industries.

The Commission's vigilance in monitoring State aid is evident in a wide variety of areas, as may be seen from its prohibition of tax aid for exports in Greece, operating aid for the paper industry in Italy and regional aid outside assisted areas in Germany and France. Particular mention should be made of the motor vehicle industry, where, leaving aside the Community framework which entered into force in January, major decisions were adopted in cases such as Enasa, Alfa Romeo and Renault. In addition to these decisions prohibiting or granting conditional authorization for aid, the Commission decided not to raise any objections in 216 aid cases examined during the year which did not pose any problems of compatibility with the competition rules.

The Court of First Instance began its work at the end of the year. As far as competition is concerned, the main effect of this will be the transfer to it of cases arising from appeals against Commission decisions.

The judgments delivered by the Court of Justice in competition cases, of which there were 10 in 1989, were particularly illuminating in the light they shed on defining the commission's powers in anti-trust proceedings.

In two judgments, [1] the Court confirmed the wide scope of the Commission's powers of investigation while at the same time stressing that the Commission cannot compel an undertaking to confess its participation in an agreement. Three other judgments handed down by the Court [2] dealt with the Commission's powers of investigation. These judgments stipulate in particular that the Commission must clearly indicate to the undertakings the presumptions which it intends to investigate, that the powers to investigate may include active inquiries in pursuit of evidence and that, where the company refuses to submit to the investigation, the Commission officials may seek   all the necessary information with the help of the national authorities. The Court points out that it is for national law to define the procedural safeguards that ensure the protection of companies' rights during investigation procedures, it being understood that Member States are required to ensure the effectiveness of the Commission's action.

As the deadline for completing the internal market approaches, economic operators, producers and consumers are entitled to expect a competitive

---

[1]   *CdF Chimie* v *Commission, Solvay SA* v *Commission*. See Part Two, Chapter III of this Report.
[2]   *Hoechst AG* v *Commission, Dow Chemical* v *Commission, Dow Benelux NV* v *Commission*. See Part Two, Chapter III of this Report.

environment in which trade is carried out in accordance with the common interest. International developments, such as the forthcoming completion of negotiations in the Uruguay Round and the steps taken to bring the Community and its partners in EFTA closer together, also require the Community to be competitive and open to the outside world. The competition policy pursued in 1989 has been in line with these twin objectives.

Part One

General competition policy

Chapter I

The contribution from socio-economic and political circles

§ 1 — European Parliament

1. During the latter half of 1989, the newly elected European Parliament considered a number of different aspects of Community competition policy. In preparing its resolution on the Eighteenth Competition Report, the Parliament once again took the opportunity to examine and discuss current competition issues as well as recent developments. [1] In addition, it scrutinized in more detail both the progress of the proposal for a Council regulation to establish a Community system of merger control, [2] and the directive recently adopted under Article 90(3) of the EEC Treaty aimed at liberalizing telecommunications services within the Community. [3] At its November session, the Parliament passed a resolution in which it stated its view that the appropriate legal base for the latter should be Article 100a of the EEC Treaty. [4]

During the Parliament's examination of the Eighteenth Competition Report, the crucial importance of maintaining an effective competition policy was reiterated. It was emphasized that such a policy was a basic prerequisite for a genuine European internal market. Issues of particular concern to the Parliament included:

(i) the continuing growth of mergers in the period leading up to the establishment of the single market;

(ii) the high level of government subsidy and other forms of support within the Community as revealed in the Commission's 'First survey' on State aids, which was issued in 1988;

---

[1] See the Annex to this Report.
[2] See point 14 of this Report.
[3] See points 31 and 226 of this Report.
[4] OJ C 323, 27.12.1989.

(iii) the rate of progress in applying competition policy in a variety of service sectors;

(iv) certain aspects of the Commission's internal procedures, in particular as regards investigations under Regulation 17/62, and the responsibilities of the Hearing Officer.

A number of these concerns are addressed later in this Report. In particular, the Commission's activities aimed at enhancing competition in the various service sectors is highlighted. The adoption of a more stringent policy in the field of State aids, with a new emphasis upon re-examination of existing State aids, is also outlined.

As regards mergers, the Commission shares the Parliament's view that the Community was in need of an effective system for controlling operations which have a significant impact upon the wider market. Very considerable efforts went into achieving a regulation which was capable of obtaining unanimous approval in Council while at the same time making a positive contribution to the Community's legislative framework in the competition field. The Parliament played a constructive role in the process leading to the adoption of the text. Its opinions and criticisms were taken into account by the Commission. The regulation was finally adopted by the Council on 21 December.

As regards procedural questions, the Commission has noted the comments and criticisms raised by the Parliament. These will be taken into account in any future alterations of internal procedures and the Commission will strive to ensure that such changes reflect its twin obligations to respect the rights of the defence and to maintain the strict application of the Treaty rules.

2. In the course of 1989, the Parliament submitted 162 written questions to the Commission on competition matters (170 in 1988). A further 54 questions were submitted for oral reply (34 in 1988).

§ 2 — Economic and Social Committee

3. The Economic and Social Committee, which brings together representatives of workers, employers and consumers, provides an important forum within the Community's institutional framework for discussing the development of Community competition policy. In its opinion on the Eighteenth Report on Competition Policy, which was adopted in plenary on 19 December, the Committee focused on a number of specific issues and made suggestions for

certain policy guidelines to be adopted in the run-up to the single market. Its main concerns were in the following areas:

(i)   the current legal position regarding mergers;

(ii) the inadequacy of resources in the Competition Directorate-General of the Commission;

(iii) the application of the competition rules in cases involving copyright.

The Commission welcomes the constructive comments put forward by the Economic and Social Committee, including the various policy suggestions set out in its opinion. These will be taken into account in the formulation of future policy. The full opinion of the Committee is reproduced in the Annex to this Report.

On 18 October, the Economic and Social Committee adopted an own-initiative opinion on the social consequences of cross-frontier mergers. [1]

§ 3 — Advisory Committee on Restrictive Practices and Dominant Positions

4.   During 1989, the Advisory Committee met 10 times to consider preliminary draft decisions of the Commission in individual cases applying Articles 85 and 86 of the EEC Treaty. It delivered a total of 15 opinions. It was also consulted in three cases where the Commission envisaged sending an administrative letter to the companies concerned, following the publication of a notification, in conformity with Article 19(3) of Regulation 17. The Committee was informed, furthermore, about the state of progress in a number of current cases of importance. The 200th meeting of the Committee took place in October.

Conference of National Government Experts

5.   A meeting of government experts was convened in Brussels on 20 July for a preliminary discussion on the possibility of establishing a group exemption in the insurance sector. [2]

---

[1]   OJ C 329, 30.12.1989.
[2]   See point 30 of this Report.

§ 4 — Other contacts

6.   The Commission maintained contact with a variety of different organizations which have a particular interest in Community competition policy or aspects of it. A meeting was held with representatives of businesses at the European level (Unice) to discuss merger control, and there were a number of bilateral exchanges with national employers' organizations. In September, discussions took place between the Commission and representatives of professional associations in the insurance sector, in the framework of the Commission's preparations for block exemption legislation in this field.

Chapter II

International contacts

§ 1 — OECD

7.   The Committee on Competition Law and Policy met on several occasions in 1989. It took note of the work carried out by various working groups, in particular as regards the deregulation of international trade and in the field of intellectual property rights. At the October plenary session of the Committee, it was the turn of Community competition policy to be the subject of a detailed presentation.

The Industry Committee continued with its task of identifying and quantifying different types of publicly funded aid schemes. The Secretariat of the Organization aims to present a report to the OECD Council during 1990, drawn up on the basis of the contributions which have been submitted to it.

In the Shipbuilding working party, the main emphasis was on examining the possible strengthening of the General Arrangement on the progressive elimination of obstacles to normal conditions of competition in this sector.

A symposium involving third countries as well as the Member States of the OECD was held in October, providing an opportunity for detailed exchanges of view on the theme of 'Competition and economic development'.

§ 2 — Unctad

8.   During its seventh session, which took place from 27 February to 3 March, the Intergovernmental Group of Experts on Restrictive Business Practices was presented with a further request from the Community seeking participation, on the same basis as Member States, in the work of the Group. This request was sent to the Trade and Development Board which decided on 15 March, during its 35th session, to accord to intergovernmental organizations competent

in the matter of restrictive business practices the same rights of participation as States, voting rights excepted.

During its eighth session, which took place from 23 to 27 October 1989, the Intergovernmental Group dealt, in particular, with the following:

(i)   application of the 'Set of principles' [1] and experience of its implementation;

(ii) study on the concentration of commercial power through mergers, take-overs, joint ventures and other forms of acquiring control;

(iii) programmes of technical assistance and training;

(iv) manual of restrictive trade practices legislation;

(v)   model laws for the control of restrictive trade practices.

§ 3 — GATT — Uruguay Round

9.   Following on from the mid-term review held in Montreal in December 1988, work has continued in the various negotiating groups. The ideas developed within the framework of the Interservices Group of the Commission have focused on achieving the closest possible coherence between competition policy and the other policies of the Community. Exchanges of view within the Interservices Group were particularly useful in respect of 'trade related investment measures' (TRIMs), 'services', 'natural resource-based products', 'safeguards' and 'subsidies and countervailing measures'. Bearing in mind the continuing negotiations in Geneva, however, it would be premature to draw conclusions about the disciplines which might finally be included in this area, whether on the basis of ideas put forward by the Community or by its partners in GATT.

§ 4 — EFTA

10.   As was foreseen by President Delors in his inaugural speech to the European Parliament, 1989 saw important developments in relations between the Community and the EFTA countries.

Discussions on the development of a policy governing Community/EFTA relations focused particularly on the way in which basic economic freedoms

---

[1]   The Set of multilaterally agreed equitable principles and rules for the control of restrictive business practices.

could be guaranteed at the level of the 'European economic space'. As regards competition policy, it became clear from the exploratory talks that analogous rules were needed on both sides, and that practices incompatible with such rules would have to be dealt with rigorously. The next requirement is for more detailed work to be undertaken to assess the full implications of establishing equivalence in competition rules, in the Community and in EFTA.

In conformity with the conclusions of the Tampere meeting, arrangements for the exchange of information on States aids were established. The first meeting of experts on this topic was held in Brussels in March.

§ 5 — Cooperation between the Commission and the anti-trust authorities of non-member countries

11.   During a visit to Tokyo, Commission Vice-President Sir Leon Brittan had discussions with various government ministers as well as taking part in a number of meetings with other interested parties. In a speech to the Confederation of Japanese Industry (Kaidanren), Sir Leon drew attention to the problems arising from the Japanese distribution system and underlined the need for steps to be taken providing for more effective action against restrictive and anti-competitive practices.

A meeting was also organized with the Japanese Fair Trade Commission within the framework of existing annual bilateral contacts. The main emphasis of the discussion was upon recent developments in competition policy, notably as regards the distribution system, and the deregulation taking place in a number of economic sectors as part of the process of 'administrative reform' in Japan. A further meeting provided, for the first time, an opportunity for an exchange of views with representatives of MITI (the Ministry for Industry and International Trade).

On the occasion of the meeting of the OECD Committee on Competition Law and Policy, bilateral discussions were held with the Federal Trade Commission and the Department of Justice of the United States. These concerned mainly the Community proposal for a merger control Regulation, and the participants' respective competition policies in the air transport sector.

Elsewhere, in the course of a fact-finding mission, a representative of the Commission made contact with the Turkish authorities with a view to assessing from the competition standpoint, Turkey's application for membership of the Community.

Finally, Commission officials participated in two seminars on the subject of competition policy in developing countries. These took place in Peru (organized by the Junta del Acuerdo de Cartagena) and in Cameroon (at the initiative of France and of Unctad).

Chapter III

Small and medium-sized enterprises

12.   In the field of State aids,[1] a number of programmes designed specifically to help small and medium-sized enterprises, or of particular benefit to them, were approved by the Commission. Included among these were:

(i)   a Spanish Government scheme offering one-off grants for small companies in the autonomous region of Castilla-La Mancha to invest in new plant and equipment or to extend or modernize existing plant and equipment;[2]

(ii)   a scheme of assistance introduced by the autonomous region of Madrid which is designed to help finance technological and innovative research as well as the acquisition of scientific infrastructures, and which is only available to firms with fewer than 100 staff and with a turnover of less than ECU 10 million;[3]

(iii) the financing by the Italian authorities of feasibility studies by small firms connected with international projects, including those arising from the Eureka programme;[4]

(iv)   a French aid scheme enabling small businesses to call in outside consultants, subject to limits which vary according to the region;[5]

(v)   a French Government proposal to establish a fund for the purpose of supporting individual investment projects and joint operations in favour of SMEs, particularly in areas which have undergone major industrial restructuring;[6]

(vi)   an aid scheme in the *Land* of Hamburg, providing assistance towards the cost of consultancy services in order to facilitate the transfer of know-how, for industrial and commercial enterprises whose annual turnover

---

1   See also Part Three, Chapter I of this Report.
2   Bull. EC 1-1989, point 2.1.33.
3   Bull. EC 2-1989, point 2.1.57.
4   Bull. EC 2-1989, point 2.1.58.
5   Bull. EC 5-1989, point 2.1.86.
6   Bull. EC 7/8-1989, point 2.1.75.

does not exceed DM 15 million (ECU 7.2 million) and which are not controlled, through a majority shareholding, by another company; [1]

(vii) the extension of a Belgian scheme providing tax relief for new companies in the high-technology sector, which employ no more than 200 people and which establish themselves in regions experiencing serious economic problems. [2]

13.   On two occasions during the year, officials from the Competition Directorate-General delivered talks on the principles of Community competition policy to 'Euro Info Centre' (EIC) representatives. These took place within the framework of seminars organized by Directorate-General XXIII (Enterprise Policy, Distributive Trades, Tourism and Cooperatives). The establishment of EICs throughout the Community was conceived in particular to respond to the needs of SMEs for information concerning Community rules, policies and programmes.

---

[1]   Bull. EC 6-1989, point 2.1.76.
[2]   Bull. EC 7/8-1989, point 2.1.73.

Part Two

Competition policy
towards enterprises

Chapter I

Main developments in Community policy

§ 1 — Merger control

14.   On 21 December, the Council adopted the Commission's proposal on the control of concentrations between undertakings. [1] The Regulation will form a cornerstone of competition policy and make a major contribution to ensuring success in the completion of the internal market.

Given the inadequacy of the existing competition rules in dealing with the entire concentration phenomenon at Community level, the need for such a Regulation was recognized as early as 1973 in the wake of the Continental Can judgment. [2] However, at that time, the Council did not give serious consideration to the new draft Regulation. The Commission tabled an updated proposal in the autumn of 1987. At its meeting on 30 November 1987, the Council adopted a generally positive attitude on the main lines of the Commission's approach. [3]

The progress made towards completing the internal market and the new political environment provided a key impetus towards approval of the merger control Regulation. The logic of the single market prompted Member States to agree unanimously on a system of merger control at Community level for Community-scale mergers.

15.   Merger control is necessary for both economic and political reasons. The process of restructuring European industry has given rise and will continue to give rise to a wave of mergers. Although many such mergers have not posed any problems from the competition point of view, it must be ensured that they do not in the long run jeopardize the competition process, which lies at the

---

1   OJ L 395, 30.12.1989. See the Annex to this Report.
2   See Third Competition Report, pp. 15-16.
3   See Seventeenth Competition Report, points 49-51.

heart of the common market and is essential in securing all the benefits linked with the single market. In addition, it has become ever more clearly apparent that national rules are inadequate as a means of controlling Community-scale mergers, mainly because such rules are restricted to the respective territories of the Member States concerned. Clearly, Community law must be applied in controlling and examining large-scale mergers, where the reference market is increasingly the Community as a whole or a large part of it. The new Regulation also introduces a system of control for Member States which do not have any specific rules in this area.

16.   The fundamental principles of the Regulation are as follows:

(a) The basic concept underlying the Regulation is to establish a clear allocation between Community-scale mergers, for which the Commission is responsible, and those whose main impact is in the territory of a Member State, for which the national authorities are responsible.

(b) In its scope, the new Regulation covers mergers having a Community dimension, which are defined on the basis of three criteria, namely:

(i)   a threshold of at least ECU 5 000 million for the aggregate world-wide turnover of all the undertakings concerned. This figure reflects the aggregate economic and financial power of the undertakings involved in a merger. In the case of financial institutions and insurance companies, specific criteria are laid down;

(ii)   a threshold of at least ECU 250 million for the aggregate Community-wide turnover of each of at least two of the undertakings concerned. Thus, only undertakings with a specified level of activity in the Community are covered by the Regulation;

(iii) a transnationality criterion. Community control does not apply if each of the undertakings concerned achieves two thirds of its turnover within one and the same Member State. This criterion allows mergers whose impact is mainly national to be excluded from the Community control system.

(c) The current thresholds were set at a high level for an initial stage in implementing the Regulation. However, this represents an important first step in establishing Community merger control and will probably result in some 50 cases being examined a year, on the basis of an extrapolation of the statistics for the last few years. The thresholds are to be reviewed by the Council, acting by a qualified majority on a proposal from the Commission, in the light of experience, no later than four years after the adoption of the Regulation. The Commission's declared intention is that the thresholds will be revised downwards: the objective is to lower the overall threshold to ECU 2 000 million and to reduce the Community threshold similarly.

(d) All mergers falling within the scope of the Regulation will be assessed on the basis of clearly defined criteria. The basic concept is that of 'dominant position'. The creation or strengthening of a dominant position will be declared incompatible with the common market if effective competition is impeded to a significant extent, whether within the common market as a whole, or in a substantial part thereof; conversely, a merger which does not impede effective competition will be declared compatible with the common market. The assessment process will take various aspects of competition into account. These will include the structure of the markets concerned, actual and potential competition (from inside and outside the Community), the market position of the undertakings concerned, the scope for choice on the part of third parties, barriers to entry, the interests of consumers, and technical and economic progress. This overall list will be used in assessing the impact of a merger on competition.

(e) For the purposes of the Regulation, a 'concentration' is defined as the acquisition of control and covers both mergers and acquisitions. The definition includes partial mergers and merger-type joint ventures, but it does not cover the coordination of the behaviour of undertakings which remain independent.

(f) So as to ensure that control is effective and that undertakings enjoy legal certainty, the merger control arrangements include the following:

(i) The principle of mandatory prior notification by the undertakings concerned. This has a suspensory effect on the concentration for a period of three weeks (suspension of the concentration may be extended or, in some cases, dispensed with). However, the validity of stock exchange transactions will not be affected.

(ii) The setting of strict deadlines to be met by the Commission in its proceedings:
— the Commission has one month following notification within which to initiate proceedings. [1] In cases where the Commission does not raise any objections (this is likely to be the general rule), the parties will receive the go-ahead within one month;

---

[1]   This period is increased to six weeks if the Commission receives a request from a Member State that a notified merger case be referred to it (see below).

— four months after the initiation of proceedings, the Commission must take its final decision on the concentration. During that period, the parties are free to propose adjustments to the concentration so as to avoid a negative decision.

(iii) The Commission's powers of investigation and the fines provided for in the Regulation are similar to those applicable to restrictive practices. Furthermore, the Commission may require undertakings or assets unlawfully merged to be separated.

(g) The Regulation is based on the principle of exclusivity, but provision is made for a few limited exceptions to this rule. The principle of exclusivity applies as follows:

(i) All decisions relating to Community-scale mergers falling within the scope of the Regulation will be taken by the Commission. The Member States have undertaken not to apply their national law to such cases. There will, therefore, be no need for concurrent proceedings.

(ii) There are two derogations from the principle of exclusivity:

— The Regulation provides for referral to the national authorities of a Member State where a problem of a dominant position arises on a distinct market within its territory and where application of the Regulation would not achieve a satisfactory solution to the particular problem. This mechanism would normally apply to local markets, for example in distribution or hotels; exceptionally, the provision could also apply to a national market which is to some extent isolated from the rest of the Community, for example, because of high transport costs.

— In cases where Member States may invoke legitimate interests other than those protected by the regulation. These include public security, plurality of the media and prudential rules. Exceptionally, other legitimate interests may be recognized by the Commission after an assessment of their compatibility with Community law; certain such legitimate interests may be protected by the provisions of national law. In such cases, a Member State may take appropriate measures to protect such interests, which means that they have the power to prohibit a concentration or to make its approval subject to additional conditions or requirements. However, a Member State may not under this heading, authorize a concentration which has been prohibited by the Commission.

(h) Concentrations which are not covered by the Community Regulation fall in principle within the jurisdiction of the Member States. However, the

Regulation gives the Commission the power to take action with regard to concentrations that do not have a Community dimension at the request of a Member State concerned, in cases where a problem involving a dominant position arises within the territory of that Member State.

(i) The Regulation will enter into force nine months after its adoption (on 21 September 1990). There will be no retroactive examination of mergers implemented before that date. The nine-month period is intended to allow firms to familiarize themselves with the Regulation and to allow the Commission to draw up its implementing rules. These will include the arrangements for notification and for hearings, and guidelines on joint ventures. The nine-month period will also give the Commission time to reorganize its departments and its methods.

§ 2 — Application of the block exemption Regulations

Exclusive distribution agreements

17.   During the period covered by the Report, the Commission continued its examination of exclusive distribution agreements notified, to see whether they fell within the scope of Regulation (EEC) No 1983/83. [1]

The Commission also had to deal with questions relating to the interpretation of the Regulation in response to specific queries from firms.

An agreement concluded by a manufacturer of pharmaceutical products with several traders, relating to the distribution within one and the same Member State of identical products which had been registered under separate, new, brand names, was judged not to be covered by the block exemption. The Commission reiterated its position [2] that it did not consider agreements, under which a manufacturer appoints more than one sole distributor for a given territory, to be covered by the block exemption. However, such agreements may often fulfil the requirements for an individual exemption.

Specialization and research and development

18.   The Commission received only one notification in 1989 under Article 4 of Regulation 417/85 [3] on specialization agreements and only one other notification under Article 7 of Regulation 418/85 [3] on research and development agreements.

In both cases, the relevant Regulations were considered to be inapplicable. In the first case, there was no reciprocal undertaking on specialization, such undertakings being required under Article 1, if the Regulation on specialization agreements is to apply.

In the second case, the Commission found that, in view of the situation on the market concerned, there was no need for it to take any action on the agreement under Article 85.

---

[1]   OJ L 173, 30.6.1983.
[2]   Seventeenth Competition Report, point 28.
[3]   OJ L 53, 22.2.1985.

Patent and know-how licensing

19.   In 1989, the Commission examined a number of notifications of agreements coming under the provisions of Regulation (EEC) No 556/89 on know-how agreements and mixed know-how and patent licensing agreements. [1] It requested the undertakings concerned to bring their agreements into line with the conditions laid down in the Regulation.

The Commission also began examining seven recent notifications in which the parties requested the opposition procedure, either under Article 4 of Regulation 556/89 or under Article 4 of Regulation 2349/84 on patent licences. [2] Although the cases are still under examination, it is already apparent that at least three of them cannot be automatically exempted, since they contain clauses included in the blacklist set out in Article 3. In addition, in one of the cases, the notification does not comply with the conditions stipulated in Article 4 of the exemption Regulation and in Regulation No 27, [3] which stipulate in particular that the information to be provided with the notification must be complete.

Franchise agreements

20.   During the period covered by the Report, the Commission examined a number of notifications of agreements covered by Regulation (EEC) 4087/88 on franchise agreements. [4] In some of the cases examined, the Commission asked the undertakings concerned to comply with the conditions laid down in the Regulation.

It also examined a number of agreements which do not fall within the scope of the Regulation, namely wholesale franchise agreements, which are not included in the definition given in Article 1 of the Regulation.

The Commission also very recently received five notifications in which the parties requested the opposition procedure provided for in Article 6 of the Regulation. In the two cases which it has already examined, the Commission found that the opposition procedure could not properly be requested because the agreements contained blacklisted clauses.

---

[1]   OJ L 61, 4.3.1989.
[2]   OJ L 219, 16.8.1984; Corrigendum OJ L 113, 26.4.1985.
[3]   OJ 35, 10.5.1962 amended by Regulation (EEC) 2526/85 of 5.8.1985.
[4]   OJ L 359, 28.12.1988.

Motor-vehicle distribution

21.   During the year, the Commission did not have to take a decision to withdraw the exemption granted by Regulation 123/85 [1] in any individual case. However, in dealing with complaints which it received, it reminded   the undertakings concerned of the principles set out in the notice [2] which it published at the same time as the Regulation. These concern the thresholds (price differentials exceeding 12% over sufficiently long periods) beyond which the Commission deems it necessary to initiate proceedings for withdrawal of the block exemption. Although at first, in implementing the Regulation, the Commission took the view that such differentials were not on a scale that might justify withdrawal of the block exemption in specific cases, there have for some time been a number of indications that this might no longer be the case. The Commission is keeping a careful eye on developments in this area. On the basis of its five years of experience in this matter, the Commission would not hesitate to take all necessary measures, including amendment of the notice, or indeed of the Regulation itself, should the situation so require.

Air transport

22.   The block exemption Regulations adopted last year [3] seem to be achieving their objective of enabling airlines to adjust to a more competitive environment. The Regulations meet a real need for legal security on the part of air carriers and other operators on the market and at the same time encourage them to abandon earlier, more restrictive practices.

During the year, the Commission published a notice [4] on the conditions under which the block exemption for agreements on consultations on tariffs applies to inclusive tour and group inclusive tour fares.

The Commission also began examining the application of the block exemption Regulation to agreements on tariff consultations so as to determine the effect of the conditions laid down in the Regulation. The Commission will take account of the results of its examination in presenting proposals on the block exemptions that will be applicable after 31 January 1991. Such proposals could make the notification requirements more specific and easier to comply with.

---

[1]   OJ L 15, 18.1.1985.
[2]   OJ C 17, 18.1.1985.
[3]   Eighteenth Competition Report, point 28.
[4]   OJ C 119, 13.5.1989.

§3 — Transport

Air transport

Liberalization programme — second phase

23.   As part of the first package of liberalization measures in the air transport sector, Council Regulation (EEC) Nos 3976/87 [1] empowered the Commission to adopt for a limited period, a number of block exemptions to the competition rules. This was to allow for the gradual introduction of the changes required in bilateral and multilateral agreements between air carriers, thus enabling them to adapt progressively to the more competitive environment.

The Commission initially adopted three block exemption regulations which are due to expire on 31 January 1991. [2] These appear to satisfy a genuine need for legal certainty among air carriers and other market operators, while at the same time providing an incentive for them to abandon previous more restrictive agreements.

With a view to developing the liberalization process, the Commission is now proposing a second package of measures [3] which will allow it to pursue the objectives of the block exemptions beyond 31 January 1991. Thus the Commission has proposed that the Council adopt a regulation modifying Council Regulation (EEC) No 3976/87 so as to grant the Commission the power to continue the group exemptions and to review their contents in the light of the progress achieved in the liberalization process.

Commission proposals following the Court's judgment in Case 66/86.

24.   The Commission has also proposed that the Council extend implementation of the EEC competition rules to air transport between Member States and third countries and in respect of air transport within Member States. These areas were not covered by Council Regulations (EEC) Nos 3975/87 and 3976/87. [1]

---

[1]   OJ L 374, 31.12.1987.
[2]   OJ L 239, 30.8.1988; Eighteenth Competition Report, point 28.
[3]   OJ C 258, 11.10.1989.

In its judgment in the *Ahmed Saeed* Case,[1] the Court of Justice confirmed the position it took in the *Nouvelles Frontières* Case[2] as regards the application of Article 85 of the EEC Treaty. It ruled furthermore, that Article 86 is directly applicable by national courts, even in the absence of an implementing regulation under Article 87, or of action by a competent national authority or by the Commission (under Articles 88 and 89 respectively). The Court's judgment means that where a dominant airline succeeds, other than by normal competitive means, in distorting competition, even on a domestic or on a Community/third country route, this behaviour is to be considered an abuse. The Court also ruled that a Member State is in breach of its Treaty obligations if it approves fares which infringe Articles 85 or 86. Such would be the case, for instance where a uniform agreed price structure results from consultations which have not been exempted pursuant to Article 85(3).

Since, in respect of both domestic and EC/third country air transport the Commission is not in a position to grant exemption under Article 85(3), or to use normal procedures to rule on possible abuses of dominant position under Article 86, there is now a climate of damaging uncertainty in which air carriers do not know what practices and arrangements they may legitimately engage in on such routes. Even if they breach the rules inadvertently, they run the risk of actions in national courts leading to the payment of damages. Moreover, Member States face comparable uncertainties when approving the fares filed by carriers on such routes. In order to establish a framework of certainty, the Commission is seeking the necessary enabling powers with a view to defining the way in which Articles 85 and 86 apply to domestic and to extra-Community air transport.[3]

Horizontal cooperation

25. Between May and September 1988, 12 joint venture agreements were notified to the Commission pursuant to Article 5 of Council Regulation (EEC) 3975/87, for the purpose of benefiting from the application of Article 85(3), of the EEC Treaty. The agreements provide for the joint operation of certain intra-Comunity routes, the flights being operated by one of the two companies. Programmes and timetables are decided jointly, commercial cooperation is established and costs and revenues shared.

---

1   Judgment of 11 April 1989 in Case 66/86 *Ahmed Saeed Flugreisen* v *Zentrale zur Bekämpfung unlauteren Wettbewerbs*, not yet reported. See also point 90 of this Report.
2   Judgment of 30 April 1986 in Joined Cases 209-213/84.
3   OJ C 248, 29.9.1989.

Of the 12 agreements, three were terminated following discussion with the Commission. The Commission published a summary of the remaining nine in accordance with Article 5(2), of Regulation 3975/87[1] and invited other interested parties and the Member States to submit their comments.

The Commission took a favourable view of three agreements which involved cooperation between a small company operating a new route and a large airline providing its marketing network. The Commission, however, intends to re-assess these agreements after two or three years of operation, with a view to ensuring that the cooperation is still indispensable and that sufficient competition remains.

In the six other cases, the Commission raised doubts concerning the applicability of Article 85(3), because the agreements did not appear to be indispensable to the exploitation of the services involved and because they appeared substantially to eliminate actual or potential competition on the market for transport between the cities concerned.

Sea transport

Consortia

26. The shipping industry has finally provided the Commission with a sufficient number of texts of consortia agreements to form a basis for analysis. The examination of these agreements and of other available information has led the Commission to draw the following main conclusions:

(i)   There are many different types of agreement. In practice, the only common factor is that they involve groupings of several independent shipping lines who wish to cooperate in order to achieve profitability through rationalization in the widest sense, and to spread investment costs in container transport operations.

(ii) The information available to the Commission suggests that consortia in liner shipping are not to be regarded as mergers between the parties.

(iii) Consortia are not, in most cases, purely technical arrangements; there are few, if any agreements whose sole object or effect is merely to achieve technical (i.e. non-commercial) improvements or cooperation within the meaning of Article 2 of Council Regulation 4056/86.

---

[1]   OJ C 204, 9.8.1989.

(iv) Consortia are not covered by the block exemption for liner conferences under Article 3 of Council Regulation 4056/86. They differ from conferences in that they pursue other objectives and are different in organization. Moreover a considerable number of consortia agreements contain restrictive arrangements which go beyond the scope of the liner conference block exemption.

(v) Consortia deal increasingly with combined sea/land door-to-door transport.

The Commission is considering in its report, which it has promised to submit to the Council, the possibility of granting a block exemption from the prohibition of restrictive practices under Article 85(3), of the Treaty. The Commission also envisages submitting a proposal for a Council regulation empowering the Commission to adopt a block exemption. The main conclusions in this respect are that:

(i)   the development of containerized transport services has increased pressures for cooperation and rationalization between shipping lines;

(ii) consortia can help to provide the necessary means for improving the productivity of liner shipping services and promoting technical and economic progress;

(iii) users of the shipping services offered by consortia can obtain considerable benefits — including, for example, economies of scale in the use of ships and on-shore facilities. They can accordingly reduce costs, increase reliability and improve the quality of shipping services by providing multimodal services which meet the needs of efficient door-to-door transport;

(iv) however, to ensure that the conditions of Article 85(3), of the Treaty are fulfilled, it would be necessary to attach to a block exemption certain obligations.

Multimodal transport

27. The question of multimodal transport price fixing which includes not only rate fixing of the maritime carriage of cargo but also land transport is viewed with great concern by carriers and shippers.

The Commission has taken the view that multimodal transport price fixing is not covered by the block exemption for liner conferences, of Council Regulation 4056/86.

The Commission is studying this problem carefully in order to work out a solution with regard to the possible repercussions on other transport markets. The Commission will report to the Council and make appropriate proposals where necessary.

West and Central Africa

28. The Commission continued to study, with the African countries in question, ways of ensuring access to traffic between Europe and West and Central Africa, in compliance with the international treaties which link the two regions and on the basis of general principles confirmed by the ACP/EEC Council in May 1988. [1]

Additionally, the Commission conducted investigations, on the basis of complaints made to it in 1987 under Article 12(2) of Regulation (EEC) No 4056/86, in particular at the premises of maritime conferences operating between Europe and the west and central coast of Africa.

Passenger transport

29. In accordance with Article 12(2) of Regulation (EEC) No 4056/86 the Commission published the agreements concluded between ferry companies operating between the United Kingdom and the Netherlands. [2]

Elsewhere, the Commission was approached by the ferry companies operating in the Pas-de-Calais which are proposing to cooperate in response to the envisaged opening of the Channel Tunnel in 1993. As no agreement had been formally notified, the Commission was restricted to gathering, with the cooperation of the companies concerned, the information required for an initial assessment of the case.

In addition, the Commission established contact with the Monopolies and Mergers Commission which was looking at the case on the basis of domestic UK law. These contacts should, in the view of the EC Commission, lead to better coordination of the work being undertaken, respecting the competences of the national authorities on the one hand and the Community on the other. In the event, the Monopolies and Mergers Commission suggested in a report published in December that the British authorities should oppose the proposal

---

[1]   Eighteenth Competition Report, point 32.
[2]   Seventeenth Competition Report, point 47.

put forward by the shipping companies. The British Government accepted these conclusions while at the same time declaring itself willing to consider a new proposal to cooperate, nearer the time to the planned opening of the tunnel. In these circumstances, the EC Commission does not envisage any change in its position on this case in the coming months.

Finally, the Commission had its attention drawn to difficulties being encountered by an Irish ferry operator in obtaining commercially attractive landing times at a British port. The company also raised the question of port charges which it felt were excessive. Following contacts between the Commission, the firm in question and the port authority, an amicable agreement was reached. The agreement enters into force in January 1990.

§ 4 — Insurance

30. In its judgment delivered on 27 January 1987 in Case 45/87 (*Verband der Sachversicherer* v *Commission*),[1] the Court held that Articles 85 and 86 of the EEC Treaty and Regulation 17 applied fully to the insurance sector. The Commission has, since then, received some 300 notifications of agreements and recommendations from insurers and their associations.

So as to avoid being overwhelmed by an influx of notifications that cannot be dealt with on the basis of individual procedures, the Commission favours an overall solution in the form of a block exemption Regulation.

It is apparent from the notifications so far received that a number of agreements, decisions by associations of undertakings and concerted practices frequently encountered could be covered by an exemption. These include recommendations on pure premium tariffs and standard policy conditions, agreements on the common coverage of certain types of risks, agreements on the settlement of claims and on the testing and acceptance of security devices, and registers of and information on aggravated risks. The Commission accordingly intends to seek agreement from the Council, pursuant to Article 87 of the EEC Treaty, on the adoption of a Regulation empowering the Commission to set the conditions under which such agreements, decisions by associations of undertakings and concerted practices may be declared compatible with the provisions of Article 85. It is only on the basis of such authorization given by the Council that the Commission will be able to adopt a block exemption Regulation.

The Commission decided, on 18 December 1989,[2] to present to the Council a proposal for a Regulation giving it such authorization. The adoption of the Regulation would create an appropriate legal framework which would allow insurers sufficient freedom to pursue a flexible policy on contracts while a the same giving them a maximum amount of legal security.

---

[1] See Seventeenth Competition Report, point 102.
[2] OJ C 16, 23.1.1990.

§ 5 — Telecommunications

31.   The Commission Directive of 26 June, based on Article 90 of the EEC Treaty, concerns competition in the markets for telecommunications services. The Directive, which was announced in 1987 in the Green Paper on the development of the common market for telecommunications services and equipment, [1] identifies the services which Member States may reserve exclusively to the public telecommunications authorities and those which must be opened up to competition, thus avoiding any restriction of competition that is not justified by public service requirements.

The procedure for implementing the Directive is linked to the adoption of the Council Directive on a Open Network Provision (ONP). Consequently, the two Directives will be notified to the Member States at the same time. [2]

---

[1]   COM(87) 290 final, 30.6.1987, p. 65.
[2]   See also, point 226 of this Report.

§ 6 — Energy

32.   The competition rules also apply to the energy sector. The fact that, in the case of certain types of energy such as electricity and gas, the central governments or local authorities grant special or exclusive rights to companies operating in these sectors [1] does not mean that such companies are not also subject to the competition rules and, in particular, to Articles 85 and 86, though within the limits of the specific derogations provided for in this connection in Article 90(2). Articles 85 and 86 and Council Regulation 17 of 6 February 1962 [2] apply to the extent that restrictions of competition are liable to affect trade between Member States and result from the behaviour of one or more undertakings, whether private or public. The derogations provided for in Article 85(3) and Article 90(2) allow the particular features of the sector to be taken into account.

In cases where the agreements or concerted practices between undertakings that are liable to affect trade between Member States are the result of public measures (whether laws or administrative provisions) or of recommendations by the public authorities, they may be caught by Article 5 of the EEC Treaty in conjunction with Article 85. Article 5 stipulates that Member States must abstain from any measure which could jeopardize the attainment of the objectives of the Treaty.

In its working document entitled 'The internal energy market', [3] the Commission emphasized its determination to apply the competition rules in this sector more strictly than in the past, with a view to achieving gradual integration of the energy market.

In 1989, the Commission accordingly began an investigation into the vertical agreements between electricity generators and coal producers that exist in certain Member States. Such agreements may be caught by Article 85 where they are liable significantly to affect trade between Member States.

The Commission takes the view that, in certain clearly defined cases and subject to certain conditions, the existing competition rules, and in particular Articles 85 and 86, may require access to the network to be granted to third parties.

---

[1]   See Chapter II of Part Three of this Report.
[2]   OJ 13, 21.1.1962, p. 204.
[3]   COM(88) 238 final, 2.5.1988.

The Commission has continued its examination of the possible general application at Community level of the principle of allowing third parties access to networks ('Common carrier' principle) in the electricity and natural gas sectors. It decided to examine more closely, in collaboration with the Member States and all the parties concerned, whether rules should be laid down on the access of third parties to the transmission network and, if so, under what conditions.

§ 7 — Audiovisual media

33. Developments in the audiovisual media have resulted in a significant change in competitive conditions in recent years.

As a result of the deregulation of broadcasting in most Member States and the new technical possibilities opened up by satellite and cable television, a large number of new, mostly commercial, broadcasters have entered the market, in competition with the established public broadcasting organizations. Satellite and cable television have furthermore resulted, not only in the use of these media to broadcast in other Member States, programmes produced by established national stations, but also in the emergence of new transnational or pan-European satellite channels. The programmes of these channels are targetted at audiences in more than one Member State and are already to some degree, distributed in a variety of languages. This has created strong competition among the broadcasting stations for both advertising business and programmes which have mass appeal, the latter being required to ensure high viewing figures. This, in turn, has resulted in increased involvement by press undertakings in the audiovisual media, leading to more cross-media ownership and the development of multinational media groups.

The market for the production and distribution of feature fims has, by contrast, been suffering for a number of years from declining cinema audiences and box-office receipts as well as from a sharp increase in production costs. Measures to rationalize production and distribution have consequently been necessary. The same period has seen the development of a new and rapidly increasing market for the production and distribution of video cassettes.

In the light of these changes, the Commission has increasingly focused on the audiovisual media in recent years, from the standpoint of competition policy. Its main concern has been to keep markets open and to prevent or reduce barriers to market entry.

As far as television is concerned, the main area of interest at present is the programme procurement market. As Commission studies on the impact of new technologies on television revealed in 1988, [1] this market is characterized by steadily growing demand for a limited supply of programmes. The Commission aims to ensure that all broadcasting organizations have appropriate access to

---

[1] See Seventeenth Competition Report, point 330 and the annex to the Eighteenth Competition Report at Part IV.

attractive programmes and it is therefore endeavouring above all to prevent programme material being withdrawn from the market as a result of long-term exclusive contracts. In a decision adopted on 15 September 1989, [1] the Commission for the first time made it clear that the simultaneous granting of a large number of long-term exclusive television rights in feature and television films may be covered by Article 85(1) and that exemption is possible only if sufficient scope remains for third parties to have access. Other proceedings relating to long-term exclusive television rights in sporting events are currently pending.

In a decision adopted on 12 July 1989, [2] the Commission indicated that it takes a positive view of rationalization and cost-saving measures in the distribution of feature films, given the structural peculiarities of the film industry. Thus, joint ventures set up for the joint distribution of feature films may be exempted if they do not unduly restrict the competitive room for manoeuvre of the undertakings concerned.

With regard to the production of feature and television films, the Commission has repeatedly stated that it takes a positive attitude in principle to State aids, and that these may be deemed to be compatible with the common market provided they meet the conditions laid down in Article 92(3)(c). This approach is due to the difficult situation facing the industry, in particular as a result of strong competitive pressure from US films, as well as because of the particular cultural importance of the sector. The Commission must, however, ensure that trade between Member States is not adversely affected to an undue extent.

Lastly, the Commission has been considering the increasing trends towards cross-media ownership, in particular the formation of transnational multimedia groups and the resulting dangers not only for competition, but also for pluralism and variety of opinion in the political and cultural spheres. With the adoption of the Regulation on merger control, the Commission will be able to take action on large mergers which have an adverse effect on competition. However, in order to safeguard pluralism and freedom of expression, additional legal measures will, in certain circumstances, be necessary at national or Community level. The merger Regulation gives Member States the right to continue to apply national legal provisions for the protection of pluralism and freedom of expression where the Commission does not take action against mergers in the media sector.

---

[1]   Film purchases by German television stations, OJ L 248, 3.10.1989, p. 36 et seq. See also point 52 of this Report.
[2]   UIP, OJ L 226, 3.8.1989, p. 25 et seq. See also point 51 of this Report.

§ 8 - Computer software

34. The Directorate-General for Competition is actively involved in the development of the legislative process with regard to the Directive on the legal protection of computer programmes, the proposal for which was adopted by the Commission in December 1988.[1] Computer programs are an essential component in the information technology sector, which has grown very rapidly in recent years.

The proposal for a Directive sets out to harmonize Member States' copyright legislation so as to ensure that computer programs, whose preparation often requires very considerable investment, are adequately protected. At the same time, the Commission is endeavouring through the adoption of the proposal, to maintain effective competition in the sector. The area of protection in itself and the definition of the acts exclusively reserved to the copyright owner directly affect the conditions of competition.

In assessing these various interests, account should be taken of the particular nature of computer programs which differ from other works traditionally protected by copyright. The most important aspects from the competition policy point of view are the extension of copyright protection of interfaces and the risk of extending protection beyond the objective aimed at, with the result that access to unprotected parts of programs would be legally blocked.

The Directorate-General for Competition, in conjunction with the department most directly concerned, the Directorate-General for the Internal Market and Industrial Affairs, will continue to underline the importance of these aspects relating to competition policy and will contribute constructively to the discussion that will take place within the Council.

---

[1] Eighteenth Competition Report, point 42.

Chapter II

Main decisions and measures taken by the Commission

35.   In 1989, the Commission adopted 15 decisions on substantive matters under Articles 85 and 86 of the EEC Treaty. The 13 decisions taken on the basis of Article 85 of the EEC Treaty are broken down as follows: 2 prohibition decisions accompanied by fines, 1 prohibition decision without fine, 1 negative clearance, 6 exemption decisions under Article 85(3) and 3 decisions rejecting complaints. The two decisions adopted under Article 86 of the EEC Treaty were decisions rejecting complaints.

In addition, 46 procedures were terminated by administrative letter, including three following publication of a notice pursuant to Article 19(3) of Regulation No 17.[1] The procedures concerned notifications which did not result in a formal decision, the undertakings concerned being satisfied with a written statement of position from the Directorate-General for Competition.

A further 382 cases were settled either because the agreements in question were no longer in force (284), or because the Commission considered their impact too slight to warrant further consideration (98).

The Commission also adopted 15 decisions under Articles 65 and 66 of the ECSC Treaty.

36.   On 31 December 1989, there were 3 239 cases pending (as against 3 451 on 31 December 1988), of which 2 669 were applications or notifications (206 submitted in 1989), 359 were complaints from firms (93 made in 1989) and 211 were proceedings initiated by the Commission on its own initiative (67 commenced in 1989).

---

[1]   Council Regulation No 17 of 6 February 1962, OJ 13, 21.2.1962.

A — APPLICATION OF ARTICLES 85 AND 86 OF THE EEC TREATY

§ 1 — Horizontal agreements in the industrial and commercial areas

Welded steel mesh [1]

37.   The Commission fined 14 undertakings a total of ECU 9.5 million for having engaged from 1981 to 1985 in a series of agreements or concerted practices between the main welded steel mesh producers in the six original Member States (Belgium, France, Federal Republic of Germany, Italy, Luxembourg and the Netherlands) designed to fix prices or delivery quotas and to share markets. Welded steel mesh is widely used in the building industry, in civil engineering and in many other industries. The companies concerned, which are the main producers, accounted for 47% of total output in 1985.

In determining the amount of the fines, the Commission took into account the relatively long duration of most of the infringements (between two and five years), their serious nature and the fact that they involved practices such as export bans, market partitioning and price fixing, which have been outlawed by the Commission in many previous cases. The Commission, nevertheless, took into account the fact that at the time when the cartel was operating, the industry was going through a period of crisis and had been suffering from problems of excess capacity.

Three undertakings have paid the fine. Eleven undertakings have appealed against the Commission's Decision to the Court of First Instance [2] after having deposited a bank guarantee.

Sugarbeet [3]

38.   In a case concerning supplies of sugarbeet to Belgian sugar refineries, the Commission found in a Decision that the priority for national producers provided for in an inter-trade agreement and the exclusion of foreign producers

---

[1]   Decision of 2 August 1989, OJ L 260, 6.9.1989.
[2]   OJ C 306, 5.12.1989.
[3]   Decision of 19.12.1989, OJ L 31, 2.2.1990.

from the network of traditional suppliers constituted infringements of Article 85(1) of the EEC Treaty.

From 1976 to 1980, because of a shortfall in Belgian production of sugarbeet compared to the sugar quotas allocated to Belgian sugar manufacturers, the Raffinerie Tirlemontoise (RT) concluded with the sugarbeet growers in the Bavay-Maubeuge region, in northern France, a series of supply contracts providing for the same purchasing terms and conditions as those granted to national suppliers.

The subsequent increase in Belgian sugarbeet production and fall in world sugar prices meant that, after 1980, all of the sugar produced could not be marketed profitably. The Belgian associations of sugarbeet producers and sugar manufacturers then decided, in December 1985, to conclude new inter-trade agreements providing for the imposition of quota restrictions on sugarbeet supplies accompanied by priority for supplies from national growers, culminating in 1986 in the exclusion of the Bavay-Maubeuge suppliers.

In August 1987, a complaint was lodged by some of the excluded suppliers, and, in a statement of objections, the Commission challenged the priority clause and the exclusion of the French suppliers. Negotiations were then begun which resulted, in June 1989, in an arrangement under which RT and the Confédération des Betteraviers Belges (CBB) re-established the initial pattern of supplies from the complainants. In addition, in November 1989, the CBB passed on to the Commission a new version of the inter-trade agreements that no longer contained the priority clauses for sugarbeet grown in Belgium.

In its Decision the Commission found that the priority clause and the exclusion of the French suppliers were covered by the prohibition laid down in Article 85(1) of the EEC Treaty and that they could not be justified by the system of national quotas provided for under the common organization of markets in the sugar sector. Such restrictions are wholly at odds not only with the principles of the single market, but also with the rule laid down in Article 40(3) of the Treaty that there should not be any discrimination between producers within the Community.

Perlite

39.   A unilateral specialization agreement which had been notified under the non-opposition procedure provided for in Article 7 of Regulation 417/85 [1] was finally considered not to be liable to restrict competition to a significant extent

---

[1]   OJ L 53, 22.2.1985.

following the removal of a clause which prevented the party which had agreed not to manufacture the product in question from asking the other party for supplies beyond a certain ceiling. The clause, which was linked to the requirement to make purchases solely from the other party, was equivalent to a quantitative restriction. Following amendment of the contract, the purchaser became free to obtain supplies from other suppliers in quantities exceeding the agreed ceiling. The case was consequently closed without any formal decision.

Shotton Paper Company

40. The Commission took a favourable view of a standard form forestry management agreement notified by Shotton Paper Company plc, a British producer of newsprint. In order to meet its expanding requirements for pulpwood, Shotton wished to enter into agreements with forest owners in Britain. Under the agreements, it would provide forest management and contract supervision services and have the right, and obligation, to purchase the timber produced at a negotiated price, with provision for verifying the market price in case of disagreement, by sale of part of the produce on the open market.

In view of the small area of woodland which would be affected by the agreements, the Commission informed the parties that the agreements did not call for intervention under the Treaty competition rules.

Allied/VIL

41. The Commission adopted a decision, in the form of a letter,[1] rejecting a complaint by Allied Products Corp. (Allied) against the Verson International Group (VIL) that the agreements on the sale to VIL of the overseas interests of Verson Allsteel Press Co. (VASP) contained obligations that infringed the Community competition rules. When Allied took over VASP, it also took over the obligations which bound VASP as a buyer.

Allied complained that the five-year ban on competition between Allied and VIL on the Community market went beyond the restrictions allowed in respect of the sale of a business.

The Court in the *Remia* Case[2] and the Commission in the same Case and in its Reuter/BASF decision[3] held that a non-competition clause may fall outside

---

[1] Bull. EC 9-1989, point 2.1.45.
[2] [1985] ECR 2545.
[3] OJ L 254, 17.9.1976.

the scope of Article 85(1) provided that it is necessary in order to ensure that the seller fulfils his undertaking to sell his business at its full commercial value. However, protection of the purchaser must be limited to the minimum that is objectively necessary for the purchaser to assume by active competitive behaviour, the market previously occupied by the seller.

In rejecting the complaint, the Commission decided that Article 85 had not been infringed since:

(i)   the five-year non-competition clause was necessary in order to enable VIL to take over VASP's customers, to establish itself as a credible manufacturer and to set up its own R&D facilities;

(ii) VIL needed protection against competition, since it did not have the necessary know-how and the R&D facilities to develop it;

(iii) contrary to Allied's allegations, the scope of the business sold both geographically and as to products was as VIL had claimed.

Hudson's Bay/Finnish Fur Sales

42.   On 1 April 1987, Hudson's Bay (Canada) (HBC) and Finnish Fur Sales Co. (FFS) notified agreements relating to the sale of Hudson's Bay and Annings Ltd (HBA) as a going concern. Amongst other stipulations, the agreement contained a five-year non-competition covenant between HBC and FFS on the Community furs market.

In May 1988, FFS agreed in principle to sell 50% of its HBA shareholding to three competitors (including 35% to its largest competitor, Danish Fur Sales).

Under the abovementioned Community case-law (*Remia* and *Reuter/BASF* Cases), a non-competition clause may escape the ban laid down in Article 85(1) provided that certain objective criteria are met. However, the agreement in principle by FFS to sell 35% of its shares to its main competitor appeared to the Commission to be such as to exclude FFS as an active competitor from the market.

A statement of objections was sent to FFS with a view to the adoption of a Commission decision under Article 15(6) of Council Regulation No 17/62 (removal of protection from fines).

Since the sale of shares by FFS was not carried out, the file was closed in so far as it related to the Article 15(6) procedure.

National Sulphuric Acid Association [1]

43.   The Commission extended until 31 December 1998 the exemption granted since 1980 [2] to the rules of the joint buying pool of the National Sulphuric Acid Association in the United Kingdom.

When taking its decision in 1980, the Commission stipulated that pool members must be free to acquire 75% of their annual requirements of imported sulphur outside the pool, but the Commission also stated in the decision that any member could continue to purchase through the pool. In fact, with only a very few exceptions, pool members have continued to purchase all their requirements of imported sulphur for sulphuric acid production through the pool. This appears to have been due solely to the advantageous conditions which the pool was able to negotiate for its members with the few major world suppliers of sulphur.

At present all the producers of sulphuric acid in the United Kingdom (12 as against 19 in 1980) are members of the pool.

The Commission concluded that the advantages of the activities of the pool (i.e. price and transport advantages, more flexibility in distribution, greater security of supply) still constitute a sufficient basis for the application of Article 85(3).

---

[1]   Decision of 9 June 1989, OJ L 190, 5.7.1989.
[2]   Decision of 9 July 1980, OJ L 260, 3.10.1980.

§ 2 — Distribution agreements

Finnpap

44.   Following discussions with the Commission, the joint sales organization for newsprint operated by the Finnish Paper Mills Association, Finnpap, agreed in June 1989 to refrain from requiring firms using the joint sales organization to sell their production exclusively via that organization. Buyers in the Community may now make direct approaches to member producers, who are free to handle business themselves with such customers.

Following publication of a notice inviting comments from third parties,[1] the Commission concluded that the operation of the Finnish joint sales organization for newsprint was not liable to affect substantially trade between Member States and that it did not therefore give rise to any infringement of the competition rules laid down in the Treaty. The case was therefore closed.

AKZO Coatings

45.   The Commission accepted from the Dutch firm AKZO Coatings BV, one or Europe's largest paint manufacturers, unilateral undertakings which will ensure that competition in the sector of car refinish products, and in particular parallel trade, will not be restricted in future.

Following a number of investigations in 1986, the Commission found that the prices of car refinish products were persistently higher in the United Kingdom than in other Member States of the Community.

During the course of the proceedings, AKZO Coatings submitted that it was its policy not to hinder parallel trade in its products. It nevertheless recognized that it had on occasions departed from its policy in this respect. However, even before the Commission's intervention in the case, AKZO Coatings had taken all necessary steps to ensure full compliance with the Community competition rules. As to the future, AKZO Coatings gave several unilateral undertakings. These concern in particular the free provision of 'essential services' to body shops using AKZO refinish systems irrespective of the country of purchase of the AKZO products. Such 'essential services' are those necessary to enable a reasonably competent user (a body shop) to obtain the desired result (new coat

---

[1]   OJ C 45, 24.2.1989.

of paint). For this purpose, the user must be provided with the following information:

(a) specification of the paint and additive depending on the vehicle (and its existing finish or refinish) to be repaired and instructions on appropriate use of the selected colours in a safe way; this information is included in the technical data sheets;

(b) the exact composition of the colour that must be used for a vehicle, by reference to the base colours in the AKZO Coatings range of colours; this information is contained in the colour delivery programme and the colour mixing system formula, regularly updated by AKZO Coatings.

These undertakings contribute significantly to the opening up of the markets concerned. The sale of products is often linked with the provision of services. One example is consumer products for which guaranteed services are offered. The Commission has made it clear on a number of occasions that the guarantees provided by producers as part of after-sales service must be valid throughout the entire Community, [1] irrespective of the Member State in which the product was purchased. The Commission has in a large number of cases made authorization of distribution agreements subject to this condition being met. [2] The provision of after-sales service and the provision of 'essential services' seem, however, to be equally necessary to the free movement of goods in the Community.

Association Pharmaceutique Belge [3]

46.   The Commission decided to grant negative clearance under Article 85 of the Treaty to a standard agreement concluded or intended to be concluded by the Association Pharmaceutique Belge (APB) and individual Belgian or foreign manufacturers of pharmaceutical products.

The standard agreement relates to the distribution of parapharmaceuticals in Belgian pharmacies. The contract gives manufacturers the right to place on such parapharmaceutical products the APB stamp, which is a guarantee that the products have been checked and approved by the APB. In return, the manufacturers undertake to sell the products bearing the APB stamp only through pharmacies.

---

[1]   Most recently in the Seventeenth Competition Report, point 67 — 'Sony'.
[2]   See Sixteenth Competition Report, point 56 — 'Consumer guarantees'.
[3]   Decision of 14 December 1989, OJ L 18, 23.1.1990.

In the initial version of the contract, which was notified by the APB on 1 December 1986, manufacturers were not allowed to sell directly or through intermediaries the pharmaceutical products concerned, whether bearing the APB stamp or not, through distribution channels other than pharmacies.

On 26 October 1988 the Commission sent a statement of objections informing the APB that the exclusivity clause infringed Article 85(1) of the EEC Treaty and that it could not exempt the agreement under Article 85(3). The APB then amended the agreement so that the exclusivity requirement applied only to products bearing the APB stamp. Manufacturers are now free to sell the same product both to pharmacies and to retail outlets; however, they may place the APB stamp only on products intended for sale through pharmacies.

The Commission took the view that the amended agreement could still restrict competition, not because distributors other than pharmacies are excluded from the distribution of parapharmaceutical products checked and approved by the APB, but because they are excluded from participation in the APB quality stamp system. However, the Commission felt that this restriction of competition was not appreciable, since distributors other than pharmacies were free to create their own quality stamp and since the quality of pharmaceutical products was only one means of competition among others.

Fluke/Philips

47.   Under agreements concluded between the Dutch Philips Group and the American company John Fluke Manufacturing Company, the latter became the exclusive distributor of certain Philips testing and measurement products in the United States, Canada, Mexico and a number of other countries, while Philips became the exclusive distributor of certain Fluke test and measuring products in all remaining countries, including Member States of the European Communities.

Although their respective product ranges are largely complementary, the parties remain in direct competition in respect of certain types of multimeters, products for which their combined market shares amount to some 20% of the Community market. The distribution agreement concerning sales in the Community is thus not covered by Regulation (EEC) No 1983/83 on the application of Article 85(3) to categories of exclusive distribution agreements. It was for this reason that the parties requested individual exemption.

The reasons underlying the application for individual exemption were set out in a notice published by the Commission [1] in which the Commission announced

---

[1]   OJ C 188, 25.7.1989.

its intention to grant exemption. Since no objections were raised by third parties, the Directorate-General for Competition closed the file by sending a comfort letter.

Volkswagen

48. This case arose from a number of complaints from consumers in the United Kingdom who wanted to benefit from the lower prices in certain Member States, but met with difficulties in ordering cars on the Continent and in obtaining delivery of them with the specifications necessary and customary in the UK market. In accordance with the Community rules and with the previous case-law of the Court of Justice, the Commission had made it a condition that car manufacturers should make right-hand-drive cars available to meet orders from authorized dealers within their distribution networks, to the extent that the model ranges in the countries of proposed import and export correspond to each other. [1] As a result of the Commission's intervention, Volkswagen AG adjusted its ordering and production processes so as to ensure that right-hand-drive car customers could obtain cars with UK specifications within the normal delivery period on the Continent. Any order of a right-hand-drive car with extra specifications must be treated in the same way as the usual local orders received directly by distributors in a country in which right-hand-drive cars are used. The order must be met from among the pre-planned production volume for the right-hand-drive country or from any central stocks that may exist.

Bayer AG [2]

49. The Commission imposed a fine of ECU 500 000 on Bayer AG, a chemicals undertaking, as a result of agreements concluded between Bayer and its customers operating in the feedstuffs industry.

Under the agreements, Bayer's customers were obliged to purchase the product 'Bayo-n-ox Premix 10%' exclusively to cover their own requirements in their own premises. 'Bayo-n-ox Premix 10%' is a growth promoter containing an active substance which leads to an improvement in feed conversion and in daily weight gain.

---

[1] See:
  (i) Regulation 123/85 of 12 December 1984, OJ C 15, 18.1.1985, p. 16. (Regulation on the block exemption of motor-vehicle distribution and servicing agreements), Article 5(1), point 2(d);
  (ii) Commission notice concerning Regulation (EEC) No 123/85, OJ C 17, 18.1.1985, p. 4.
[2] Decision of 13 December 1989, OJ L 21, 26.1.1990.

The product was protected by patents relating to the various qualities of the product and to the finished product itself. In Germany, patent protection expired in 1985. Consequently, the price of the product in the Federal Republic of Germany had fallen, and Bayer AG's German customers became an economically attractive source of supply for Bayo-n-ox purchasers, at least in the adjacent Member States.

The object and effect of the obligation on the undertakings concerned to use the product exclusively for their own requirements were to prevent the German purchasers of Bayo-n-ox from re-selling and exporting the product to other Member States of the EEC in which patent protection still existed and where prices were higher.

Following the intervention by the Commission, Bayer AG terminated the agreements.

Coca Cola

50. On 19 December 1989, following a unilateral undertaking given by The Coca Cola Export Corporation (Coca Cola Export), the Commission terminated the proceedings which it had initiated in September 1987 under Article 86. The undertaking commits Coca Cola to comply with its specific obligations in regard to cola-flavoured soft drinks and to implement a compliance programme regarding its commercial behaviour in the Community as a whole.

The proceedings were initiated as a result of a complaint that Coca Cola Export's Italian subsidiary had concluded distribution agreements with a large number of Italian firms under which it granted a fidelity rebate to distributors who did not sell cola-flavoured soft drinks other than 'Coca-Cola'. The amount of the rebates was set individually for each distributor. The contracts often included specific clauses extending the exclusivity to other drinks.

During the proceedings, the Commission had informed Export Italia that it considered that Export Italia held a dominant position on the Italian market for cola-flavoured soft drinks and that, in the Commission's view, the fidelity rebates infringed Article 86 of the EEC Treaty, since their effect was to get distributors to sell only 'Coca-Cola' and, consequently, to prevent competing producers from having access to a substantial part of the Italian market for cola-flavoured soft drinks. In addition, the Commission had pointed out that the rebates linked to the distributors achieving a given target calculated on the basis of the level of purchases made the previous year and the rebates linked to the purchase of several products belonging to separate markets were also contrary to Article 86. By contrast, the Commission had taken the view that the rebates linked to the purchase of different packagings of the same product and the rebates linked to the distributors promoting the product in various ways were admissible.

Though it denied that it held a dominant position or had abused a dominant position, Coca Cola Export agreed to amend the agreements concluded with the distributors. The amended agreements, which entered into force on 1 January 1988, no longer included fidelity rebates or other rebates challenged by the Commission. Consequently, in October 1988, the Commission informed Coca Cola Export that the amended agreements were compatible with the Community competition rules.

Subsequently, within the framework of the proceedings, Coca Cola Export proposed an undertaking which was accepted by the Commission. In particular, Coca Cola Export undertook not to include the following provisions in the agreements to be concluded with distributors in the Member States of the Community:

(a) clauses which require the joint contracting party not to buy other cola-flavoured beverages or which grant him a rebate (or other benefits) if he does not purchase such drinks;

(b) clauses which make the granting of rebates subject to the joint contracting party's purchasing quantities of 'Coca-Cola' set individually during a period of more than three consecutive months;

(c) clauses which make the granting of rebates subject to the joint contracting party's purchasing a given quantity of 'Coca-Cola' along with other beverages produced by Coca Cola Export;

(d) clauses which make the supply of 'Coca-Cola' or the granting of rebates subject to the joint contracting party's purchasing other beverages produced by Coca Cola Export along with the purchase of 'Coca-Cola'.

In addition, Coca Cola Export undertook not to engage in any restrictive practices having an effect equivalent to the clauses mentioned above in points a, b, c and d.

The undertaking will have the effect of ensuring that competition on the soft drinks market in the European Community will be strengthened to the benefit both of Coca Cola Export's competitors and consumers as a whole.

Coca Cola Export's competitors will have greater access to distribution networks and can launch new products, thus enabling consumers to choose among a wider range of drinks.

§ 3 — Agreements in the service sector

Media

UIP [1]

51.   By Decision of 12 July 1989, the Commission granted a five-year exemption to a series of agreements entered into between Paramount Pictures Corporation, MCA Inc., and MGA/UA Communications Co. regarding the creation of a joint venture, United International Pictures (UIP). Within the Community, UIP distributes and licenses feature films produced by its parent c_____ ___ showing in cinemas.

Before UIP was set up, Paramount, MCA, Metro-Goldwyn-M_____ _____ed Artists distributed their films within the Community through ____ _____rate organizations. So as to gain efficiencies by avoiding adminis_____ ____ation, the parent companies pooled their distribution activities in th_____ ____ity and granted UIP exclusive rights to their respective productions.

The agreements notified were substantially amended at the C_mmission's request. The amendments made were designed to ensure the highest possible degree of autonomy for the parent companies in the conduct of their business and the marketing of their products, taking into account the specific characteristics of the industry. The changes should allow wider distribution of films, especially to smaller cinemas and cinemas away from the main population centres.

The changes affected UIP's operating committees by limiting their powers in the preparation of release plans for the individual films of the parent companies. The Commission also required, and obtained, an amendement to the provisions regarding co-production agreements to ensure that the parent companies remained independent from each other and from UIP and could enter into co-production agreements with third parties in the Community.

The exclusivity provisions were limited in their effect by allowing UIP only to have the right of first refusal to the parent companies' films. This means that the parent company concerned must offer its product for distribution in the Community first to UIP. Should UIP elect not to distribute a picture, the parent

---

[1]   Decision of 12 July 1989, OJ L 226, 3.8.1989.

company would be entitled to impose its distribution on UIP or to distribute the film on its own or through a third party.

The companies concerned also gave several undertakings to the Commission as to maintenance of approriate records and the establishment of an arbitration procedure for solving problems common to the cinema industry such as film allocation and access to the exihibitors' screen space.

It should be noted that UIP is not comparable to a traditional sales outlet, since it distributes non-homogenous products on a very specific market and since the prices and terms are set by the producer companies; furthermore, each parent company receives the net profits resulting from the distribution of its own films.

Film purchases by German television stations [1]

52.   In 1984, the Association of Public Broacasting Organizations in Germany (ARD) concluded with a subsidiary of the American Company Metro-Goldwyn-Mayer/United Artists (MGM/UA) agreements on television broadcasting rights and all new feature films to be produced by MGM/UA from 1984 to 1988.

The Commission objected to the agreements, considering that the number and duration of the exclusive rights acquired by ARD rendered access for third parties unreasonably difficult. The ARD organizations agreed to allow the licensing of the films to other television stations during so-called 'windows'. The windows designate certain periods relating to individual films during which the exclusivity granted to the ARD organizations is lifted, and during which the ARD organizations themselves will not use the films. The windows vary in length between two and eight years.

In addition, the ARD organizations now allow licensing throughout the contract territory to other television stations wishing to show non-German versions, which was previously prohibited under the agreements.

In view of the new scope for third parties to gain access to the films, the Commission exempted the agreements under Article 85(3). The Decision is the first of its kind to make clear that agreements relating to exclusive television rights can be contrary to the Community competition rules because of the number and duration of the rights and that an exemption is possible only if suitable access facilities are available to third parties.

---

[1]   Decision of 15 September 1989, OJ L 284, 3.10.1989.

Banking

Dutch banks [1]

53.   As a result of action by the Commission, several associations of Dutch banks abandoned in 1988 and 1989 a series of agreements providing in particular for:

(i)   uniform minimum commissions for several banking services between banks and to private and business customers;

(ii)   uniform value dates for debit and credit operations;

(iii)   uniform exchange rates and margins for foreign currency transactions;

(iv)   uniform commissions and exclusive arrangements for foreign currency brokers in relation to certain financial services.

The banks involved account for more than 90% of total deposits and assets of banks operating in the Netherlands. The Commission had objected that the agreements restricted competition and could not be exempted under Article 85(3), notably because they limited the scope for the banks concerned to develop their own commercial and financial policy independently and because they were discriminatory in that they required different charges to be made in certain situations for similar banking services.

The Commission Decision in this case states that a number of technical agreements which remained in force did not come under Article 85(1), either because they do not, or not appreciably, restrict competition, or because they do not appreciably affect trade between Member States.

The Decision also granted exemption under Article 85(3) to two circulars concerning simplified clearing procedures for cheques denominated in guilders or foreign currencies.

However, the Decision does not provide for any exemption for agreements on banking commissions. As regards agreements on commissions for services to clients, the Decision confirms the Commission's position in earlier Decisions, namely that agreements on commissions for services between banks may be exempted only in exceptional cases where they are really necessary for the successful implementation of certain forms of cooperation between several banks. This was not the case with the amended agreements as proposed by the parties.

---

1   Decision of 19 July 1989, OJ L 253, 30.8.1989.

The Decision does not relate to agreements on electronic transactions and bank cards, on which the Commission reserves its position.

Insurance

AMB/La Fondiaria

54. In November 1988, the German company Aachener und Münchener Beteiligungsgesellschaft (AMB) and the Italian company La Fondiaria Assicurazioni SpA each acquired 25% plus one of the shares of Volksfürsorge Deutsche Lebensversicherung AG from Beteiligungsgesellschaft für Gemeinwirtschaft (BGAG), which itself kept the remainder of the shares.

BGAG is a holding company belonging to the German trade unions. AMB, La Fondiaria and Volksfürsorge are the parent companies of insurance groups operating in the various branches of their respective national markets.

The acquisition of the shares in Volksfürsorge forms part of a general plan of cooperation between AMB and La Fondiaria intended to help strengthen their competitiveness and to develop new activities in other Member States. For this purpose, they concluded a cooperation agreement under which each party offers the other party the opportunity of participating in its activities, including new business initiatives in other Member States. AMB and La Fondiaria also agreed to collaborate in the management of Volksfürsorge with AMB acting as lead-manager. In addition they concluded an agreement with BGAG providing for cooperation in the management of Volksfürsorge.

After publishing a notice inviting interested parties to submit their observations,[1] the Commission decided that the agreements could be exempted under Article 85(3). It informed the parties of this conclusion in an administrative letter stating that, with the agreement of the parties, the file had been closed without any formal decision being taken.

Concordato Incendio[2]

55. The Commission granted exemption under Article 85(3) to an agreement between insurance companies in Italy concerning a non-profit-making association of insurance companies known as the 'Concordato Italiano Incendio Rischi Industriali'.

---

[1]   OJ C 210, 16.8.1989.
[2]   Decision of 20 December 1989, OJ L 15, 19.1.1990.

The activities of the Concordato concern fire insurance in respect of industrial risks located in Italy and supplementary cover, including consequential loss insurance.

At the time of notification, the list of members comprised 28 companies established in Italy, whose combined share of the industrial fire insurance market was at least 50 %. Members are invited to quote risks on the basis of the risk rates of the tariff, to which they add commission and overheads calculated on the basis of their own viability. They are provided with a model fire insurance policy containing definitions and standard general conditions.

They may depart from these standard general conditions, but if such departure is likely to affect the uniformity of the statistics, it must be notified to the Concordato.

TEKO [1]

56.   On 20 December, the Commission adopted a Decision granting an exemption to the operation of TEKO (Technisches Kontor für die Maschinen-Betriebs-unterbrechungs-Versicherung), a pool set up for the purpose of joint and mutual reinsurance of insurance policies covering loss of profits from machine breakages. TEKO consists of 20 insurance companies which together have a market share of about 20%. The companies may if they wish bring their policies into TEKO for reinsurance, but are under no obligation to do so. TEKO concludes on behalf of the companies common reinsurance contracts which it administers itself.

With regard to premiums and conditions for their direct insurance policies, the individual companies in each individual case may ask TEKO to carry out a risk assessment and a premium calculation, without being obliged to do so. Once a calculation has been carried out by TEKO, the common reinsurance is subject to the application of the premium and conditions calculated by TEKO. Insurance in the aerospace sector was recently added to the cooperation agreements.

In the Commission's opinion, the cooperation between the companies concerned within the framework of TEKO results in substantial rationalization and cost saving. Because of the small number of contracts and the diversity of the risks, the individual companies do not have the specialized experience required for

---

[1]   Decision of 20 December 1989, OJ L 13, 17.1.1990.

the conclusion and processing of direct insurance contracts, nor are they able individually to negotiate favourable terms and conditions for reinsurance.

Under these circumstances and taking into account the fact that the participating companies face strong competition from other undertakings operating on the relevant markets, the Commission decided to grant an exemption. The Decision shows that a reinsurance pool which allows members to take out reinsurance outside the pool and to calculate premiums and terms and conditions for direct insurance themselves may be granted exemption.

§ 4 — Agreements in the transport sector

Eurotunnel II

57.   On 16 February 1989, the Commission decided not to object to a utilization agreement concluded between Eurotunnel and the French and British railways SNCF and British Rail, concerning the Channel Tunnel. The Agreement, which was concluded on 29 July 1987, is intended to share transport markets and to establish traffic forecasts and utilization rules for the tunnel. Pursuant to Regulation (EEC) No 1017/68 of 19 July 1968,[1] the agreement, which was notified on 2 November 1987, is exempted for three years as from 16 November 1988, when the request was published in the Official Journal.[2] The granting of exemption for a longer period is currently being examined.

IATA

58.   The Commission examined the IATA passenger agency programme in respect of which IATA had applied for an individual exemption.

The programme lays down the criteria for IATA accreditation of agents and the terms on which IATA carriers are to deal with travel agents. It also imposes various conditions on accredited agents.

The Commission did not object to the purposes of the agency programme in so far as they involve objective selection criteria for travel agents, security documents and professional training. These are legitimate objectives, which can certainly contribute to consumer satisfaction by ensuring that travel agents provide an efficient service.

The Commission was, nevertheless, concerned that the current systems, basically contained in IATA Resolutions 800, 802 and 808, tended to eliminate competition between agents and between airlines in a number of important respects and were liable to operate against the interests of consumers, especially by unduly limiting the number of accredited agents and by prohibiting agents from sharing their commission with their clients. Moreover, a number of restrictions did not appear to be necessary to achieve the benefits of the programme: for example, some accreditation criteria and procedures were

---

[1]   OJ L 175, 23.7.1968.
[2]   OJ C 292, 16.11.1988.

unnecessarily strict, and there were restrictions on the carriers' ability to deal with other agents and on the terms on which they could deal with agents.

Accordingly, on 15 June 1989, the Commission sent a statement of objections to IATA.

Following this statement of objections, IATA drew up Resolution 814, which establishes a new system to operate within the European Community. The new Resolution, which is currently being examined by the Commission, reduces the barriers to IATA accreditation, allows carriers to deal with IATA agents and with other agents on an unrestricted basis and does not prohibit commission splitting.

§ 5 — Agreements relating to industrial property rights

Syntex/Synthelabo

59. Following intervention by the Commission, Syntex, a United States health-care company, and Synthelabo, a French manufacturer of various pharmaceutical and parapharmaceutical products, amended a geographical delimitation agreement concluded in order to end litigation between the two companies on the validity of their trade marks in a number of Community countries. The Commission had taken the view that the agreement infringed Article 85(1) of the EEC Treaty.

In principle, national jurisdictions usually have the right to decide regarding the existence or non-existence of the risk of confusion between different trade marks. However, when individuals sign delimitation agreements and in particular when such agreements effectively divide the common market into a number of territories, the Commission must have a right to intervene.

The Commission is more often likely to intervene in cases where available evidence points to the inability of a party to legally enforce its claim of invalidity of the other party's trade mark. If it is evident that through such actions one party may legally exclude the other from selling in certain Member States, an agreement between the two companies having the same effect would not restrict competition.

The parties are obliged to examine all options available to them before signing an agreement that would effectively partition the common market. In particular, less restrictive solutions should be examined to determine if, for example, an agreement on how a trade mark should be used would succeed in eliminating the risk of confusion. Having examined the agreement in question, the Commission considered that any risk of confusion did not justify the partitioning of markets. Once the agreement was amended, the Commission closed the file.

Pilkington/Covina

60. A patent and know-how licensing agreement granted by Pilkington (United Kingdom) to Covina (Portugal) on the float glass process was deemed to be in line with Regulation No 2349/84[1] after it had undergone a number of amendments.

---

[1] Regulation No 2349/84 on the application of Article 85(3) of the Treaty to certain categories of patent licensing agreements, OJ L 219, 16.8.1984.

In the version initially notified, the agreement prohibited the licensee, Covina, from exporting to certain Community countries for the whole period of the licence (10 years) and for 10 years after the agreement expired, irrespective of the protection afforded by registered patents in such countries. The Commission took the view that these provisions breached Article 3(10) of the block exemption Regulation. The Commission also pointed out that a patent holder who had granted sales licences within certain protected territories to licensees producing within other territories cannot be deemed to have reserved such territories for himself within the meaning of Article 1(1)(3) of the Regulation.

Following intervention by the Commission, the parties amended their agreements so that the territorial restrictions apply only where patents are enforced in the territories concerned, and for as long as the patents remain valid, and only restrict the licensee from pursuing an active sales policy in those territories. This brought the agreement into line with Article 1(1)(5) of the Regulation.

A comfort letter was sent terminating the case.

§ 6 — Abuse of a dominant position

Filtrona/Tabacalera

61.   On 26 April, the Commission adopted a Decision under Article 86 of the EEC Treaty rejecting a complaint made by a Spanish cigarette filter producer, Filtrona Española, against the Spanish tobacco monopoly holder, Tabacalera. Filtrona accused Tabacalera of abusing a dominant position as a purchaser of cigarette filters by increasing its own production of ordinary cigarette filters from 44% to 100% of its own requirements. After examination, the Commission concluded, firstly, that Filtrona was not dependent on Tabacalera for its sales of cigarette filters, since Filtrona exports its filters to other markets and can change its production from ordinary filters to special filters and, secondly, that Tabacalera's decision to produce all the ordinary filters it needed was not an abuse of a dominant position, since a company's production of its own requirements is not in itself an abnormal act of competition. Production by cigarette manufacturers of their own filters is common practice in the industry. In addition, Tabacalera justified its vertical integration on economic grounds: production of all its filter requirements allows it to achieve economies of scale and generally to reduce its production costs. There were no special circumstances suggesting that Tabacalera's decision was part of an abusive behaviour or strategy.

Industrial gases

62.   Following an investigation and proceedings conducted by the Commission in the industrial gas sector, L'Air Liquide SA, AGA AB, Union Carbide, BOC Ltd, Air Products Europe Inc., Linde AG and Messer Griesheim GmbH, which are the major producers of industrial gases on the world and European markets, each agreed to amend clauses in their sales contracts for oxygen, nitrogen and argon supplied in piped and bulk form. In addition, L'Air Liquide, AGA, Linde and Messer dissolved their joint subsidiaries operating in the sector.

The Commission had objected that some of the clauses in the gas sales contracts infringed Article 85 and constituted an abuse of a dominant position, contrary to Article 86 by L'Air Liquide in France, Belgium, Luxembourg and Italy and by BOC Ltd in the United Kingdom and Ireland. The Commission objected in particular to the exclusivity clause obliging customers to cover all or most of their gas requirements from one supplier and to the duration of the contracts, which had the effect of tying customer and supplier for a long period and of preserving established positions.

The producers, acting on their own behalf and on behalf of their subsidiaries in the Community countries, each undertook separately and individually to amend their contracts.

In the case of tonnage, on-site or pipeline contracts, supplying and purchasing obligations must be restricted to 15 years and must relate only to quantities falling within a fixed minimum/maximum range. In the case of liquid in-bulk contracts, supply and purchasing obligations must be restricted from five to three years and must relate only to quantities up to a fixed maximum. Any clause which obliges customers to obtain all or a fixed percentage of their requirements of any gas (whether or not the subject of the contract) from one supplier must no longer be used. The 'English clause', which allows the supplier to be informed in detail on competitors offering more favourable terms, must cease to be used.

However, in view of the safety arguments put forward by the producers, it was agreed that suppliers could have the exclusive right to fill and maintain customers' tanks, with customers remaining free to purchase the tank from other suppliers; consequently, if the customer prefers to have more than one supplier, he must have more than one tank.

Furthermore, L'Air Liquide SA and AGA AB agreed to separate their interests in their joint subsidiaries. As from 1 January 1987, L'Air Liquide Belge and L'Air Liquide Luxembourg became wholly-owned subsidiaries of L'Air Liquide SA, while AGA Gas (Germany) and AGA Gas (Netherlands) became wholly-owned subsidiaries of AGA AB. Linde AG and Messer Griesheim GmbH also separated the interests which they held in their joint subsidiaries Airgaz SARL, Airgas Nederland BV and L'Oxhydrique Internationale SA.

In view of the results obtained and the undertakings given by the producers concerned, the Commission decided to close the case.

Gestetner/Rank Xerox

63.   In January 1989, the Commission decided to reject the complaint lodged by the British undertaking Gestetner Holdings plc against the American company Xerox Corporation.

Gestetner argued that, through its majority control in the joint subsidiary Rank Xerox, Xerox held a dominant position on the Community market for photocopiers using ordinary paper and in particular for high-speed photocopiers. The complainant also alleged that Xerox had abused its dominant position through conduct intended to exclude competition.

The Commission rejected the complaint, on the grounds that Xerox Corporation did not in fact enjoy a dominant position on the market concerned, accounting for only about one quarter of the market for machines serving the same purpose, namely photocopiers and offset printing machines.

§ 7 — Mergers and concentrations

TWIL/Bridon

64.   Following investigations by the Commission into TWIL Ltd (United Kingdom), SA Bekaert NV (Belgium), British Steel plc (United Kingdom) and Bridon plc (United Kingdom), Bridon has agreed to dispose of its entire shareholding in, and to sever all its links with, TWIL Ltd, the largest UK producer of steel wire products. TWIL was a long-standing joint venture, owned by Bekaert, British Steel and Bridon. As Bekaert and Bridon are also producers of steel wire products, this has led to the danger of a degree of commercial cooperation between the parties that was unacceptable under the competition rules. Under the new structure, Bekaert will own 60% and British Steel 40% of TWIL. As part payment of its shareholding in TWIL, Bridon will acquire three TWIL subsidiaries. One of these, Fox Wire Ltd, has a substantial position in the UK market for stainless steel wire, a market in which Bridon already holds a small share. However, there are at least five other UK producers of this product and substantial imports from the rest of the Community, with the result that this increase in market share is acceptable. The Commission therefore closed the case in February 1989.

Ibercobre/Outokumpu

65.   In August, the Commission terminated, without any formal decision, proceedings which it had initiated in respect of a set of cooperation agreements concluded between Outokumpu and Iberica del Cobre. Outokumpu is the only Finnish producer of semi-manufactured copper and copper alloy products and controls two of the three other largest producers in Scandinavia. Iberica del Cobre is the largest Spanish producer of such products.

The cooperation agreements provided for Outokumpu to acquire a minority interest in Iberica del Cobre as well as production rationalization plans, marketing agreements and the setting up of a joint venture to distribute Outokumpu's products in Spain. The agreements also provided for Outokumpu to acquire subsequent control of Iberica del Cobre through options on Ibercobre's remaining stock.

The Commission wanted to make sure that such a minority interest, together with the agreements in question, was not in fact a means of allowing the two competitors to concert their investment policies and business activities, an arrangement which could become long-term or indeed permanent in the event of the initial concentration project being delayed or abandoned.

After Outokumpu had announced its decision to raise its stake in Ibercobre to 51% with the intention of subsequently raising it to 80.4%, the Commission decided to close the case, having concluded that the transaction was unlikely to prevent the maintenance of effective competition on the market.

The Commission concluded that there were on the market in the products concerned, which were standard intermediate products, no real barriers either to entry into the EEC of products from third countries, or to trade between Member States. Furthermore, producers have long since ceased to enjoy patent protection, and brand loyalty is weak. On the Community market, competition is sufficiently guaranteed by the presence of other large producers and by opportunities for consumers to obtain supplies outside the Community.

Plessey/GEC-Siemens

66. On 1 September, the Commission formally rejected the complaint from Plessey plc, the British electronics manufacturer, that the proposed joint take-over by GEC-Siemens infringed the EEC competition rules. The complaint concerned the agreement between GEC and Siemens to purchase Plessey, combined with plans for the future joint and/or separate management of certain assets.

The Commission considered that certain elements of the agreement might constitute appreciable restrictions of competition within the meaning of Article 85(1) of the EEC Treaty, particularly concerning telecommunications and integrated circuits. However, in the light of the particular circumstances of the case, it considered that an individual Article 83(3) exemption could be envisaged regarding these aspects of the agreement. With regard to these sectors, it was expected that the transaction would produce advantages in the form of economic and technical progress thanks to the pooling of research and development resources in markets where there was a sharp and steady rise in R&D costs. Moreover, a number of international competitors that were more powerful than the companies in question existed on the markets.

In relation to the other areas covered by the complaint, i.e. traffic control systems and defence equipment, the Commission found no appreciable restriction of competition in the context of Article 85(1).

The Commission adopted the decision as a matter of urgency following the renewed bid by GEC-Siemens on 17 August 1989, so that Plessey could exercise its right of appeal. On 16 April, the Commission had already announced the initiation of formal proceedings with a view to approval of the transaction.

Rhône Poulenc/Monsanto

67.   In February, the French company Rhône Poulenc and the US company Monsanto informed the Commission that they had come to a preliminary understanding concerning the acquisition by Rhône Poulenc of all Monsanto's production units in the United States, the United Kingdom and Thailand involved in the manufacture of two lines of products. The products in question are salicylic acid, methyl salicylate and acetylsalicylic acid on the one hand and acetyl para amino phenol on the other. These are intermediates used chiefly by the pharmaceuticals industry in the manufacture of analgesic and anti-pyretic compounds.

Following its analysis of the product markets concerned, the Commission concluded that Rhône Poulenc did not hold a dominant position within the Community and that it was not therefore necessary to apply Article 86 to the proposed acquisition. Despite the large market shares held by Rhône Poulenc, notably in the acetylsalicylic acid sector (pre-product of aspirin), the independence of the French company remained limited. The Commission noted in particular that there were no real barriers either to the entry of these products into the EEC from third countries or to trade between Member States. They are common intermediate products, for which the manufacturing technology is now easily accessible, even in newly industrialized countries. Furthermore, the patents protecting them expired many years ago and their marketing is not dependent on user brand loyalty. There is also considerable overcapacity worldwide in the products in question and a growing number of producers. The combination of all these factors has led to a constant growth in imports into the Community from third countries and increased pressure on prices.

The same case was referred by the British Secretary of State for Trade and Industry to the United Kingdom Monopolies and Mergers Commission (MMC), which examined the acquisition with reference to the British market. Having noted the substantial overcapacity on the world market, the competition from non-Community sources of supply and the lack of technical barriers to entry, the MMC decided not to raise any objections to the acquisition, thus confirming the conclusions already arrived at by the Commission. The French authority responsible for competition matters, to which the case was also referred, took a similar decision.

Consolidated Gold Fields/Minorco

68. Following a complaint by Consolidated Gold Fields plc against a takeover bid for its shares by Minorco SA, the Commission received formal assurances from Minorco that, in the event of the bid succeeding, it would, within a specified period of time, sell the platinum interests of Consolidated Gold Fields. So as to prevent any strengthening of a dominant position in the sector, the sale would not be to Anglo-American Corporation of South Africa Ltd, De Beers Consolidated Mines Ltd or parties associated with them.

The Commission would be consulted before the sale was concluded, and, meanwhile, neither Minorco nor any associated party would interfere with the running of Consolidated Gold Fields' associates in the platinum sector — Gold Fields of South Africa and Northam Platinum. On the basis of the information in its possession, the Commission concluded that Consolidated Gold Fields' complaint should be rejected. In the event, the bid was prevented from going ahead by an action before the courts in the United States by a US affiliate of Consolidated Gold Fields.

The Commission was particularly concerned in this case to ensure the maintenance of competition in the supply of platinum to the Community, especially in the light of growing demand from manufacturers of catalytic converters, which are used to reduce car exhaust pollution. The Commission announced that it would closely monitor developments in the platinum industry.

Carnaud-Metal Box, Pechiney-American Can

69. In February, the Commission announced that, following examination of two recent mergers in the European packaging industry, namely Carnaud-Metal Box and Pechiney-American Can, it would not oppose the two mergers since they were not such as to constitute an abuse of a dominant position. Particular attention was paid to the fact that several major customers of the companies concerned were large companies with considerable market power.

However, in view of the level of concentration in the European metal packaging industry, the Commission will follow market developments with particular vigilance and will examine carefully any further merger activity in areas where the companies concerned already hold strong market positions. The Commission drew attention to the obligation of companies in a dominant position not to commit abuses by engaging in discriminatory or predatory behaviour against smaller purchasers or competitors.

Stena-Houlder Offshore

70.   Following a complaint made by Comex SA, the Commission objected to the terms of acquisition of Houlder Offshore Ltd by Stena UK Ltd.

Firstly, the Commission noted that the acquisition gave Stena control over two diving support vessels used by Comex for inspection, maintenance, repair and construction work in offshore stations, Stena being a competitor of Comex in subsea works, its acquisition of the two vessels on which Comex largely depended was likely either to restrict access by Comex to the vessels, or to increase the cost of such access.

Secondly, the acquisition gave Stena control over shareholdings of 13% and 50% owned by Houlder Offshore Ltd in two competing companies, i.e. in Comex SA and in Comex Houlder Ltd. The creation of this structural link between two important competitors, Stena and Comex, was likely to affect competition in a highly concentrated market. Following the Commission's intervention, Stena and Comex agreed to become completely independent. Stena will sell the shareholdings previously owned by Houlder Offshore Ltd to the Comex group and will hire one of the diving support vessels to Comex for two years. This undertaking guarantees Comex access to an essential input for the execution of its subsea diving services. Comex believes that, after that period, other opportunities will be available. In view of this settlement, the Commission closed the case without taking a formal decision.

B — APPLICATION OF ARTICLES 65 AND 66 OF THE ECSC TREATY

§ 1 — Concentrations in the steel industry

Usinor-Sacilor/Lutrix [1]

71.   Acting under Article 66 of the ECSC Treaty, the Commission authorized Usinor-Sacilor SA to acquire a 24.5% minority shareholding in Lutrix SRL, Brescia. Usinor-Sacilor is a major Community steel producer which, through its subsidiary Sollac, produces cold-rolled sheet and coated sheet. Lutrix is a holding company belonging to the Italian private sector group Lucchini, which controls La Magona d'Italia, whose main activity is in cold-rolled coated sheet, with a production of some 450 000 tonnes a year. There are several large producers on the market for coated steel as well as a number of smaller producers. There will therefore be little change in the two companies' position on the market after the concentration.

ASD/Welbeck International [2]

72.   The Commission authorized ASD plc, Leeds, United Kingdom, to acquire the entire share capital of Welbeck International Ltd, Barking, United Kingdom. Both companies are engaged in the distribution of steel products. The transaction will strengthen ASD's position on the United Kingdom market without allowing it to impede competition, since it has to compete with two other larger distributors.

British Steel/Bore Steel Group [3]

73.   The Commission authorized British Steel plc, London, United Kingdom, to acquire the entire share capital of Bore Steel Group Ltd, Walsall, United Kingdom. Besides being one of the largest European steel producers, British Steel is a steel stockholder. The acquisition of Bore Steel Group will strengthen British Steel's position as stockholder on the United Kingdom market, but

---

[1]   Decision of 3 April 1989, Bull. EC 4-1989, point 2.1.71.
[2]   Decision of 24 April 1989, Bull. EC 5-1989, point 2.1.84.
[3]   Decision of 6 June 1989, Bull. EC 6-1989, point 2.1.75.

owing to the presence of a number of rival stockholders, including one larger firm, it will not have the effect of restricting competition.

United Engineering Steels/Bird Group of Companies [1]

74. The Commission authorized United Engineering Steels Ltd, Rotherham (UES) and Bird Group of Companies Ltd, to form a new company under the name of Hyfrag Ltd. Hyfrag, which will be jointly owned by UES and BIRD, will operate a ferrous scrap fragmenting plant in Rotherham (South Yorkshire), supplying UES with shredder scrap. Plant production will be some 100 000 tonnes a year, equivalent to less than 2% of shredder scrap production. This will not have any significant impact on the scrap market.

Neue Maxhütte Stahlwerke [2]

75. The Commission authorized Mannesmannröhrenwerke AG, Klöckner Stahl Gmbh, Krupp Stahl AG, Lech Stahlwerke GmbH, Thyssen Stahl AG, Thyssen Edelstahlwerke AG and the *Land* of Bavaria to form a new company under the name of 'Neue Maxhütte Stahlwerke Gmbh'. The new company will take over part of the facilities and workforce of Eisenwerk Gesellschaft Maximilianshütte mbH, which was declared bankrupt on 16 April 1987. The *Land* of Bavaria owns 45% of the shares in the new company, the remaining 55% being divided among the other shareholders. A restructuring plan providing for production cuts and closure of the Haidhof works should help the company to return to viability while at the same time contributing to the restructuring of the Community steel industry.

Hüttenwerke Krupp Mannesmann [3]

76. The Commission authorized Krupp Stahl AG and Mannesman röhrenwerke AG to set up a joint venture under the name of 'Hüttenwerke Krupp Mannesmann GmbH' (HKM). HKM will operate the Huckingen blast furnace and rolling mill previously owned by Mannesmann and supply crude steel and semi-finished products to the parent. Krupp will close down its Rheinhausen plant at the end of 1990 and transfer production of crude steel to Huckingen.

---

[1] Decision of 19 June 1989, Bull. EC 6-1989, point 2.1.72.
[2] Decision of 27 June 1989, Bull. EC 6-1989, point 2.1.74.
[3] Decision of 27 June 1989, Bull. EC 6-1989, point 2.1.73.

Parallel to this, it will withdraw from the market for long products. The measures as a whole will allow Krupps production to be restructured and consolidated and to optimize the efficiency of the Huckingen plant as regards the production of cast iron and crude steel. In a Community context, the measures contribute considerably to restructuring, since they will lead to a considerable reduction in production capacity for crude steel and sections.

Special Products Lemforder [1]

77. The Commission authorized United Engineering Steels Ltd, Rotherham (UES) and Lemforder Metallwaren AG (Lemforder) to form a new company under the name of Special Products Lemforder Ltd (SPL). SPL will manufacture and market ball-joint assemblies in the United Kingdom and Scandinavia. It will be owned by UES and Lemforder. UES is one of Europe's largest producers of engineering steels, while Lemforder is a major producer of high-precision motor vehicle components. The transaction is an example of cooperation between a steel products producer and consumer who are not in competition with one another. It will not have any effect on the markets in question.

Dillinger Hütte-Saarstahl [2]

78. The Commission authorized Usinor/Sacilor to acquire a 70% majority interest in a new holding company Dillinger Hütte-Saarstahl AG, which will control Saarstahl (formerly Saarstahl Völklingen GmbH) and Dillinger Hütte (formerly Dillinger Hüttenwerke AG). Usinor/Sacilor already holds 58% of the capital of Dillinger Hütte AG. Usinor/Sacilor, Dillinger Hütte and Saarstahl are major steel producers in the Community. The Saarland government will have a blocking minority interest of 27.5% in the new holding company, whilst Arbed will have 2.5%. The new holding company will control two subsidiaries, one for flat products (Dillinger Hütte), the other for long products (Saarstahl). The new concentration resulting from the agreements will have a market share of between 8.2% in the case of concrete reinforcing bars and 26.5% in the case of machine wire. However, it will have to face competition from the other major Community producers, and also from a large number of smaller producers. It will not therefore be in a position to determine prices or to restrict competition on the Community market in any other way.

---

[1] Decision of 24 July 1989, Bull. EC 7/8-1989, point 2.1.68.
[2] Decision of 11 September 1989, Bull. EC 9-1989, point 2.1.48.

§ 2 — Agreement in the coal and steel industry [1]

Ruhrkohle steelworks agreement

79. The Commission authorized the Essen based Ruhrkohle AG and six German steelworks to apply a collective set of agreements ('Hüttenverträge' or steelworks agreements) under which Ruhrkohle is to supply most of the steelworks' solid fuel requirements from 1 January 1989 to 31 December 1997. Such agreements were first concluded in 1969, when the steelworks concerned undertook to buy their solid fuel requirements exclusively from Ruhrkohle, which in turn guaranteed to supply such requirements, amounting in recent years to some 16 to 18 million tonnes per annum of coal equivalent. Under the new agreements, the exclusive procurement obligation is dropped, and the steelworks are free to use other solid fuels for specific purposes, for example petroleum coke, which can replace coking coal, and pulverize lignite, which can be injected into blast furnaces, thus replacing coke. The actual use of these fuels will be restricted only by technical requirements and price competitiveness. In addition, another German coal mine (Auguste Victoria) will to some extent participate in the scheme. The Commission recognized that the agreements meet the rationalization requirements set out in Article 65(2). The agreements were authorized for nine years. However, as Ruhrkohle receives State aid, authorized by Commission Decision 2064/86/ECSC, the decision stipulates that the authorization does not prejudice the Commission's position regarding State aids when the current State aids Decision expires of 31 December 1993.

---

[1] Decision of 30 March 1989, Bull. EC 3-1989, point 2.1.60; OJ L 101, 13.4.1989.

§ 3 — Concentrations in the coal industry

Raab Karcher/Cory Coal Trading [1]

80.   The Commission authorized the coal traders Raab Karcher, London, a wholly owned subsidiary of Raab Karcher, Essen, to acquire all the issued share capital of the London company Cory Coal Trading Ltd. As a result of the transaction, Raab Karcher's sales in the United Kingdom will increase significantly. However, the merger will not have any adverse effect on competition, since the nationalized producer, British Coal, has a very large share of the market, which amounted to 114 million tonnes in 1987. Raab Karcher is part of the VEBA group, which mainly trades in third country coal. Since this is frequently cheaper than Community coal, there may even be increased competition as a result of the merger.

Coalite Group/Anglo United [2]

81.   The Commission authorized Anglo United to acquire the entire share capital of Coalite Group. Anglo United is a coal distributor and has an important holding in a coal producer. Coalite is a manufacturer of smokeless fuels and a distributor of liquid and solid fuels. The acquisition will not have any effect on competition as regards the production of ECSC products. So far as distribution is concerned, the merger of Anglo United and Coalite will create one of the largest distributors in the United Kingdom. However, competition will continue to be assured by a large number of smaller wholesalers and by distributors owned or controlled by British Coal. The combined operations of Anglo United and Coalite will be equivalent to less than half those of British Coal, the nationalized coal producer.

---

[1]   Decision of 20 January 1989, Bull. EC 1-1989, point 2.1.31.
[2]   Decision of 24 July 1989, Bull. EC 7/8-1989, point 2.1.70.

§ 4 — ECSC inspections

82.   As in the past, a series of ECSC inspections were carried out on coal and steel productions subject to the levy (Articles 49 and 50 of the ECSC Treaty) and on the application of the pricing rules in the steel sector.

A total of 89 checks were carried out on declared production by coal and steel undertakings (Articles 49 and 50 of the ECSC Treaty), while 58 checks were carried out on the application of the pricing rules by steel undertakings (Article 60 of the ECSC Treaty). Each of the checks was followed up by a report, which was sent to the Directorates-General concerned, namely DG XVIII in the case of the levy and DG III in the case of prices.

Chapter III

Main cases decided by the Court of Justice

83. This report covers a total of 10 judgments, of which six were delivered in actions brought by firms against a formal decision of the Commission under Article 173 of the EEC Treaty, whilst the others were delivered under the preliminary ruling procedure of Article 177 of the EEC Treaty. The report does not cover orders of the President of the Court in competition matters.

§ 1 — Commission's powers regarding requests for information

84.   The two cases in question [1] relate to the inquiry which the Commission carried out in the thermoplastics sector. After having undertaken investigations based on Article 14(3) of Council Regulation No 17 of 6 February 1962 and having requested information under Article 11(1) of that Regulation, the Commission called upon the plaintiffs, by decisions taken pursuant to Article 11(5), to answer the questions asked in the request for information.

The two decisions were appealed against by the companies CdF Chimie and Solvay under Article 173 of the EEC Treaty.

Although the decisions were partly annulled, the judgments confirm the wide scope of the Commission's investigating powers. The Court rejected the argument put forward by the plaintiffs that the Commission, by adopting the decisions under Article 11(5) of Regulation No 17, had made illegal use of its power to request information from the firms that were the subject of the inquiry, since it was for the Commission to assess whether information was necessary in order to be able to identify an infringement of the competition rules. Even if the Commission already had evidence of an infringement, it could legitimately deem it necessary to request additional information that would allow it to identify more clearly the extent of the infringement, by determining its duration or the number of undertakings involved. In the case in point, the Court held that the Commission had not exceeded its discretionary powers of assessment.

In the light of these criteria, the Court then examined the questions which the Commission required the plaintiffs to answer. It concluded that most of the questions, notably those relating to the meetings of producers, which were designed merely to obtain factual information on the holding of the meetings and on the participants, were unobjectionable.

However, it took a different view of the questions which were such as to oblige the plaintiff to admit having participated in an agreement aimed at fixing selling prices so as to prevent or restrict competition or to declare having had the intention of achieving that objective, and of the questions that were such as to induce the plaintiff to admit participation in an agreement intended to restrict or control output or outlets or to share markets.

---

[1]   Case 374/87 *CdF Chimie* v *Commission,* judgment of 18 October 1989 and Case 27/88 *Solvay SA* v *Commission,* judgment of 18 October 1989.

The Court held that, through these latter questions, the Commission was obliging the firms to admit an infringement of Article 85 of the EEC Treaty. In so doing, the Commission infringed the plaintiff's right of defence and disregarded the rules on the burden of proof.

In the light of this judgment, it is clear that firms do not have a 'right to silence', nor even the right to refuse to reply to a request for information on the grounds that their answers would facilitate the Commission's task in demonstrating the existence of an infringement.

§ 2 — Investigating powers of the Commission

85.   This question was dealt with in three judgments.[1] Some factual background is required before analysing the significance of the judgments.

On 15 January 1987, pursuant to Article 14(3) of Regulation No 17 of 6 February 1962, the Commission adopted a series of decisions ordering various firms to submit to investigations into their possible participation in agreements or concerted practices under which prices and quotas or sales objectives for PVC and polyethylene in the Community had been fixed.

Hoechst categorically refused on several occasions to submit to the investigation on the grounds that what was involved was a search that violated the rights of defence and the inviolability of domicile, protection of which meant that the investigation could take place only on the basis of a prior court order.

It was not until 2 April 1987 that the company complied, after the Commission, acting on the basis of Article 14(6) of Regulation No 17, had requested assistance from the Bundeskartellamt, which obtained a search warrant for the Commission from the Frankfurt Amtsgericht.

In the meantime, by decision of 3 February 1987, adopted pursuant to Article 16(1)(d) of Regulation No 17, the Commission imposed on Hoechst a periodic penalty payment of 1 000 ECU per day in order to compel it to submit to the investigation ordered. The final amount of the periodic penalty payment was fixed at ECU 55 000 by decision adopted by the Commission pursuant to Article 16(2) of Regulation No 17.

Dow Benelux for its part expressed objections against an investigation decision taken by the Commission, but did not oppose its implementation. Indeed, it provided assistance to the Commission officials.

After the Commission officials had outlined to them orally and in writing their rights and duties as set out in Articles 14, 15 and 16 of Regulation No 17, the companies Iberica, Alcudia and EMP not only agreed to the investigation, but cooperated actively in it.

In the three judgments, the Court upheld the Commission position. The three main points brought out by the judgments are set out below.

---

[1]   Cases 46/87 and 227/88 *Hoechst AG* v *Commission,* judgment of 21 September 1989.
Cases 97, 98 and 99/87 *Dow Chemical, J. Bericau Alcudia and EMP* v *Commission,* judgment of 17 October 1989.
Case 85/87 *Dow Benelux NV* v *Commission,* judgment of 17 October 1989.

(i) The degree to which grounds should be provided for an investigation decision

86. In the *Hoechst* Case, the plaintiff argued that the investigation decision infringed Article 190 of the Treaty and Article 14(3) of Regulation No 17, since it lacked precision, notably as regards the subject matter and purpose of the investigation.

In this respect, the Court pointed out that the requirement incumbent on the Commission, pursuant to Article 14(3), to specify the subject matter and purpose of the investigation constituted a fundamental guarantee of the rights of defence of the undertakings concerned. It followed that the extent of the requirement to specify the grounds for investigation decisions could not be restricted on the basis of considerations relating to the effectiveness of the investigation. On this subject, the Court held that, while the Commission was not required to communicate to the addressee of an investigation decision all the information it had concerning presumed infringements or to give a strict legal evaluation of such infringements, it did have to indicate clearly the presumptions which it intended to investigate.

The Court held that, while the grounds specified for the investigation decision were drafted in very general terms which should have been made more precise and were thus open to criticism in this respect, they did nevertheless contain the essential elements required by Article 14(3) of Regulation No 17.

In its Dow Chemical Iberica judgment, the Court, rejecting the argument that adequate grounds had not been specified for the investigation decisions, held that neither the precise definition of the market in question, nor the exact legal assessment of the presumed infringements and the indication of the period during which such infringements took place were indispensable in an investigation decision provided that the investigation decision contained the essential elements provided for in Article 14(3) of Regulation No 17.

(ii) The extent of the Commission's investigating powers

87. Pursuant to Article 14(1) of Regulation No 17, 'the Commission may undertake all necessary investigations into undertakings and associations of undertakings. To this end the officials authorized by the Commission are empowered:

(a) to examine the books and other business records;

(b) to take copies of or extracts from the books and business records;

(c) to ask for oral explanations on-the-spot;

(d) to enter any premises, land and means of transport of undertakings'.

In the cases in question, the Commission had opted for surprise investigations ordered by decision pursuant to Article 14(3). Investigating powers are the same whether ordered by decision or by authorization in writing. The main difference is that, pursuant to Article 14(3), 'undertakings... shall submit to investigations ordered by decision of the Commission'.

Pursuant to Article 14(6), where an undertaking opposes an investigation ordered by decision, the Member State concerned must afford the necessary assistance to the officials authorized by the Commission to enable them to make their investigation.

Both the purpose of Regulation No 17 and the powers conferred on Commission officials under Article 14 show that investigations can have very wide scope.

The Court firstly pointed out that the right to enter the premises of undertakings was of particular importance. Such right, if it were to be effective, implied the right to look for various items of information that were not yet known or fully identified. Without such a right, it would be impossible for the Commission to obtain the information necessary for the investigation if it were confronted with a refusal to collaborate or an attitude of obstruction on the part of the undertakings concerned.

The Court thus clearly confirmed that the powers of investigation under Article 14 were not confined to passive investigation on the part of the Commission officials, but could comprise an active search for evidence not fully known at the time the search was carried out.

In its Dow Chemical Iberica judgment, the Court held that acts preceding the adoption of a decision could not affect the validity of the decision since, even if the conduct of the Commission's officials was not in accordance with the powers they held under Regulation No 17, this fact could not affect the legality of such decisions.

In the case of investigations carried out with the collaboration of the undertakings concerned, the Commission's officials had the right to have the documents which they requested presented to them, to enter the premises which they designated and to have the content of the furniture which they indicated shown to them. However, they could not force access to premises or to furniture or compel the staff of the undertaking to afford them such access nor could they undertake searches without the authorization of the management of the undertaking (Hoechst judgment referring to above). In the case of investigations which met with opposition from the undertakings concerned, the Commission officials could, without the collaboration of the undertaking, seek all the information necessary for the investigation with the assistance of the national authorities (Hoechst judgment).

(iii) The assistance of the national authorities during investigations

88.   The court pointed out that it was for each Member State to determine the conditions under which the assistance of the national authorities was afforded to the Commission's officials. In this respect the Member States were required to ensure the effectiveness of the Commission's action. It was national law which laid down the appropriate procedural arrangements for ensuring that the rights of undertakings were observed (Hoechst judgment).

The Commission must therefore, in the such cases, submit to the procedural guarantees laid down for this purpose by national law and must make sure that the authority competent under national law had all the facts necessary to allow it to exercise its own particular control. However, the Court emphasized that such authority, whether or not judicial, could not substitute its own assessment of whether the investigations ordered were necessary for that of the Commission, whose factual and legal assessments were subject only to control as to legality by the Court of Justice. However, it did fall within the powers of the national authority to examine, after having established the correctness of the investigation decision, whether the measures of constraint envisaged were not arbitrary or excessive in relation to the subject matter of the investigation and to ensure that the rules of national law were complied with in carrying out such measures.

In the light of the above, the Court held that the investigation decision (the subject of the appeal) authorizing the Commission's officials to implement the procedure did not exceed the powers conferred on them under Article 14 of Regulation No 17.

§3 — Application of Article 85 to a national cartel and effect on trade between Member States

89.   In its Belasco judgment, [1] the court rejected all the arguments put forward by the plaintiffs in support of their appeal against the Commission Decision finding that the national cartel entered into by seven Belgian producers of roofing felt had infringed Article 85 of the Treaty. [2]

The seven producers, who together held some 60% of the Belgian market, had concluded an agreement which established production quotas for each of them and a system of checks and compensation where these were exceeded, and which also was designed to establish common price lists, terms of sale and discounts, provided for joint promotional measures, the use of a joint trade mark and the production of standardized products. The parties had also set themselves the objective of defending and promoting their interests jointly as far as possible, notably in the event of increased competition from foreign firms, the establishment of new firms or the development of substitute products.

The agreement was implemented through regular general meetings of the members and with the assistance of their professional association, Belasco, from 1 January 1978 to 9 April 1984.

On all points, the Court upheld the Commission's assessment regarding the restrictive object and effect of the various provisions of the agreement. The Commission Decision was extremely precise, particularly as regards its assessment of the effects of some of the provisions, such as the joint setting of discounts. In its decision, the Commission conceded that the parties' compliance with some of the provisions or measures decided on could not be materially proved.

Although the agreement was concluded between producers in a single Member State and concerned only the marketing of products in that Member State, the Commission had taken the view that, even though the agreement did not make any specific provision for combating foreign competition, the agreement was liable to affect trade between Member States. Since its purpose was to preserve the market shares of the parties, it was necessarily liable to affect the scope for competitors from other Member States to develop their sales.

This point was upheld by the Court. In the Court's view, the fact that an agreement had as its object only the marketing of products in a single Member

---

[1]   Case 246/86 Belasco SA v Commission, judgment of 11 July 1989.
[2]   Decision of 10 July 1986, OJ L 232, 19.8.1986. Sixteenth Competition Report, point 48.

State did not mean that trade between Member States could not be affected. The Court held that, where the market was open to imports, the members of a national price cartel could preserve their market shares only if they ensured protection against foreign competition. The Court noted in this respect the specific provisions and the measures taken to combat foreign competition and stressed that the size of the market shares held meant that such measures could be made effective.

Accordingly, although the cartel related only to the marketing of products in a single Member State, the Court held that it could have a significant influence on intra-Community trade.

§ 4 — Application of the competition rules to air transport

90.   The Bundesgerichtshof referred three questions for a preliminary ruling, pursuant to Article 177, on the interpretation of Article 5, 85, 86, 88, 89 and 90 of the Treaty, for the purposes of assessing the compatibility of certain practices regarding the setting of fares for passengers on scheduled flights.

The questions arose in proceedings against two travel agencies charged before the German courts with having infringed national law on air transport, which prohibits the charging, on German territory, of fares not approved by the relevant Federal Ministry, on the grounds that the prices of the air tickets which they sold were lower than the approved fares charged by their competitors.

Regulation No 3975/87, [1] which lays down the procedure for applying Articles 85 and 86 to undertakings in the air transport sector, covers only air transport between Community airports. However, the case in question related to air transport within one Member State and to air transport between a Member State and a non-Community country.

On this question, the Court gave the same ruling as in its Asjes judgment, [2] delivered at a time when Community rules did not exist, namely that, in such instances, the rules on the setting of fares remained subject to the transitional provisions provided for in Articles 88 and 89 of the Treaty.

The main points clarified by the judgment [3] are as follows:

(i) The direct effect of Article 86

91.   The Court must in future distinguish in accordance with the geographical scope of the agreement in question. Thus, Article 85 is directly applicable to intra-Community fare agreements.

The implementing Regulation No 3975/87, which covers international air transport between Community airports, has given Article 85 an immediate direct effect in its scope of application.

---

[1]   Council Regulation No 3975/87 of 14 December 1987 laying down the procedure for the application of the rules of competition to undertakings in the air transport sector, OJ L 374, 31.12.1987, p. 1. Seventeenth Competition Report, points 43-45.

[2]   Joined Cases 209 to 213/84 *Ministère Public* v *Asjes*, OJ C 318, 11.12.1986, p. 4. Sixteenth Competition Report, points 89-91.

[3]   Case 66/86 *Ahmed Saeed Flugreisen and Silverline*, judgment of 11 April 1989.

In the case of fare agreements within a Member State or between a Member State and a non-Community country, the Court was confronted with the situation that had prevailed before 1987, since the Regulation does not cover such cases.

The Court reverted to the line it had adopted in its judgment of 30 April 1986: 'Article 85 is applicable to such fare agreements, but national courts may find that there has been an infringement (Article 85(1)) and declare the agreement void (Article 85(2)) only if the competent authority of a Member State (pursuant to Article 88) or the Commission (pursuant to Article 89) have previously established that Article 85 is applicable.'

*(ii) The conditions for applying Article 86 outside
        the scope of application of Regulation No 3975/87*

92.   The Court's reasoning here is different, since there cannot be any exemption for an abuse of a dominant position. Consequently, Article 86 is directly applicable to the whole of the air transport sector.

The Court also gives some indication of what might be considered an abuse, within the meaning of Article 86, in the fares charged by a carrier: a fare is abusive if it involves unfair transport conditions, either in respect of travellers (the fare is too high), or in respect of competitors (the fare is too low, with the aim of eliminating from the market undertakings not party to the agreement).

It may also be concluded from the judgment that fares worked out jointly by two undertakings could involve abuse of a joint dominant position if the fares were excessively high or low.

To the extent that the new Council Regulations provide that Article 86 may be applicable to a concerted practice that had initially been granted either a block exemption or an individual exemption obtained under the position procedure, Article 86 may in certain cases apply to the charging of fares on a given route or routes involving scheduled flights, where such fares have been set on the basis of bilateral or multilateral agreements concluded between air carriers, if the conditions laid down in Article 86 are met.

*(iii) The legality of the approval procedure in the light
        of Articles 5 and 90 of the Treaty*

93.   The third question referred by the Bundesgerichtshof concerns the legality of the approval granted by the supervisory authority in a Member State for fares that are contrary to Article 85(1) or Article 86 of the Treaty. The

Bundesgerichtshof asked in particular whether such approval was not incompatible with the second paragraph of Article 5 and with Article 90(1) of the Treaty, even though the Commission has not criticized such approval on the basis of Article 90(3).

In this respect, it should be noted firstly that, in accordance with well-established case-law of the Court, [1] although the competition rules provided for in Articles 85 and 86 concern the conduct of undertakings and not measures taken by the authorities of Member States, Article 5 of the Treaty nevertheless requires the authorities of the Member States not to take or maintain in force measures which could thwart the full effectiveness of such rules. This would be the case if a Member State imposed or promoted the conclusion of agreements, decisions and concerted practices that were contrary to Article 85 or reinforced their effects.

It must be concluded from this that the air transport authorities' approval of tariff agreements that are contrary to Article 5(1) is not compatible with Community law, and in particular with Article 5 of the Treaty. It also follows from this that the air transport authorities must abstain from any measure which could be seen as encouraging the airlines to conclude tariff agreements that infringe the Treaty. In the particular case of fares for scheduled flights, this interpretation is confirmed by Article 90(1) of the Treaty.

If, consequently, the new rules laid down by the Council and by the Commission allow the Community institutions and the authorities of the Member States the freedom to get airlines to hold reciprocal consultations on the fares to be charged on certain scheduled services, the Treaty formally prohibits them from promoting, in whatever form, the carrying out of agreements or concerted practices on air fares that are contrary to Article 85(1) or, as the case may be, Article 86.

Similarly, Article 90(2) could have consequences for decisions taken by the air transport authorities regarding the approval of fares. Article 90(2) may apply to air carriers which are obliged by the public authorities to operate routes which are not commercially profitable, but whose operation is necessary in the general interest. In each particular case, it is for the competent national administrative authorities or courts to check whether the air transport company concerned has actually been entrusted with the operation of such routes by an act of the public authorities.

---

[1]   On this point, see the *Asjes* judgment, Joined Cases 209 to 213/84, 30.4.1986. Sixth Competition Report, point 93, and Fifteenth Competition Report, points 91 to 93.

However, in order that the effect of the competition rules may be restricted, in accordance with Article 90(2), by the needs arising from the performance of a task in the general interest, the national authorities responsible for approving fares and the courts to which disputes in such matters are referred must be able to determine what is the exact nature of the needs in question and what is the impact of these on the structure of the fares charged by the airlines concerned.

Unless there is effective transparency in the structure of fares, it is difficult, or indeed impossible, to assess the influence of a task in the general interest on the application of the competition rules to fares.

§ 5 — Application of Articles 85(1) and 86 to the exercise of copyright

94. In its judgments in the *Ministère public* v *Tournier*[1] and *Lucazean/Sacem*[2] Cases, the Court gave a ruling, at the request of the Cour d'Appel of Aix-en-Provence and the Cour d'Appel du Tribunal de Grande Instance of Poitiers, on the compatibility with Article 85(1) of the reciprocal representation agreements concluded between copyright management societies of the Member States and on the applicability of Article 86 to the fees imposed by a society in a dominant position.

The Court of Justice held that such contracts were contracts for the performance of services and were not in themselves restrictive of competition within the meaning of Article 85(1) of the Treaty. They could be if it were established that, through concerted practices, national copyright management societies refused users established in another Member State direct access to their own repertory. Assessment of this was for the national courts.

The mere fact of finding that copyright management societies refused in parallel to this to license their repertory directly to discotheques in another Member State did not allow it to be inferred that there was a concerted practice between the copyright management societies. Any parallel features in the conduct could be explained by reasons other than concerted practices.

As regards Article 86, the questions referred for a preliminary ruling were what criteria should be applied in determining whether a copyright management society was imposing unfair conditions and whether, in the case in point, the rate of 8.25% of turnover set by Sacem in respect of a discotheque could be regarded as an abuse. The Court confirmed that comparison with the rates applied by copyright management societies in other Member States was an acceptable method for deciding on the fairness of a condition applied by a society in a dominant position. The Court held that, if the charges applied by such a society were significantly higher than those in the other Member States, the comparison between charge levels being carried out on a homogeneous basis, such difference must be regarded as evidence of abuse of a dominant position. It was then for the undertaking in question to justify the difference,

---

[1] Case 395/87, judgment of 13 July 1989.
[2] Joined Cases 110/88, 241/88, and 242/88, judgment of 13 July 1989.

on the basis of the objective divergences between the situation in the Member State concerned and that prevailing in all the other Member States.

This judgment follows on from the case-law already laid down by the Court of Justice, [1] in which it established the principle that the level of the fees to be paid to Sacem by way of copyright for the public performance of musical works could constitute an abuse if it proved to be unfair. ·

---

1   Case 402/85 *Basset* v *Sacem*, judgment of 9 April 1987, Seventeenth Competition Report, point 108.

§ 6 — Application of Article 85(1) to certain clauses in patent licensing agreements

95.   In its judgments in the *Kai Ottung* v *Klee and Weilbach* Case, [1] the Court of Justice gave a ruling, at the request of the Sø-og Handelsret, on the compatibility with Article 85(1) of a clause under which the grantee of a patent licence is required to pay royalties for an indeterminate period, even after the expiry of the patent. The Court held that, as such, an obligation to continue to pay royalties after the expiry of the patent can only result from the licensing agreement where the agreement either does not give the licensee the right to terminate the agreement subject to a reasonable period of notice or tries to restrict the licensee's freedom of action after termination. If such were the case, the agreement could, in the light of its economic and legal context, restrict competition within the meaning of Article 85(1).

However, where the licensee is free to terminate the agreement subject to a reasonable period of notice, an obligation to pay royalties throughout the period of validity of the agreement does not fall within the scope of the ban laid down in Article 85(1).

The Court also held that a clause prohibiting competition in the manufacture and marketing of the products covered by the licensing agreement imposed a competitive disadvantage on the licensee, since the prohibition placed the licensee in a less favourable position than his competitors, who, once the period of validity of the patent had expired, could manufacture and market the products concerned as they wished. Accordingly, in the light of the legal and economic contexts in which the agreement was concluded, the clause in question could restrict competition within the meaning of Article 85(1).

---

[1]   Case 320/87, judgment of 12 May 1989.

§ 7 — Procedural matters and observance of the rights of defence

96.   A number of judgments [1] dealt with important procedural matters and the Commission's observance of the rights of undertakings to defend themselves. Thus, the Court pointed out that implementation of proceedings against restrictive agreements and abuses of dominant positions must reconcile efficiency in the adducement of proof with the necessary safeguard of the rights of defence of undertakings.

Thus, certain restrictions on the Commission's powers of investigation during preliminary inquiries may result from the need to ensure observance of the rights of the defence, which the Court held to be a fundamental principle of the Community's legal order. [2]

Nevertheless, during the inquiry procedure, Regulation No 17 provides expressly for only certain specific guarantees for the undertaking which is the subject of the inquiry.

In this respect, the Court held that, [3] while the rights of the defence must be observed in administrative procedures which might lead to the imposition of penalties, it was important to ensure that such rights were not irreversibly comprised in preliminary inquiry procedures, which could be decisive in establishing proof of the unlawfulness of conduct on the part of undertakings.

It was therefore for the Commission to indicate clearly the subject matter and purpose of the investigation, so that the undertakings concerned were able to grasp the scope of their duty to collaborate, while at the same time preserving their right of defence. [4]

In addition, in the Dow Benelux judgment, [5] the Court concluded that it was not prohibited for the Commission to initiate inquiry proceedings in order to check the correctness of or to supplement information which had come to its knowledge during a previous investigation.

Furthermore, under the procedure for requesting information provided for in Regulation No 17, although the undertaking which is the subject of an investi-

---

1   Notably the Hoechst, Dow Benelux and Solvay judgments.
2   Case 322/81 *Michelin* v *Commission* [1983] ECR 3461, paragraph 7.
3   Cases 46/47 and 227/88 *Hoechst* v *Commission*, judgment of 21 September 1989.
4   Ibid.
5   See also point 85 of this Report.

gation measure cannot elude the measure requiring it to provide such information, it does not have to admit expressly the existence of the infringement, whose proof it is up to the Commission to establish. [1]

In order not to delay the date of adoption of a decision imposing a periodic penalty payment on an undertaking which had refused to submit to an investigation, the Court — upholding the Commission's position — ruled that the hearing of the undertaking and the consultation of the Advisory Committee on Restrictive Practices and Dominant Positions could take place prior to the adoption of the decision setting the final amount of the periodic penalty payment, if such hearing and such consultation had not taken place before the decision imposing the periodic penalty payment. [2]

Lastly, in the Belasco judgment, [3] the Court upheld the Commission's view in the calculation of the amount of the fines imposed. The Commission had based its calculation on the total turnover of each of the undertakings concerned and on its turnover from the supply of roofing felt in Belgium and, in the case of Belasco, on its annual expenditure. The Commission had also taken the view that, amongst the elements making up the cartel, the restrictions concerning prices and market sharing and the joint measures between the competitors were amongst the most serious infringements of free competition.

---

[1] Case 27/88 *Solvay* v *Commission,* judgment of 18 October 1989.
[2] Cases 46/87 and 227/88 *Hoechst* v *Commission.*
[3] Case 246/86 *Belasco* v *Commission,* judgment of 11 July 1989.

Chapter IV

Competition law in the Member States

§ 1 — Legislative developments in the Member States

97.   In the Federal Republic of Germany, the law against restraints of competition (Gesetz gegen Wettbewerbsbeschränkungen — GWB) was amended by the Fifth Amending Law of 22 December 1989[1] which entered into force on 1 January 1990. The amending law tightens the existing instruments of merger and conduct control in trade and industry. Special provisions that are no longer justified in the transport, banking and insurance and public utilities sectors, which enjoy exemptions from competition law are removed. In addition, the conditions for applying competition law are improved and unnecessary notification requirements abolished. In detail, the following changes have been introduced:

(i)   Control of buyer concentration of power, particularly in merger control in the distributive trades, has been improved by extending the statutory criteria for determining the existence of a dominant market position to include additional demand related elements.[2]

(ii)   The protection of small and medium-sized businesses against unfair competition by undertakings in a dominant position has been made more effective by simplifying the statutory rules and by giving the previous prohibition rules the force of *per se* illegality.[3]

(iii) The obligation to supply, to which undertakings in a strong but not dominant market position are subject, has been restricted to conduct *vis-à-vis* small and medium-sized businesses through amendment of the prohibition of discrimination.[4]

---

[1]   Kartellgesetznovelle BGB1. I S. 2486.
[2]   §22(1).
[3]   §26(4) and (5).
[4]   §26(2).

(iv)   Exemption from the ban on cartels has been introduced for cooperative joint purchasing arrangements that help to improve the competitiveness of small and medium-sized businesses. [1]

(v)   The large number of exemptions applying to transport has been reduced. [2]

(vi)   A rule of *per se* prohibition has been introduced in place of the previous principle of abuse in the banking and insurance sectors. [3]

(vii)   In the electricity supply sector, the statutory limitation of the duration of demarcation contracts has been made more effective so that such contracts no longer stand in the way of a change of supplier when concession contracts expire. The rules governing common carriage have been made more flexible. [4]

(viii)   The definition of mergers has been improved so as to prevent attempts to evade the law. [5]

(ix)   The notification requirement in company mergers has been narrowed. [6]

(x)   The procedural rules have been adjusted to help resolve conflicts between business secrecy and the right of audience in complaint proceedings. [7]

(xi)   The database of the Monopolies Commission has been improved. [8]

The new rules governing the powers of the Federal Cartel Office (Bundeskartellamt) in applying Community competition law [9] are of particular importance. The amendments were made necessary, firstly, by a decision by the Berlin Court of Appeal (Kammergericht)[10] on 4 November 1988 in which it held that the Federal Cartel did not have the power to apply Community law.

Secondly, by clarifying important questions (the role of the national authorities and the powers of the Commission) in the Hoechst Case,[11] the Court of Justice of the European Communities made it possible to establish clearer provisions governing these questions.

---

[1]   §5 c.
[2]   §99.
[3]   §102.
[4]   §103, 103a.
[5]   §23(2).
[6]   §23(1) and (5).
[7]   §70 and 71.
[8]   §24 c.
[9]   §47.
[10]   Kart. 11/88, KG WuW/E OLG 4291 'Landegebühr'.
[11]   Cases 46/87 and 227/88, judgment of 21.9.1989.

The Federal Cartel Office is now the competent authority within the meaning of Articles 88 and 89 of the EEC Treaty and in all cases in which action by the national authorities is provided for in present and future regulations based on Article 87 of the EEC Treaty.

Where it applies Community law or assists the Commission, the Federal Cartel Office has the same powers as for the implementation of national competition law. However, it cannot impose fines for infringement of Articles 85 and 86 of the EEC Treaty.

All legal actions arising from Articles 85 and 86 of the EEC Treaty come under the exclusive competence of the Regional Courts (Landgerichte), then of the Cartel Panels (Kartellsenate) in the Higher Regional Courts (Oberlandesgerichte) and Federal High Court (Bundesgerichtshof). These courts must inform the Federal Cartel Office of all such cases. The latter has the right to take part in the proceedings. These rules improve the transparency of the implementation of Community competition law by the German civil courts. In particular, it enables the Federal Cartel Office to contribute its experience in such proceedings.

The law on the implementation of Regulation No 17 of the Council of the European Communities, which had been superseded as a result of the new rules on the powers of the Federal Cartel Office, was repealed.

98.   In Belgium a new draft law on concerted practices, abuses of dominant positions and mergers, embodying and extending the previous draft which had lapsed, [1] is currrectly being examined by the Belgian Council of Ministers.

99.   In June 1989, a new Competition Act was passed by the Danish Parliament. [2] The Act came into force on 1 January 1990, and from the same date, the Monopolies Act and Prices and Profits Act were repealed. The administration of the Competition Act is the responsibility of the Competition Board (Konkurrenceradet) consisting of a chairman appointed by the King and 14 members appointed by the Minister for Industry.

The purpose of the new legislation is to increase competition and hence to strengthen the effectiveness of production and distribution of goods and services. Thus, in the light of increasing internationalization of business, the wider aim

---

[1]   See Seventeenth Competition Report, point 112.
[2]   Law No 370 of 7 June 1989. The law is based upon Report No 1075 'From the Monopoly Act to the Competition Act — a Modernization of the Monopoly Act and the Prices and Profits Act', published by the Minister for Industry in August 1986.

is to support the development of a market structure based on competition and efficiency.

The principal means identified for achieving this aim is by ensuring transparency — providing easy and equitable access to information about prices, business terms and other matters — for manufacturers, dealers and consumers. With this objective in mind, the Act on Public Access to Documents and Administrative Files applies to the administration of the Competition Act with only a few exceptions.

The Competition Act applies to private enterprises (including financial institutions and insurance companies), associations of enterprises and, with certain limitations, public and publicly regulated companies.

As with the Monopolies Act, the Competition Act respects the fundamental right to enter into agreements. Accordingly, it is based upon the concepts of 'abuse and control'. Agreements and decisions, including tacit agreements and concerted practices, which exert or may exert a dominant influence on a market must be notified to the Competition Board within 14 days of their being concluded. Changes to such agreements are subject to the same notification requirement. Lack of notification entails invalidity and the Competition Board may, in such instances, impose a daily or weekly fine on the parties concerned. Fines may also be imposed for infringements of other provisions of the Act.

In accordance with the principle of transparency, the Competition Board may publish the results of its investigations into markets and their structure, as well as information about prices, discounts, and other relevant facts, where this will assist the strengthening of competition. The Board may, furthermore:

(i)   order an undertaking within a specified time-limit and for a period not exceeding two years, to supply up-to-date reports containing information on prices, profits, discounts, bonuses, business terms, financial relations etc.;

(ii) lay down requirements for invoicing and the documenting of price calculations;

(iii) lay down requirements for the marking and display of prices and quantities.

The Board is empowered to demand information and, on obtaining a court order, to carry out the necessary on-the-spot investigations.

The essential condition for intervention is that a restrictive practice in a particular market has or may have a harmful effect upon competition which adversely affects efficiency in the production or distribution of goods or services, or which amounts to a restraint of trade.

Further powers conferred on the Board allow it to take measures against the harmful effects of anti-competitive practices. Thus, the Board may make an order annulling an agreement. Orders for total or partial annulment may only be made if the Board has first attempted to terminate the harmful effects through negotiation. Where annulment does not have the desired effect, the Board may, in the alternative, order an undertaking to supply goods or services to another, even where this overrides existing rights under a sole agency agreement, if such a measure is found to be necessary to create effective competition.

Also in the alternative, the Board may stipulate, for periods of up to one year at a time, maximum prices, maximum profits or calculation requirements where a price or profit clearly exceeds what would be obtainable in a market with effective competition.

The prohibition of resale price maintenance is continued under the new legislation with infringements punishable by fine. In order to emphasize that resellers are free to fix their prices, it is provided that where recommended prices are indicated, the fact that they are recommended shall be stated.

As regards public, and publicly regulated enterprises, the Competitive Board may apply to the competent public authority drawing attention to the potentially anti-competitive effects of the practice in question. Such applications will be published.

Decisions of the Competition Board may be appealed to the Competition Appeals Tribunal within a time-limit of four weeks. The Tribunal consists of a Supreme Court judge as chairman and two other members with proficiency in economics and law respectively. Decisions not to deal with particular cases, and regarding the publication of investigations, and of price information cannot be appealed. Decisions of the Competition Appeals Tribunal may be brought before the High Court within a time-limit of eight weeks. The limitation period for criminal liability is five years.

100.   In March, the Danish Parliament enacted a law [1] amending the 1972 Law on the control of the observance of EEC rules on monopolies and the anti-competitive practices. [2] The legal changes should be seen against the background of Council Regulations 4056/86 and 3975/87 which laid down the procedures for the application of Articles 85 and 86 of the EEC Treaty to

---

[1]   Law No 160 of 15 May 1989.
[2]   Law No 505 of 29 November 1972.

maritime transport and air transport respectively. These regulations provide for the designation in each Member State of a competent authority to assist the EC Commission in control investigations.

Under the 1972 law, the Monopolies Control Authority (Monopoltilsynet) was designated to assist the European Commission in investigations. The successor to this authority, the Competition Board (Konkurrenceradet) is made responsible for this task under Law No 160, although work on legal proposals must be undertaken in consultation with the Ministry of Traffic and Communications in respect of air transport and with the Industry Ministry in respect of sea transport.

101.   In Spain, Law 16/1989 of 17 July 1989 [1] on the protection of competition which replaced the previsious law against anti-competitive practices, [2] entered into force on 8 August 1989. The.purpose of the new law is to adjust to the changes which have taken place in recent years in the field of competition policy in Spain. The differences between the old and the new law as regards substance, procedures and powers are summarized below.

As regards substance the following changes are introduced:

(i)   a ban on restrictive agreements between undertakings, even if they are not put into effect;

(ii)   the possibility of block exemption for certain specified types of agreement;

(iii) a ban on abuses of dominant position;

(iv)   extension of the scope of the law to unfair acts which affect the public interest;

(v)   the establishment of merger control;

(vi)   the possibility of intervention in the field of State aids.

As regards powers, two separate bodies are maintained: one for examining matters and the other for taking decisions ('Servicio de Defensa de la Competencia' and 'Tribunal de Defensa de la Competencia'). The Tribunal is independent of the government with judges appointed for fixed periods of six years, i.e. for a longer period than the term of the Parliament. The 'Consejo de Defensa de la Competencia' is abolished.

---

[1]   Published in the *Boletin Oficial del Estado* of 18.7.1989.
[2]   Law 110/1963, 20.7.1963.

Lastly, the following differences should be noted in terms of procedure:

(i)   investigatory powers lie with the 'Servicio de Defensa de la Competencia';

(ii)   the two abovementioned bodies may impose fines on parties which refuse to provide information or which supply incorrect or misleading information;

(iii) a limitation period is introduced;

(iv)   appeals to the Tribunal sitting in plenary session are abolished;

(v)   provision is made for the adoption of preventive measures;

(vi)   the Tribunal may itself impose fines for infringements of Law 16/1989 without government intervention;

(vii) the processing of cases during the two phases of examination and decision-making has been simplified.

102.   During 1989, the following regulatory or legislative changes took place in the field of competition in France:

(i)   Law No 89-421 of 23 June 1989 on certain commercial practices (door-to-door sales, credit transactions). The purpose of the law is to reinforce consumer protection and to bring French law into line with the Community Directives of 20 december 1985 and 22 December 1986.

(ii)   Decree of 22 December 1989 on clearance sales, adopted on the basis of Article 28 of Order No 86-1243 of 1 September 1986. The Decree supplements the provisions of Decree No 89-690 of 22 December 1989, wich lays down a period of two months for clearance sales. The Decree is designed to ensure better information for consumers and to limit the use of the term 'sales' to transactions which actually fulfil the conditions associated with a clearance sale.

(iii) Decree of 17 April 1989, wich transposed into French law the Community Directive of 22 March 1988 on the opening up of public supply contracts to competition. A second decree is being drawn up for the purpose of implementing the Community Directive of 18 July 1989 on public works contracts.

(iv)   Decree of 26 April 1989 concerning the initial placing on the market of sea fisheries products and the rules governing the communication of statistics. The decree was adopted pursuant to the Community Regulations on the common organization of fishery products.

The public authorities also continued to examine the closed professions so as to promote competition in cases where long-established rules tend to prevent free competition, and in order to adapt such professions to the single market. These have included pharmacists (method of remuneration, scope of monopoly) and lawyers/legal advisers in respect of which a draft law is being drawn up.

103. No legislative changes were made in Ireland in the competition field during 1989. However, the programme for government contains a commitment that legislation will be introduced to give effect in domestic law to provisions similar to Articles 85 and 86 of the EEC Treaty. The Fair Trade Commission has furnished a report to the Minister for Industry and Commerce on this issue and preparation of the legislation is proceeding.

104. In Luxembourg, the Law of 20 April 1989 [1] reorganized the powers of investigation into restrictive trade practices. Otherwise, the Law of 17 June 1970 remained unchanged. In addition, the Law of 27 November 1986 on unfair competition and the Law of 16 July 1987 on door-to-door trading, itinerant trading, display of goods and soliciting for orders, were implemented.

105. In the Netherlands, a law extending the scope for appeal by affected third parties against arrangements established under the Law on economic competition entered into force on 24 March 1989. The new law also allows such persons to appeal in cases of failure to exercise decision-making powers.

On 14 November 1989, a law was adopted amending the Law on economic competition with regard to resale price maintenance. The new law prohibits collective resale maintenance, though exemptions may be allowed where required by the general interest. Individual resale price maintenance is prohibited in respect of such goods as are to be specified by administrative measure. The law is to enter into force by 15 June 1990.

106. In Portugal, Decree-Law No 329-A/89 amending Decree-Law 422/83 was approved on 26 December. Under the new provisions, minimum prices may not be imposed for the sale of those schoolbooks and related materials which require to be used during the period up to the statutory school-leaving age. The aim is to extend the benefits of competition to consumers of the end product in this area.

---

[1]   See Eighteenth Competition Report, point 145.

107.   In the United Kingdom a number of legislative changes took place in the field of competition during 1989. The Companies Act introduced improvements to the procedures for examining mergers, including:

(i)   a voluntary but formal system for prenotification to the Director-General of Fair Trading (DGFT) of proposed mergers, with clearance normally within four weeks for cases which the Secretary of State decides not to refer to the Monopolies and Mergers Commission (MMC);

(ii)   powers for the DGFT to obtain, and the Secretary of State to accept, legally binding undertakings from parties to divest part of a merged business as an alternative to a reference to the MMC;

(iii)   a power to charge fees to recover the costs of merger control.

These changes were originally proposed in a policy document 'Mergers policy: A Department of Trade and Industry paper on the policy and procedures of merger control' published in March 1988.[1] This followed a review of UK mergers policy, which concluded that the main criterion in deciding whether to refer mergers to the MMC for detailed examination should continue to be their effect on competition. The Companies Act also introduced:

(i)   a prohibition on the acquisition by parties to a proposed merger, of shares in one another during the period of an MMC investigation, other than with the consent of the Secretary of State;

(ii)   improved provisions for examining cases where there is a gradual build-up of shareholdings and it is not obvious when the crucial degree of control is reached;

(iii)   a new offence of giving false or misleading information to the competition authorities;

(iv)   improved requirements relating to company accounting for mergers and acquisitions;

(v)   pursuant to the Eighth Directive on Company Law, new provisions for the regulation of auditors and for assessment of the effects on competition of the rules made by accountancy bodies under the Act;

(vi)   changes to the test applied for recognition of a self-regulating organization or professional body under the Financial Services Act 1986.

A policy document entitled 'Opening markets: New policy on restrictive trade practices',[2] which was published in July, proposed a fundamental reform of

---

[1]   See Eighteenth Competition Report, point 158.
[2]   Cm 727.

UK restrictive practices legislation. The existing system, which requires the registration of agreements which are restrictive in form, would be abolished. Under the proposed new legislation, agreements and concerted practices with anti-competitive objects or effects would be prohibited, but there would be provision for exemption of agreements with economic or technical benefits. The proposals would align UK law more closely with Article 85 of the EEC Treaty.

The Copyright, Designs and Patents Act, 1988 came into force on 1 August. The Act introduces a new right giving original designs protection against copying for 10 years, but with licences as of right being available after five years. An exception to the right permits copying necessary for a spare part to fit or match. The Act also introduces powers exercisable in consequence of reports of the MMC in respect of copyright and design right. These allow the Secretary of State to modifiy licences or to grant compulsory licences in cases where a practice has been found to operate against the public interest in either of these areas. In addition, the Act includes provisions ending the exclusive right of registered patent agents and solicitors to represent inventors in dealing with the UK Patent Office and removing restrictions on registered patent agents forming mixed practices.

The Water Act, which entered into force on 22 November, provides for the privatization of the water supply and sewerage function of the regional water authorities in England and Wales, and brings the water industry within the DGFT's responsibilities under the monopoly provisions of the Fair Trading Act 1973. The Act establishes a special merger control regime for water and sewerage undertakings, so as to preserve a sufficiently large number of separate companies to enable their efficiency to be compared for regulatory purposes. The Act also provides for the establishment of a Director-General of Water Supplies (DGWS) to operate a regulatory regime for the provision of water supply and sewerage, and to make MMC references under competition legislation in respect of these matters.

The Electricity Act 1989 provides for a restructuring of the industry prior to privatization. It introduces competition into electricity generation and supply, and provides for the appointment of a Director-General of Electricity Supply (DGES) who will regulate and promote competition within the industry. The DGES will have the authority to refer matters to the MMC. The Act also enables the DGFT to make a monopoly reference relating to the electricity supply industry.

In June orders were made modifying the application of the restrictive Trade Practices Act 1976 in relation to categories of agreements for the sale and purchase of shares in a company or of a business and agreements for the subscription of shares in a company. The orders substantially reduce the number of agreements requiring to be furnished for registration under the Act, thereby alleviating the regulatory burdens on the businesses involved (predominantly small and medium-sized firms) while allowing the OFT to concentrate on agreements and practices with potentially more significant effects on competition.

108. On 16 March 1989, the Italian Senate approved a draft law which establishes a body of rules aimed at the protection of competition and of the market.

The provisions of the draft law apply to agreements, to abuses of dominant position and to concentrations of undertakings which do not fall within the scope of Articles 85 and 86 of the EEC Treaty, Articles 65 and 66 of the ECSC Treaty or of Community regulations.

The substantive norms of the draft law are inspired largely by the principles enshrined in the Community legal regime on competition. In the first instance, the draft law forbids agreements between undertakings which have as their object or effect the prevention, restriction or distortion of competition, in an appreciable way, within the national market or within a relevant part of it. However, agreements restrictive of competition may be authorized where they give rise to improvements in supply conditions or where they result in substantial benefits for consumers.

Secondly, the draft law forbids abusive exploitation, by one or more undertakings, of a dominant position within the national market or within a relevant part of it.

Finally, the draft law forbids the operation of concentrations which result in the creation or the reinforcement of a dominant position on the national market in such a way as to eliminate or substantially reduce competition. However, there is a possibility of derogating from this prohibition where the concentration occurs in particular sectors of production specified by the Interministerial Committee for Economic Planning (CIPE).

The authority responsible for applying Italian competition law (Autorità garante della concorrenza e del mercato) will have powers of investigation (powers to request information from companies, to undertake inspections and verifications) and of decision (powers to order the ending of the infringement, to forbid concentrations and to impose financial penalties).

In addition, the authority will have the responsibility to maintain relations with European Community organs as envisaged by Community regulations in this area.

The draft law is presently being considered by the Chamber of Deputies.

§ 2 — Application of Community law by national courts

109. In a judgment delivered on 13 July 1989, the Frankfurt/Main Higher Regional Court (Oberlandesgericht) referred questions for a preliminary ruling to the European Court of Justice in proceedings relating to a beer supply contract containing exclusive purchasing clauses. The large number of questions referred to the European Court concern the application of the cumulative effects theory developed by the Court of Justice of the European Communities and interpretation of Regulation (EEC) No 1984/83.

110. The Heidelberg Regional Court (Landgericht) had to deal, as part of a petition for restraint, with a clause banning the sharing of intermediaries' commissions with clients in the field of insurance. In its judgment, which was final, the Court ruled that the clause was incompatible with Articles 5, 3(f) and 85 of the EEC Treaty, referring to the judgments of the Court of Justice of the European Communities in Cases 45/85 (Fire Insurance) and 311/85 (Flemish Travel Agencies). The clause was laid down in the general conditions governing competition drawn up by the insurance companies and in a regulation adopted by the Federal Supervisory Office for Insurance (Bundesaufsichtsamt für das Versicherungswesen).

111. In March, the Brussels Commercial Tribunal gave a ruling on the application of Articles 86 and 85 of the EEC Treaty in a dispute between two banks.

A system for the presentation and payment of cheques payable in Belgium and presented for cashing to foreign banks by their customers was introduced in 1983 by one of the parties. It disputed the charging by a Belgian bank of a commission of BFR 595 on each foreign currency cheque which it presented to it for payment under the system. Its action was based on Article 86 of the EEC Treaty primarily, and on Article 85(1) in the alternative.

The plaintiff bank alleged that the Belgian bank was abusing the dominant position which it held on the market for the cashing of foreign currency cheques by charging under the system, a commission which it does not charge foreign bankers. It argued that the Belgian bank was engaging in discriminatory practices against it. Article 86 was deemed not to apply for two reasons:

(i) the absence of any dominant position: it had not been established that the relevant market was restricted to the market for the cashing of cheques and not to a wider market;

(ii) the absence of any discriminatory measures: it had not been established that the services for which different charges were made were identical. In the alternative, the bank alleged that the amount of the charge was the result of a restrictive agreement. The Tribunal held that infringement of Article 85(1) had not been established since the alleged restrictive agreement had not been proved.

112.   On 27 June 1989, the French Court of Cassation confirmed a judgment by the Paris Court of Appeal delivered on 16 January 1989 which rejected a clause in a selective distribution contract, thus disagreeing with the position adopted by the Commission with regard to Grundig, in respect of which an exemption decision had been taken. The Court of Appeal also held that a letter from the Commission indicating that the matter had been examined under the heading of agreements of minor importance could not be deemed to be equivalent to an exemption decision under Article 85(3).

113.   In a judgment delivered on 26 April 1989, the Paris Court of Appeal settled a dispute between the Société des Pompes Funèbres Générales (PFG) and various undertakers associated with Michel Leclerc. PFG are public funeral service licensees in a large number of French communes. They hold 60% of the licence contracts, giving them a 45% share of funerals in France. PFG accused the Leclerc associates in particular of having organized funerals in several communes despite the monopoly granted to PFG by the public authorities. The Leclerc associates did not deny having breached the monopoly but argued that PFG had a dominant position on the funeral market and was abusing it in violation of national and Community competition rules (Article 86).

With regard to the application of Community law, the Paris Court of Appeal based itself on a preliminary ruling given by the European Court of Justice on 4 May 1988 (Case No 30/87, Bodson), which dealt with the compatibility of the French rules on funeral monopolies with certain provisions of the Treaty, including Article 86. The Court of Appeal, endorsing the comments of the Commission of the European Communities and of the French Government before the European Court in the Bodson Case, and the comments of the Minister for Economic Affairs in the case in point, took the view that the activity of the PFG group, although extending to include several other Community countries, could have only an imperceptible influence on trade with other Member States and that it had not been established that the activities of the PFG group affected imports of goods (coffins) from other Community countries or the scope for undertakings established in such other countries to compete for funeral licences in the French communes.

Consequently, the Paris Court of Appeal held that Article 86 was not applicable, since the condition that intra-Community trade be affected was not fulfilled. However, the Court gave a very precise list of practices which could be deemed to be abuses of a dominant position on the basis of national competition law.

114. In a judgment delivered on 28 January 1988, the Paris Court of Appeal upheld the decision of the Competition Council on 8 June 1987 to prohibit the exclusive distribution system used by manufacturers of cosmetic products, on the grounds that it restricted the distribution of such products to dispensing chemists only, thereby excluding other forms of distribution also capable of adequately marketing the products. In its judgment, the Court, agreeing with the Competition Council's analysis based in particular on Article 85(1) of the EEC Treaty and on the judgment in the *Metro* Case, had taken the view that the relevant market was the market for products distributed exclusively in pharmacies and that such distribution systems constituted a restriction of competition between Member States.

In a judgment given on 25 April 1989, the French Court of Cassation rejected the appeal lodged by the companies Pierre Fabre Cosmétiques and Vichy in this case. The Court of Cassation held that the Paris Court of Appeal had correctly defined the relevant market and that the systems of exclusive distribution in pharmacies which the manufacturers had established, had an appreciable effect on intra-Community trade.

115. On 23 January 1989, the President of the Amsterdam Court rejected an action brought by an importer of foreign newspapers. The case arose out of the refusal of a newspaper distributor to agree to distribute a title imported by the applicant unless the latter agreed to an equivalent arrangement with a competing importer/distributor to which the defendant was linked as part of the same group. The defendant wished, in this way, to keep centralized the system of supply and the administration of its distribution network. The applicant accused the defendant of abusing its dominant position as a purchaser and of engaging in concerted practices with partners in order to remove from the applicant, its agency in respect of a particular foreign newspaper. The President held that the defendant was not in a dominant position on the market and that the influence of the current partners on the conduct and contractual requirements of the defendant was not significant.

116. The President of the Hague Court ruled that an agreement under which an enterprise in the hotel and restaurant business undertook for a 10-year period to sell only beers supplied by the contracting party did not meet the

conditions for non-applicability of Article 85 of the EEC Treaty under Regulation 1984/83. Regulation 1984/83 provides that Article 85 does not apply to agreements to which only two undertakings are party. However, the agreement in question will also be applicable to an establishment still to be set up.

117.   On 20 September 1989, the Hague Court ruled that in setting certain charges in the health care sector, the supervisory body responsible had not contravened its obligations under Articles 3(f), 5 and 85 of the EEC Treaty. The provisions on charges were not mandatory in character.

118.   In the case of *Ransberg-Gema and Another* v *Electrostatis Plant Systems and Others* before thet High Court in London, the plaintiffs, who had issued a writ alleging infringement of copyright in certain drawings, sought to have struck out, a number of defences claimed by the defendants under European Community law. The Court proceeded on the basis that the plaintiff occupied a dominant position in the market for electrostatic power coating equipment. The sole question before the Court was whether the so-called 'Euro-defences' constituted any defence to the allegations of infringement.

The defendants alleged five different abuses by the plaintiffs of their dominant position, namely:

(i)   threatening to institute and instituting the action with the intention of driving the defendants out of business or out of the market;

(ii)   claiming conversion damages;

(iii)   claiming an injunction to prevent the importation into the United Kingdom of goods lawfully marketed in another part of the common market (Spain);

(iv)   the bringing of proceedings against a particular defendant for what was primarily an oppressive purpose;

(v)   behaving to an appreciable extent independently of their competitors, customers and consumers.

The Court struck out each of these claimed 'Euro-defences' on the grounds that such a defence must be sufficiently particularized so as to show a nexus between the alleged actions of the plaintiff and the alleged breaches of the dominant position under Article 86 of the EEC Treaty.

Part Three

Competition policy
and government assistance
to enterprises

Chapter I

State aids

§ 1 — General policy problems and developments

The first survey on State aids

119. An important event during 1989 in the field of State aids was the decision, taken after the publication by the Commission of the first survey on State aids in the Community, [1] to review existing aid schemes more systematically under Article 93(1) of the EEC Treaty.

The Commission drew its principal conclusions from the survey on the basis of a completed internal market by 1992, in which State aids will be one of the few means available to Member States to apply protectionist policies in their intra-Community trade and where competition will be far greater owing to the single market. As a result, it has undertaken a review in cooperation with the Member States, notably at a meeting in December, in order to redirect its policy in this area under seven major headings.

Review of aid schemes in accordance with Article 93(1)

120 As most aids are granted under existing schemes, they must be examined with the Member States on a more regular basis. The Commission will endeavour to focus primarily on schemes representing the greatest threat to competition and trade, and those where the economic conditions underlying the Commission's approval have since changed.

---

[1] EN ISBN 92-825-9535-8.

General investments aid

121.   The Commission has a very clear policy in this area. [1] Despite an increase in total aid, there has not been an increase in the number of prior notifications. In view of the fact that such aid distorts competition and is generally lacking in any regional or sectoral impact, the Commission will in future take an increasingly negative attitude to this type of aid, in particular by reviewing it under Article 93(1).

Export aids

122.   Taking account of the volume of aid for exports to non-Community countries identified in the first survey, the Commission will define its policy in this area more precisely once it has obtained further details from the Member States. It will, however, continue to maintain its strict ban on aid for intra-Community exports.

Financing of public enterprises

123.   As the Treaty adopts a natural stand on private or public ownership of undertakings, the Commission has to ensure equal treatment in the award of State aids. [2] To that end it is studying, first, the criteria for more accurate definition of cases where transfers of State resources (capital contributions, loans, guarantees, dividends, etc.) to firms, constitute aid and, second, a means of monitoring such contributions.

Rescue aid [3]

124.   Experience has shown that these aids are frequently notified once they have been granted, and that in many cases they distort competition to an extent contrary to the common interest. The Commission therefore proposes to strengthen the provisions ensuring that the aids are notified beforehand and to tighten the rules on exemption.

---

[1]   Ninth Competiton Report, point 184.
[2]   OJ L 229, 28.8.1985 and Bull. EC 9-1984, point 2.1.3.
[3]   Eighth Competition Report, point 228.

Aids of minor importance [1]

125. While on the one hand, the Commission was obliged to authorize a number of cases without modification since they clearly satisfied the conditions for exemption, on the other hand, very few schemes were notified under the simplified and accelerated procedure for aids of minor importance. In a notice published in the Official Journal, [2] the Commission reaffirmed its previous position on this subject, which consists in principle of not raising objections to aid schemes of minor importance, notified pursuant to Article 93(3) of the EEC Treaty and fulfilling defined criteria. As regards criteria, the Commission at the same time, decided to raise the thresholds below which aid qualifies for the accelerated procedure.

Standardization of notifications and of annual reports

126. It was decided to speed up the decision-making procedure for aids by standardizing the notification system.

In order to analyse the effects of aid schemes on competition more uniformly, to improve monitoring of the schemes, to increase transparency and to assess the aggregate effect of various aid schemes, the Commission intends to set up a standardized system of annual reports in cooperation with the Member States. A multilateral meeting was held in September in order to explain these plans to the Member States. Definite proposals will be prepared in 1990 for each initiative.

As the results of the first survey provided a valuable means of increasing transparency in this field, the Commission decided to repeat the exercise and update it regularly. The first updating concerned 1987 and 1988. The data for Spain and Portugal will be supplied and added to the updating.

The automobile sector

127. In December 1988, the Commission decided to adopt the Community framework on State aids to the motor-vehicle industry which entered into force on 1 January 1989. [3] The framework requires, for a two-year period, all vehicle and engine manufacturers to give prior notification of plans to award aid under

---

[1] Fourteenth Competition Report, point 203.
[2] OJ C 40, 20.2.1990.
[3] OJ C 123, 18.5.1989.

approved schemes where costs exceed ECU 12 million. It also requires Member States to draw up an annual report on all aid awarded in the sector in question. On the basis of Article 93(1) of the EEC Treaty, the Commission proposed that the Member States approve the framework. Ten Member States agreed to apply it, but the Federal Republic of Germany and Spain refused. In July 1989, therefore, the Commission decided to initiate the procedure provided for in Article 93(2) of the EEC Treaty in respect of the refusal of the German and Spanish Governments to accept the Community framework on State aid to the motor-vehicle industry.

The German Government considers that the framework pursues undesirable industrial policy objectives and is liable to jeopardize the effectiveness of regional aid. In its opinion, its aid programmes have a neutral impact and do not appreciably distort intra-Community trade. The Commission believes that the aim of the framework is to introduce transparency into aid awards in this industry and to impose strict discipline in their granting to ensure that competition is not distorted by aid. Thus, far from pursuing an industrial policy, the framework aims at improving the influence of economically sound market forces.

The Spanish authorities stated that they would apply the framework provided it formed part of a Community industrial policy which extended to the whole of the sector concerned. The Commission considered that acceptance of the framework could not be subject to any preconditions whatsoever.

The purpose of the two procedures initiated by the Commission is to require the two Member States to take the necessary measures so that the framework can be applied uniformly throughout the Community. The Commission must take account of the fact that most Member States are already applying the framework and that it has a duty to place them all on an equal footing.

In September 1989, the Commission also adopted the first two decisions on notifications made under the framework.

Aid to the steel industry

128.   After consulting the ECSC Consultative Committee on 2 December 1988 and obtaining the unanimous assent of the Council on 13 December 1988, [1] the Commission adopted Decision 322/89/ECSC [2] on 1 February, establishing

---

[1]   OJ C 18, 24.1.1989.
[2]   OJ L 38, 10.2.1989.

Community rules for aid to the steel industry (aid code). The Decision renews the terms of Decision 3484/85/ECSC [1] of 27 November 1985 which allows a very limited number of certain aids for steel (R&D, environmental protection, closure under certain conditions). The new rules now apply also to Spain, whilst Portugal continues under transitional arrangements until 1 January 1991.

Under the agreement between the European Community and the United States on a two and a half year extension to the voluntary restraint arrangements (VRA) on exports of European steel to the USA, the two partners reached agreement on a code of good conduct for the award of State aid to the steel industry. This arrangement, and all the bilateral arrangements concluded between the US and other steel exporting countries were based on the steel aids code applied within the Community since 1 January 1986. The consensus is viewed as helping to create the right conditions for the worldwide liberalization of the steel trade.

Aid to shipbuilding

129.   Following its annual review of the ceiling on production aid pursuant to the Sixth Directive [2] at the end of 1988, and after consulting the Member States, the Commission decided to reduce the ceiling from 28% to 26% [3] of the contract value before aid, and to set a 16% ceiling on aid for small vessels where the production costs do not exceed ECU 6 million, for the 1989 calendar year.

At the end of December 1989, the Commission set the new ceiling at 20% from 1 January 1990. For small vessels the maximum aid rate is reduced to 14%.

On 13 April, the Commission approved the report on the application in 1987 and 1988 of Council Directive 87/167/EEC [4] of 26 January 1987 (Sixth Directive) on aid for shipbuilding. The report shows that the machinery introduced by the Directive forms a satisfactory legal framework, affording transparency and enabling all forms of aid to shipbuilding to be monitored. It also stresses that Member States should comply more fully with their obligation to notify *ex post*, all awards of aid.

By letter dated 3 January 1989, the Commission informed the Member States that according to its interpretation of Article 4(7) of the Sixth Directive, it

---

[1]   OJ L 340, 18.12.1985.
[2]   Council Directive of 26 January 1987 on aid to shipbuilding; OJ L 69, 12.3.1987.
[3]   OJ C 32, 8.2.1989.
[4]   OJ L 69, 12.3.1987.

would regard as eligible for development aid in the form of aid to shipbuilding, only the ACP countries, countries and territories associated with the Community, countries classified by the OECD as underdeveloped, low-income countries, and intermediate income countries.

State aid in the energy sector

130.   The Commission decided to increase its efforts to establish effective monitoring of State aids in the energy sector. The sub-sector of coal is already subject to a notification and analysis requirement under Decision 2064/86/ ECSC. Thus, the next most important sub-sectors to be analysed were electricity and nuclear energy. While electricity is defined as 'goods', [1] it is special because it is a homogeneous product produced from heterogeneous sources. Historically, this has allowed the sector to establish a privileged status, often combined with intense and complex intervention by the State and electricity companies. Within the Community, the special status of the nuclear industry is also tied to a specific Treaty (Euratom). Under Article 232(2) of the EEC Treaty, the latter applies only in so far as it does not derogate from the provisions of the Euratom Treaty.

The first step was to identify State transfers of resources and the associated aid elements in all the Member States. The Commission asked all Member States to complete a questionnaire on this subject.

When in future it decides on aid proposals, the Commission will take account of the specific characteristics of the sector, notably the need to plan for the very long-term. It will also take account of the requirements of a diversified energy production system.

Regional aid

131.   After the reform of the structural Funds in 1989, and in the context of the resulting new national and Community aid schemes, the Commission examined new aid awards to the regions covered by the schemes. In its review, it took account of the variety and degree of the problems encountered in each region.

---

[1]   In its judgment in Case 6/84 (*Costa* v *ENEL*), the Court ruled that electricity should be treated as 'goods'.

Overall activity (Table 1)

132.   The following table gives an overview of the control exercised by the Commission over aids granted by Member States in 1989. It also provides a comparison with previous years and confirms findings for 1987 and 1988 in relation to the period 1981 to 1986. The adoption of certain frameworks, a

TABLE 1

Activity in the control of State aids (excluding aids to agriculture and fisheries, and transport)

Year	Number of proposals notified	Action taken by the Commission[1]				Proposals notified and later withdrawn by Member States
		Raise no objection	Open the procedure of Article 93(2) EEC or Article 8(3) of Decision 2320/81/ECSC	Close the procedure of Article 93(2) EEC or Article 8(3) of Decision 2320/81/ECSC[2]	Final decision under Article 93(2) EEC or Article 8(3) of Decision 2320/81/ECSC[3]	
1981	92 (of which steel — 16)	79 (of which steel — 11)	30 (of which steel — 9)	19 (of which steel — 4)	14	—
1982	200 (of which steel — 81)	104 (of which steel — 25)	86 (of which steel — 56)	30 (of which steel — 13)	13 (of which steel — 1)	—
1983	174 (of which steel — 4)	101 (of which steel — 18)[4]	55	18	21 (of which steel — 9)	9
1984	162 (of which steel — 10)	201 (of which steel — 66)[4]	58 (of which steel — 1)	34	21[5]	6
1985	133 (of which steel — 7)	102 (of which steel — 21)[4]	38 (of which steel — 1)	31	7	11
1986	124	98	47	26	10	5
1987	326	205	27	32	10	1
1988	375	311	31	32	13	—
1989	296	254	37	27	16	7

NB: The figures in the first column do not total with those of the next four columns on account of carry-overs from one year to the next and because if the procedure of Article 93(2) EEC or Article 8(3) of Decision 2320/81/ECSC is intitiated, the Commission has to take two decisions, first to open the procedure and then a final decision terminating it.

1 For details, see the Annex to this Report. Actions in steel include both EEC and ECSC steel products, and because of the tranche system, the number of actions exceeds the number of notifications.

2 In most cases after amendments negotiated during the procedure to remove those aspects which, a priori, made the proposal incompatible with the common market.

3 Published in the Official Journal.

4 Including tranches of aid released under decisions of 29 June 1983.

5 Excludes the 'conditional' decision on French investment aids (see Fourteenth Competition Report, point 253).

better understanding of the Commission's policy in this area and the effort made by the Commission to improve compliance with Article 93(3) of the EEC Treaty have all contributed to the relatively large increase in the number of aid notifications. It is also worth noting the larger proportion of aid schemes introduced in 1989 compared with individual awards under general schemes.

In order to increase and further refine its control over aid awards in the Community, the Commission sent a letter in May in accordance with Article 169 of the EEC Treaty, to five Member States, giving them notice to inform it of the measures they planned to take to comply with the obligations imposed on them by Article 93(3). The Commission had found that in the period 1985-87, these Member States had granted a relatively large number of aids without notifying them, or had notified them after the award. In the case of France, the percentage of unnotified aids in relation to aids examined by the Commission was 37%, followed by Belgium with 32%, Greece with 28%, Spain with 23% and Italy with 16%.

The Commission then held a multilateral meeting in December with all the Member States in order to inform them in detail about its State aid policy leading up to 1992. It outlined the main points of its policy during the meeting and gave the Member States the opportunity to express their wishes on the subject. A more detailed description of its policy is set out below.

§ 2 — State aids for research and development

General policy developments

133. The Commission pursued the policy it had started in 1986 to enhance transparency in accordance with the Community framework on State aids for research and development. [1] The number of notifications and decisions taken are as follows:

	1986	1987	1988[1]	1989[2]
Notifications	26	68	64	48
Decisions	23	46	42	59

[1] The difference between the number of cases notified and the number of decisions is due partly to 10 notified Eureka cases not requiring a Commission decision as the thresholds had not been reached, and partly to the fact that several schemes were withdrawn by Member States.
[2] The difference between the number of notifications and the number of decisions is due to the fact that several cases notified at the end of 1988 were decided in 1989.

In 1989, the total value of notified aid schemes was ECU 790 million. Specific awards under the Eureka initiative, approved by the Commission in the same period, represented a total of ECU 300 million in aid. Total budgets of R&D aid schemes in force in 1989, including those previously approved by the Commission, totalled ECU 4 550 million.

The principal decisions taken in 1989 are summarized below:

134. In all the cases dealt with by the Commission, approval was subject to a twofold obligation: to notify individual awards of aid under existing schemes to projects costing more than ECU 20 million, and to send annual reports on the application of schemes.

The first obligation is a consequence of the fact that a project costing in excess of ECU 20 million is regarded as inherently liable to distort competition, which could affect trade between Member States. The question of size is such that the projects in question must be assessed on their own merits and not solely on the basis of the scheme providing the assistance.

---

[1] OJ C 83, 11.4.1986.

The Commission has also started to review the problem of R&D contracts. This will constitute one the main features of action taken in respect of R&D aid in the next few years in view of the far-reaching implications for competition resulting from extensive recourse to major contracts (see point 9.2 of R&D framework). This matter must also be examined from the standpoint of the EEC's relations with its leading trading partners, especially within the GATT.

The Commission decided to commission a study from an independent contractor to assist in assessing any possible aid elements in such contracts, in view of the diversity of situations in the Member States.

One of the main areas in which the Commission is concerned with aid for R&D is the Eureka project. Four years after its launch, nearly 300 projects are underway. Involving international cooperation in advanced technology, the projects represent a total estimated value of ECU 6 500 million, part of which is funded by public resources.

In 1989, two-thirds of the decisions adopted by the Commission on research and development aid concerned Eureka projects: the Commission approved 29 cases of aid for individual projects, four of which were exempted under Article 92(3)(b) [1] and are described below, and took a position on six schemes used to finance Eureka. Some of these schemes are specific to Eureka, as in the United Kingdom and Italy, where 10 % of the Applied Research Fund is set aside for Eureka under special arrangements. Other schemes are aimed more generally at the financing of international projects, such as the Dutch BTIP (Bedrijfsgerichte Technologiestimulering van Internationale Projecten). The Commission approved the refinancing of and certain amendments to this scheme, whose budget is allocated almost entirely to Eureka.

In Germany and France, the choice of appropriate scheme is based on the sector concerned, the type of participant or the stage of the project. Thus the German 'Verkehrsforschung' scheme (transport research), against part of which the Commission opened the Article 93(2) procedure, includes a sub-programme for road transport which the Commission approved and which was used to finance German participants in the Prometheus project. The French schemes Anvar and FRT (see below) can also be used to finance participation in Eureka, the first in the case of SMEs, the second generally during the initial phases of projects.

---

[1] Aid to promote the execution of an important project of common European interest.

Stronger links were also forged in 1989 between the Community and Eureka, notably in the form of the new framework programme for 1990-94 proposed by the Commission and the latter's decision to take part in the Jessi project.

As regards State aids, the Commission also took account of the special nature of the Eureka initiative and its contribution to Community R&D objectives (Article 130f of the EEC Treaty) by raising the individual notification threshold from ECU 20 million to 30 million. The threshold applies to the total cost of Eureka projects to which a Member State contributes at least ECU 4 million.

135. The main decisions taken in 1989 are briefly described below, under three headings:

(i)   those resulting in exemption under Article 92(3)(c); development of certain activities;

(ii)   those resulting in exemption under Article 92(3)(b); execution of an important project of common European interest;

(iii) those which resulted initially in the opening of the Article 93(2) procedure.

Decisions giving exemption under Article 92(3)(c) of the EEC Treaty

France

Anvar (Agence Nationale pour la Valorisation de la Recherche)

136. This is a general scheme in force since 1979, its 1989 budget totalling ECU 143 million; it is aimed at firms in all sectors with fewer than 500 employees involved in research and innovation comprising high technological risks.

The aid is awarded in the form of grants or, in the event of success, in the form of repayable loans, with a maximum intensity of 40% in the first case and 12-26% in the second. Direct grants cover 10% of the budget and are limited to ECU 20 000 per project.

FRT (Research and Technology Fund)

137.   The 1989 refinancing involved a budget of some ECU 170 million to finance basic and applied research projects under France's scientific policy. [1] The maximum intensity of the aid is still 25 % net grant equivalent and the other arrangements, approved by the Commission on 3 February 1988, remain the same.

FII (Industrial Innovation Fund)

138.   The new multiannual scheme of aid for R&D, with a budget of ECU 28 million for 1989, gives priority to intersectoral or cooperative research projects involving particularly high costs.

Because of the characteristics of the programme, a maximum intensity of 30% net grant equivalent was approved for applied research, to which a further 10% may be added in the case of projects financed from the basic research stage.

Federal Republic of Germany

'Arbeit und Technik'

139.   This research programme replaces the 'Humanisierung des Ärbeitslebens' scheme, and has a budget of ECU 187 million for the period 1989-92. Aid is granted to universities, research institutes and firms for fundamental, basic and applied research projects aimed at improving working conditions and prevention in the field of health through the application of new scientific knowledge.

United Kingdom

Eureka initiative

140.   The programme involves both basic and applied research, and has a budget of some ECU 18 million for 1988/89. Aid intensity may not exceed 40% of elegible costs both in the definition phase and as regards research projects.

---

[1]   All industries and undertakings are eligible for grants and/or repayable loans. Two new schemes were launched in 1989, one to encourage technological progress, the other to promote cooperation between public research bodies and companies.

In more important cases however, the rate will be fixed after negotiation at the necessary minimum.

Italy

Special Fund for Applied Research

141. The Fund awards grants and subsidized loans to Italian firms involved in research. The scheme has a budget of ECU 500 million for 1989, of which 90% is for applied research and 10% for basis research in the form of vocational training for young research workers.

Aid may not exceed a maximum level of 31.7% of elegible costs for firms in northern and central Italy and 37.6% for firms in the Mezzogiorno and for SMEs throughout Italy.

The Commission also approved Law No 346/88 which modifies the Special Fund for Applied Research by providing aid in the form of interest subsidies on loans for major projects costing in excess of LIT 10 000 million. The programme will cost approximately ECU 84 million a year.

The Italian authorities are also planning to finance feasibility studies under the same scheme for international projects carried out in cooperation with firms employing under 100 persons and with a turnover not exceeding ECU 5 million. This measure will apply more particularly to Eureka projects.

Eureka

142. This programme covers a three-year period and has an annual budget of LIT 90 000 million (approximately ECU 60 million). The projects, involving basic and applied research, will receive aid not exceeding 35% of eligible costs; only projects of common European interest under Article 93(3)(b), or involving SMEs or firms in the Mezzogiorno will be entitled to a higher level of aid amounting to 43.5% of costs.

Netherlands

Programme to promote the use of technology —
amendment and refinancing for 1989

143.   The scheme has an annual budget of ECU 47 million, whilst the gross level of aid awarded in the form of non-repayable loans totals 37.5% of project costs. The following forms of research are assisted: feasibility studies, basic industrial research and demonstration projects. Aid awarded under the programme can be cumulated with other forms of State aid or with Community financing, with a gross ceiling on cumulated aid of 50% of the cost of the project in the case of firms with over 250 workers, and 60% for those with under 250 employees.

Decisions giving exemption under Article 92(3)(b) of the EEC Treaty

144.   To date, the Commission has considered four Eureka projects as important projects of common European interest. Aid to such projects therefore qualified for exemption under Article 92(3)(b). They involved aid from France, the United Kingdom and the Federal Republic of Germany for the high-definition colour television project (HDTV), aid from France and Italy for the Eprom (semi-conductors) project, German aid to the DAB project involving the creation of an earth radio digital system and French aid for the Eureka software factory project (ESF).

In assessing the importance of the projects, the Commission took account, not only of their size, but more particularly, of their qualitative importance in terms of producing common standards, an industrial strategy and technological progress of benefit to the Community as a whole.

Decisions to open the Article 93(2) EEC procedure

Federal Republic of Germany

Transport research aid scheme (Verkehrsforschung)

145.   The Commission opened the Article 93(2) procedure in respect of the sub-programme of research on the 'Transrapid', a high-speed magnetic levitation train. The cost of the sub-programme totals ECU 410 million for the

period 1988-92. Since the prototype had already completed 50 000 km of tests, the Commission decided in its Article 93(2) procedure that the research was too close to the marketplace for it to approve aid awards to firms of up to 75% of costs. Such aids are normally reserved for fundamental research. The Commission also questioned the German Government about the precise stage of development of the conventional high-speed railway systems, the Intercity Experimental (ICE), so that it could judge whether aid representing 30% of the costs of the project was justified.

In the same decision, the Commission approved three other sub-programmes relating to public urban and suburban transport systems, motor vehicles and road traffic, and the transport of goods and 'transport chains'.

'Technologie Programme Wirtschaft' and 'Programme Zukunftstechnologien'

146. The Article 93(2) procedure was opened against both schemes since, despite two reminders, the German Federal authorities had failed to supply the information needed to assess the projects under Articles 92 and 93 of the EEC Treaty. After further negotiations, the German authorities provided the data in question and considerably reduced the levels of aid. The final version of the schemes provides for aid intensities of 25% for applied research and 50% for basic research, increases being awarded for SMEs (150 persons) and for assisted regional areas within the limits of the R&D framework. The Commission consequently closes the procedure and granted exemption under Article 92(3)(c).

§ 3 — Aid to industries with specific structural or related problems

Aid to the coal industry (Tables 2 and 3)

147.   The Commission made efforts throughout the year to ensure that Decision 2064/86 ECSC [1] on State aids in the coal industry was strictly adhered to. In particular, it approved State aid to the coal industry provided it was sufficiently degressive and accompanied by restructuring, rationalization and modernization plans.

In that context, the Commission approved aid proposals for 1989 from Spain, [2] Belgium, [3] France [4] and the United Kingdom. [5]

In its decision of 30 March 1989, [6] the Commission authorized the compensatory amounts under Article 10(2) for 1987 and 1988, awarded in the Federal Republic of Germany under the third electricity-from-coal law.

In its decision of 20 December, the Commission approved compensatory payments for 1989 and compensatory amounts for 1987 and 1988 awarded by the Spanish Government as financial assistance from Ofico. By decision adopted in February 1989, [7] the Commission approved further financial assistance for 1988 from the German Government for the sale of coal and coking coal to the Community iron and steel industry.

Several aid cases notified to the Commission in 1989, in particular by the Federal Republic of Germany, Spain and Portugal, have yet to be decided by the Commission.

The provisional volume of aid to current coal production on which the Commission adopted decisions in 1989 reached ECU 845.6 million. Aid to defray social expenditure in the coal industry totalled ECU 7 109.9 million against ECU 6 516.1 million in 1988. The amount of aid to cover inherited liabilities amounted to ECU 1 251.3 million compared with ECU 1 047.7 million in 1988.

---

[1]   OJ L 177, 1.7.1986.
[2]   OJ L 38, 10.2.1989.
[3]   OJ L 277, 27.9.1989.
[4]   OJ L 342, 24.11.1989.
[5]   OJ L 326, 11.11.1989.
[6]   OJ L 116, 24.4.1989.
[7]   OJ L 61, 4.3.1989.

TABLE 2

State aids to the coal industry:
Aid not related to current production in 1988 and 1989 [1]

(million ECU)

| | Intervention in the sector of social benefits pursuant to Article 7 of Decision 2064/86/ECSC | | | | Aid to cover inherited liabilities pursuant to Article 8 of Decision 2064/86/ECSC | | | |
| | Total | | Excess aid of Article 7 | | Total | | Excess aid of Article 8 | |
	1988	1989	1988	1989	1988	1989	1988	1989
Belgium	883.7	918.0	—	—	—	—	—	—
Federal Republic of Germany	3 334.9	3 588.5	162.7	103.8	106.3	120.0	—	—
Spain	574.1	660.7	—	—	—	—	—	—
France	1 500.6	1 776.0	—	—	719.5	772.0	—	—
Portugal	—	—	—	—	—	—	—	—
United Kingdom[2]	60.1	62.9	—	—	221.9	359.5	—	—
Community total	6 353.4	7 006.1	162.7	103.8	1 047.7	1 251.5	—	—

[1] Planned figures.
[2] The United Kingdom has an integrated social security system. The figures shown in this column cover only the special miners' pension fund, which exists side by side with the general social security system.

TABLE 3

State aid to the coal industry —
Aid for current production in 1988 and 1989

(million ECU)

Aid under Decision 2064/86/ECSC	Belgium		FR of Germany		Spain		France		Portugal		United Kingdom		Community	
	1988	1989	1988	1989	1988	1989	1988	1989	1988	1989	1988	1989	1988	1989
1 Direct aid:														
Article 3	143.1	154.2	—	—	350.2	371.1	238.3	174.6	1.7	:	—	—	733.3	699.9
Article 4	45.4	5.1	1 825.6	:	10.0	19.8	—	—			—	—	1 881.0	24.9
Article 5	14.0	—	55.5	:	4.3	:	—	—			—	—	73.8	:
Article 6	0.1	0.1	84.5	:	—	—	—	—			21.0	23.5	105.6	23.6
Other	—	—	9.7	:	2.5	—	11.5	—			—	—	23.7	:
Total	202.6	159.4	1 975.3	:	367.0	390.0	249.8	174.6	1.7	:	21.0	23.5	2 817.4	748.4
per tonne	76.59	84.56	24.91	:	19.94	21.60	20.15	15.18	6.30	:	0.21	0.24	13.23	
2 Indirect aid	—	—	2 433.3	:	80.0	97.2	—	—	—	:	—	—	2 513.3	97.2
Total	202.6	159.4	4 408.6	:	447.0	488.1	249.8	174.6	1.7	:	21.0	23.5	5 330.7	845.6
per tonne	76.59	84.56	55.59	:	24.29	26.97	20.15	15.18	6.30	:	0.21	0.24	25.03	

Aid to shipbuilding

Application of Article 4 (5) of the Sixth Directive [1]

148.   In February, the Commission closed the Article 93(2) procedure it had opened in June 1988 against Germain aid to the Armenius-Werft shipyard for the building of six to eight coasters for the German shipowner Peter Döhle, following the withdrawal of the aid proposed by the German Government. [2]

In April, the Commision adopted a negative decision in respect of German aid totalling DM 1 734 million (ECU 858 million) awarded for the construction of a 1 700 tonne wine tanker for the German shipowner Paul Häse, an order for which German and Dutch yards were competing. [2]

In June, the Commission adopted a negative decision concerning aid which the Dutch and German Governments wished to award to the building of a fishing vessel for an Irish shipowner. It decided in this particular case that the guidelines for the examination of State aids in the fisheries sector, and the Council Regulation, should prevail over provisions of the Sixth Directive. [3]

Application of Article 4(7) of the Sixth Directive

149.   Following the strengthening of the rules on aids connected with shipbuilding and ship conversion, granted as development aid, the Commission opened the Article 93(2) procedure in two cases. The first concerns a low-interest loan for the building by Howaldtswerke Deutsche Werft of three container vessels for an Israeli company. The procedure, initiated in March, was closed in July once it was determined that the economic operators had not been informed, when they signed the contract in question, that Israel was no longer on the list of countries eligible for this type of development aid.

The second case concerned the building of four fishing vessels by Sietas Werft for a Chilean company. The Commission initiated the procedure in July, but closed it in November following the withdrawal by Germany of its aid proposal.

---

1   This Article requires Member States to notify individual aid awards where there is competition between Community yards for a particular contract.
2   Eighteenth Competition Report, point 195.
3   Eighteenth Competition Report, point 194.

Belgium

150. In February, the Commission closed the Article 93(2) procedure in respect of various aid schemes applicable to companies in the maritime sector after Belgium had given an undertaking that aid awarded under these schemes would comply with the rules of the Sixth Directive. [1]

In October, the Commission opened the Article 93(2) procedure against the financial terms offered to shipowners for an LPG vessel to be built by the Boelwerf yard on the ground that the net grant equivalent exceeded the permitted ceiling of 26%.

Italy

151. In February, the Commission decided to close the procedure initiated in November 1987 [2] in respect of the refinancing of Italian Law No 111/85 concerning aid for small and medium-sized yards. In November 1987, the Commission had authorized the refinancing of the scheme for large yards, but not for small and medium-sized ones because of the budget and tonnage involved amounting to LIT 145 billion (ECU 95.4 million) and 99 800 cgt respectively, already authorized.

The Italian authorities then modified their proposal and the Commission decided to approve the refinancing, reduced to LIT 38.5 billion (ECU 25.3 million) for 60 000 cgt. These figures produce a ratio of LIT 600 million (ECU 400 000) per assisted cgt, which is comparable to aids already authorized.

In May, the Commission initiated the Article 93(2) procedure [3] in respect of a draft law establishing direct awards of production aid to the shipbuilding industry or indirect awards through the shipping lines, and measures in favour of applied research in this sector. The Commission considers that a number of elements of the proposed aid are not compatible with the Sixth Directive, in particular the cumulation of aids to yards and shipowners, the intensity of the investment aid and the level of aid for R&D. Furthermore, assistance to cover the losses of the Fincantieri Group was not justified.

---

[1] Eighteenth Competition Report, point 187.
[2] Seventeenth Competition Report, point 193.
[3] OJ C 293, 21.11.1989.

Greece

152.   In April, the Commission decided to open the procedure provided for in Article 93(2) in respect of the application of Law 1262/1982 and its amendments, to shipyards. The Commission considered that the law could infringe the provisions of the Sixth Directive, either where aid granted exceeded the ceiling fixed, or because aid would be granted only to Greek nationals for the construction of vessels in national yards. In addition, it would be possible under the law to award operating aid to ship repairs, whereas such activities are eligible only for investment aid.

Spain

153.   In July, the Commission decided to open the Article 93(2) procedure with a view to continuing its examination of the aid which the Government proposed to award to shipbuilding and an additional aid in the form of loss compensation for public yards. The Sixth Directive provides for a special transitional system for Spain and Portugal which authorizes operating aid provided that the shipbuilding industry has adopted a restructuring programme comprising capacity cuts capable of restoring competitiveness to the industry within four years (i.e. before the end of 1990), and on condition the aid is progressively reduced.

The Commission considers that the plan communicated is inadequate and that additional restructuring measures may be required to allow Spanish yards to operate competitively by the end of 1990.

Aid to the steel industry

Federal Republic of Germany

154.   In July, the Commission decided, on the basis of Article 6(2) of Decision 322/89/ECSC, that the capital contribution of DM 145 million (ECU 71.8 million) from the Saarland to the holding company Dillinger Hütte Saarstahl Beteiligungs AG did not contain any element of State aid. The new holding company controls two steel manufacturing undertakings, Saarstahl and Dillinger Hüttenwerke, both in Saarland, which decided to merge their steel activities. The value of the two companies was estimated by independent auditors and was analysed by the Commission. The capital contribution of DM 145 million

from Saarland, which had a majority holding of 76% in the former Saarstahl GmbH, is intended to enable Saarland to retain a 27.5% blocking minority in the new company. The Commission considers that the capital injection by Saarland reflects the true value of the additional shares acquired in the new company.

In November, the Commission approved both the extension to the end of 1991 of North Rhine-Westphalia's R&D scheme concerning basic material and its widening to cover new sectors. At the same time it approved the scheme's application to the steel sector.

The scheme, originally approved in 1987, will in future have an annual budget of DM 30-35 million (ECU 14.9 to 17.3 million), of which approximately 15% will be for the steel industry, 65% for the metals industry and 20% for the non-metals sector (ceramics, fibres).

Italy

155.   In March the Commission decided to initiate the procedure provided for in Article 6(4) of the aids code in respect of a subsidized loan of LIT 6 billion (ECU 3.9 million) granted by the regional authorities of the province of Bolzano to the Bolzano steelworks. The loan relates to a LIT 23 billion (ECU 15.1 million) investment decided in 1983 as part of the restructuring of Falck. The loan, however, had not been notified in advance to the Commission and it does not qualify for any of the exemptions in the aids code.

In June, the Commission, in response to a request made by the Italian Government in March, approved the postponing of certain dates stipulated in Decision 89/218/ECSC[1] for the closure of a number of steel plants in Italy. While a substantial number of the planned closures had been carried out, the Italian Government had, on account of particularly favourable market conditions and also for technical and commercial reasons, applied for postponement of the closure or selling dates fixed for the following facilities: liquid phase at Bagnoli, cold-rolling mill at Turin, merchant bar mill at Sesto San Giovanni, steel shop at Lovere.

The Commission decided to approve part of the Italian request, namely a six-month extension for Sesto San Giovanni and, with the unanimous assent of the Council, a nine-month extension for the closure of the liquid phase at Bagnoli,

---

[1]   Eighteenth Competition Report, point 203, OJ L 86, 31.3.1989.

a 21-month extension to the closure date for the cold-rolling mill at Turin and a six-month extension to the selling date for the plant at Lovere.

After consulting the Consultative Committee in June, the Council discussion of the draft Commission decision was postponed owing to the Government crisis in Italy. The draft received the unanimous assent of the Council required by Article 95 of the ECSC Treaty only on 14 November. The agreement included the Commission proposals, and gives a further nine-month extension on the closure date for the Bagnoli liquid phase, i.e. to 31 December 1990.

The Italian Government undertook to make no further requests for extensions to the closure dates provided for in Decision 89/218/ECSC.

Spain

156. In March 1989, the Commission decided to close both the procedure under Article 6(4) of the aids code and the Article 93(2) procedure opened in July 1988 [1] in respect of an aid awarded without prior notification to the steel manufacturer Patricio Echeverria SA. The aid was in the form of an interest subsidy of 3.5% on a loan of PTA 1 200 million (ECU 9.2 million) to finance an investment and R&D programme coating PTA 5 374 million (ECU 41.0 million). It was finally considered compatible with the common market as it was awarded solely for investments in areas covered by the EEC Treaty and for research and development expenditure in areas covered by both the EEC and the ECSC Treaty.

Investment aid in areas covered by the EEC Treaty could qualify for exemption under Article 93(3) (c) whilst aid for R&D in EEC areas satisfies the criteria laid down by the Community framework for State aids for research and development. [2] As regards R&D in ECSC areas, the aid satisfies the tests of Article 2 of Decision 3484/85/ECSC since it is aimed at reducing production costs and improving product quality, and its intensity is below the 25% ceiling.

In December, the Commission decided to close the procedure under Article 6(4) of Decision 3484/85/ECSC opened in December 1988 in respect of two unnotified grants awarded to the Basque steel manufacturer Altos Hornos de Vizcaya. The aid, to defray expenditure on environmental protection, complied both with the objective defined in the aids code and with the intensity ceiling laid down therein.

---

[1]   Eighteenth Competition Report, point 201.
[2]   OJ C 83, 11.4.1986.

France

157. On 15 November, the Commission decided not to object to social aid for closures notified by France. The closures affected various Usinor facilities (Caen, Gandrange, Longwy, Dunkerque, St Etienne, Suzange and Joeuf), and involved 4 535 job losses, the workers concerned being the recipients of the aid. The total cost of these measures is FF 1 027 million (ECU 148.4 million) of which 50% is to be borne by the French Government in accordance with the aids code.

Portugal

158. In March, the Commission decided to close the infringement procedure provided for in Article 88 of the ECSC Treaty which it had opened in July 1988 [1] against the Portuguese Government in respect of an aid to Fabrica de Aços Tomé Feteira, a steel undertaking. The aid consisted of a non-repayable loan of ESC 92.84 million (ECU 528 000) to support a capacity-increasing investment programme.

It emerged in the course of the procedure that entitlement to the aid had been acquired by the undertaking in December 1985, i.e. prior to accession. The Commission therefore found that the ECSC Treaty had not been infringed.

Luxembourg

159. In July, the Commission decided not to object to four Luxembourg aid programmes to promote R&D in the steel industry. The programmes, which comprise 203 projects undertaken in the period 1986-88, grant aid under the framework Law on Economic Expansion of 14 May 1986, approved by the Commission on 24 October 1985. [2] A total of LFR 246.5 million (ECU 5.8 million) was awarded in the form of grants, and LFR 210 million (ECU 4.9 million) in the form of subsidized loans. Because it had interpreted the relevant rules incorrectly, the Luxembourg Government had failed to notify the cases as it should have done under the aids code. It had nevertheless complied with the conditions relating to the purpose and intensity of the aid and with the Community framework on State aids for research and development. [3]

---

[1] Eighteenth Competition Report, point 205.
[2] Bull. EC 10-1985, point 2.1.50.
[3] OJ C 83, 11.4.1986.

Steel manufacturing industries

France

160. In June, the Commission decided to approve part of the aid which the French Government planned to award to eight subsidiaries of Usinor-Sacilor. The eight first-stage steel processing firms operate in the tubemaking, wire-drawing, off-shore and structural engineering, foundry and forging sector.

In opening the Article 93(2) procedure,[1] the Commission had taken account of existing overcapacity at Community level in those sectors and of the large amount of aid proposed. It also wished to establish that the restructuring referred to was distinct from that invoked to justify aid in a previous case. In this case, by a decision of 25 March 1987,[2] the Commission had deemed the aid to be incompatible with the common market. Lastly, in so far as the firms in question are subsidiaries of a steel group, it wished to ensure that the aid would not filter through to that group, which would have been in breach of the ECSC Treaty.

Having completed its examination, the Commission confirmed that the aids in question were new, restructuring measures which were likely to restore the viability of the six firms remaining in operation (two others were closing down). It also considered that they contributed to the improvement of the Community markets for the products concerned since they were accompanied by substantial reductions in capacity.

The Commission therefore decided to authorize aid amounting to FF 1.625 billion (ECU 234.8 million) to finance social measures to assist 5 129 workers made redundant, the direct costs of closure and the reorganization of production. It considered, on the other hand, that other aids related to expenditure which should normally be borne by the undertakings. These were the payment of wages due to beneficiaries of the social measures between the time when the works councils agreed to the measures and their actual implementation, investment costs not connected with the closures, and aid to cover earlier losses. The Commission decided to prohibit these aids (FF 1.1 billion, or ECU 159.0 million) in view of their incompatibility with the common market under Article 92(1).

In July, the Commission decided to close the Article 93(2) procedure it had initiated[3] against aid for exports of French foundry products because of the

---

[1] Eighteenth Competition Report, point 209.
[2] OJ L 90, 14.10.1987.
[3] OJ C 125, 20.5.1989.

method of levying the parafiscal charge used to finance the aid. In the course of the procedure, the French authorities recognized the need for French foundry products to be treated uniformly throughout the Community and abolished the differences, to which the Commission had objected, between taxes on products sold on the French market and taxes on products sold in other Community markets.

Italy

161.   In July 1968, the Commission had opened the Article 93(2) procedure in respect of aid contained in a scheme to recapitalize the company Dalmine operated by its majority shareholder Finsider/Ilva.

The Article 93(2) procedure was opened by the Commission in October against a possible award of aid for the installation of a 12 000 tonne forging press at Foggia. Because of the very low take-up rate in the Community of existing capacity in this sector and the large rise in capacity resulting from the investment, there is a risk of distortion of competition, contrary to the common interest.

The procedure was initiated chiefly as a result of the failure of the Italian authorities to reply to the request for information from the Commision.

Aid to the synthetic fibres industry

162.   In view of the situation in the synthetic fibres industry, the Commission decided to prolong the control system set up in 1977 [1] for a further two years ending on 19 July 1991. In accordance with Article 93(1) of the EEC Treaty, the Commission informed the Member States that it would continue to view unfavourably all aid proposals, irrespective of their type, having the effect of increasing net production capacity among firms in the synthetic fibres sector (which includes the manufacture of all acrylic, polyester, polypropylene and polyamide yarns and fibres and the texturing of such yarns), regardless of the nature or type of product.

The Commission reminded the Member States that it must be informed of all plans to grant aid to firms in this sector and also that it would continue to give favourable consideration only to aid measures designed to resolve serious social or regional problems by speeding up or facilitating conversion from synthetic

---

[1]   Seventh Competition Report, point 204.

fibres production to other activities or by restructuring leading to a reduction in capacity.

§ 4 — Investment, sectoral and horizontal aid schemes

General investment aids

163.   In November, the Commission opened the Article 93(2) procedure against the Sicilian regional Law of 27 October 1988 on industrial development measures, which provides for a considerable number of aid awards to public and private bodies. The Commission had informed the Italian authorities of its difficulties in assessing the law and had on several occasions requested further details. In the continuing absence of such data, the Commission decided to open the procedure because of its doubts as to the compatibility of the Sicilian scheme with the common market, and also in view of the large amount involved (LIT 323 billion, i.e. ECU 212 million).

Sectoral aid

Engineering and metal recycling industries

France

164.   In June, the Commission decided not to object to the renewal for five years of the parafiscal levy scheme imposed in France on products of the engineering and metal recycling industries which partly finance the operating expenses of specialized technical centres in the industries concerned. The rate of the charge is fixed annually by Ministerial decree and is subject to two ceilings: 0.35 % for structural, hydraulics and thermal engineering, and 0.112 % for the products of the engineering, metal recycling, machine tool, welding and free-cutting industries. The Commission checked that the conditions for compatibility, with which numerous parafiscal charge schemes had had to comply in the past, had been respected, i.e. no individual aid for undertakings, no taxation on imported products and no support measures for intra-Community exports.

Non-ferrous metals and minerals

Greece

165. In March, the Commission decided to open the Article 93(2) procedure in respect of aid awarded by the Greek Business Reconstruction Organization (BRO) to Fimisco, a magnesite and chromite mining company.

In December, the Commission decided to close the Article 93(2) procedure opened on 21 December 1988 against an aid of DR 2 700 million (ECU 14.4 million) granted by the BRO to Elbaumin, a bauxite producer. Having examined the company's restructuring plan, the Commission considered the aid was compatible with the common market. The plan includes a new investment programme, the closure of uneconomic mines and the financial restructuring of the firm through the sale of land owned by it.

Portugal

166. At the end of October, the Commission decided not to object to the extension of an aid scheme to keep certain tin and wolfram mines in operation. Under the scheme, a number of mining companies which have temporarily ceased operation will receive subsidies to cover part of their maintenance costs, wages of maintenance staff and allowances for workers temporarily laid off.

In view of the temporary halt to production, the Commission considered that the aids in question were not liable adversely to affect trade to an extent contrary to the common interest.

Italy

167. In May, the Commission took a final negative decision requiring the public aluminium producers Aluminia and Comsal to repay the aid awarded illegally by the Italian Government. The aid, in the form of an interest-free loan to be converted into equity capital, totalled LIT 70 billion (ECU 46.1 million) for Aluminia and LIT 30 billion (ECU 19.7 million) for Comsal. The Commission considered that both aid measures were incompatible with the common market, not only because they had been awarded without the prior approval of the Commission, but also because they had been awarded in breach of the Commission Decision of 17 December 1986,[1] under which no new aid

---

1   Sixteenth Competition Report, point 231.

could be granted to the public aluminium sector at least until the end of 1988. On 17 August 1989, the Italian Government appealed to the Court of Justice against the Commission's Decision of 24 May 1988.

France

168.   In October, the Commission decided that the capital contribution of FF 1 000 million (ECU 144.5 million) awarded by the French Government to Pechiney was not State aid but an injection of venture capital in accordance with the normal practice of companies in a market economy.

The Commission also examined the conditions in which the State-owned electricity company EdF will provide Pechiney with electricity under a joint venture contract valid for 25 years. The electricity is for a new aluminium smelter to be built at Dunkirk which will be partly owned by Pechiney. The Commission concluded that the minimum price of the electricity to be supplied to the smelter should be increased by 10 % in 1997, 1998 and again in 1999, in order to eliminate any aid elements in the agreement in question. Since the directors of the smelter and EdF agreed on an amendment incorporating these price rises, the Commission was able to conclude its investigation.

Federal Republic of Germany

169.   On 6 January, the Commission instituted proceedings before the Court of Justice against the Federal Republic of Germany, the latter having failed to fulfil its obligation to implement the Commission Decision of 17 November 1987. [1] This Decision concerned the recovery of DM 2 million (ECU 1 million) awarded illegally as aid in April 1985 in the form of a grant to BUG Alutechnik, a manufacturer of aluminium finished and semi-finished products. [2]

Italy

170.   In June, the Commission took a decision concerning the new Italian five-year plan for mining. It did not object to the award of certain aids for basic research, applied research and prospecting in non-Member countries. However, it opened the Article 93(2) procedure in respect of aid for the environment, operating aid and reconversion aid. It considered that some of the award

---

[1]   OJ L 79, 24.3.1988.
[2]   See point 239 of this Report.

procedures, the destination of the aids, their excessive amount in relation to the objectives and the lack of any guaranteed restructuring plans meant that the aids in question were liable adversely to affect intra-Community trade and distort competition.

Textiles and clothing

France

171. In March, the Commission took a negative decision at the end of the procedure it had opened in 1988 under Article 93(2) in respect of a proposal to grant aid amounting to FF 5.3 million (ECU 0.76 million) to Caulliez Frères, a manufacturer of combed cotton at Prouvy (northern France).

The Commission considered that the aid enabled the firm to increase its capacity by some 70% in a sector suffering from structural overcapacity, falling demand, a fall in prices and severe competition both in and outside the Community. In such conditions, the proposed aid would be liable adversely to affect trade to an extent contrary to the common interest.

Aviation industry

Federal Republic of Germany

172. In March, the Commission decided to approve a series of aids proposed by the German Government for a new subsidiary of Messerschmidt-Bölkow-Blohm (MBB), the German Airbus consortium. The aid awarded to the first private firm participating in Deutsche Airbus formed part of the State's policy of putting an end to direct public aid for Airbus and was intended to promote the restructuring of the German civil aviation industry in order to improve its efficiency and international competitiveness. The Commission checked that Daimler Benz AG, which will be the new majority shareholder of MBB, will be unable to use the aid for any of its other industrial activities. In view of the economic and technological importance of the aviation industry to the Community, the Commission considered that the proposed measure would strengthen the overall competitiveness of the sector and thus concretely serve the general interest. It also took account of the fact that the State aids would decrease over the years and, in particular, of the fact that the Airbus was being produced and marketed in cooperation with several Member States. It therefore

considered that the aids qualified for exemption under Article 92(3)(b) (execution of an important project of common European interest).

United Kingdom

173.   In March, the Commission decided to approve a proposal from the United Kingdom to grant aid to Short Brothers plc Belfast (Northern Ireland). The aid, in the form of a short-term loan of UKL 390 million (ECU 527 million) should enable the company to remain viable during the restructuring preceding the privatization of Shorts. The loan is to take the place of existing bank loans, interest being payable at market rates. As the aid is to be awarded to a company whose principal activities are in the aircraft, aerostructures and missiles sector and which, with 7 700 employees, is the largest employer in manufacturing in Northern Ireland, the Commission considered that it satisfied the Community tests for rescue aid and that trade would not be affected to an extent contrary to the common interest.

In July, the Commission also decided to approve the award to Short Brothers plc, on the occasion of its sale to the Canadian firm Bombardier, of an aid package totalling UKL 731 million (ECU 988 million), of which UKL 289 million (ECU 391 million) concerned its military activities. The aid was intended to facilitate the sale of the firm through a write-off of debts accumulated in the past, a restructuring of the balance sheet and coverage of future losses linked to existing operations. As these operations are important to several customers and partners in the Community owing to their involvement or dependence on Shorts, the Commission considered that Community interests would be better served by keeping Shorts in business and restoring its competitiveness with the help of State aid than by allowing market forces to act, which could result in the disappearance of this major aerospace firm. It also considered that the aids proposed were needed for the financial restructuring of the firm, that Shorts would retain a considerable proportion of its activities, that future losses should greatly exceed the proposed contributions and that, in addition, Bombardier would be implementing a major investment programme. The State aid was therefore commensurate with the problems it was intended to resolve. The Commission also bore in mind that Short Brothers plc is by far the largest supplier of industrial jobs in Northern Ireland. The social and economic consequences of closure would have been very severe and would inevitably have led to a loss of confidence among potential outside investors who are crucial to Northern Ireland's economic development.

Chemicals

Portugal

174. In July, the Commission initiated the Article 93(2) [1] procedure in respect of an aid measure notified by the Portuguese Government involving the award of ESC 48 000 million (ECU 268 million) to the public chemicals undertaking Quimigal (Quimica de Portugal), to reduce the debts resulting from unprofitable investments which had led to the closure of some plants (pyrite pellets and fibreglass) and the rationalization of others (ammonia).

On the basis of the information in its possession and with a view in particular to the financial position of the firm, the Commission considered that the aid proposal was not compatible with the common market within the meaning of Article 92 of the EEC Treaty.

France

175. In December, the Commission decided to approve aid granted by the French Government to Orkem (formerly CDF-Chimie) in 1986 and 1987; the aid, which includes a FF 4 366 million (ECU 681 million) debt and loan write-off and two capital injections of FF 2 000 million (ECU 448 million), was to assist the recovery of the firm by financing major capacity cuts in the convenience products sector (fertilizers and petrochemical products).

The Commission decision follows a detailed examination, from which it was concluded that the aid in question does not affect trade to an extent contrary to the common interest. The capacity cuts are in a sector with serious Community-wide structural problems and they contribute accordingly to its improvement.

Pharmaceuticals

Belgium

176. In December, the Commission considered that the aid resulting from permission to make selective price increases through programme agreements concluded between the Belgian Government and certain Belgian pharmaceutical

---

[1]   OJ C 295, 23.11.1989.

companies was incompatible with the common market. The negative decision taken by the Commission orders the Belgian Government not to conclude any more programme agreements. Under the agreements, price increases are allowed under the existing pricing system in exchange for certain undertakings given by the beneficiary, without the medicaments concerned losing entitlement to reimbursement under the sickness insurance scheme.

The companies concluding a contract had to give an undertaking concerning investments and research projects, job creation and/or an increase in exports — normal and typical activities for all firms in the pharmaceuticals sector. Authorizing aid in the form of selective price increases under a strict price-fixing system would be to put the recipient firms' competitors at a disadvantage which could force them to withdraw from the market.

Since only pharmaceutical companies located in Belgium could meet the conditions required for concluding a programme contract, an infringement procedure under Article 30 of the EEC Treaty was initiated at the same time and the case is now before the Court of Justice.

Household appliances

France

177.   In November, the Commission decided to close the Article 93(2) procedure opened in July 1986 [1] against three aids to Usines et Fonderies Arthur Martin (UFAM), a household appliances manufacturer. In the course of the procedure, the French authorities provided detailed information concerning UFAM investments at Revin and the relevant aids. The information enabled the Commission to determine that the investment in question comprised innovatory elements and contributed to a substantial reduction in production capacity. The Commission also took account of the fact that the intensity of the three aids did not exceed the regional aid ceiling which the Commission had approved for Revin. It therefore decided that the aid qualified for exemption under Article 92(3)(c).

Spain

178.   In December, following the procedure of Article 93(2) of the EEC Treaty, the Commission adopted a final negative decision regarding aid which had been granted to Magefesa, the Spanish producer of stainless steel household

---

[1]   Sixteenth Competition Report, point 234.

goods and small electric appliances. The aid in question had been provided in 1986-87 by the Spanish Government and by the governments of the autonomous regions of Andalusia, Cantabria and the Basque country, following serious financial difficulties which had been encountered by the companies in the group. The aid formed part of a package of rescue aids which consisted of: credit guarantees to the value of PTA 1 830 million (ECU 14.0 million); a PTA 2 085 million (ECU 15.9 million) subsidized refinancing for Fogasa; subsidies totalling PTA 1 095 million (ECU 8.4 million); and a credit interest discount of PTA 9 million (ECU 68 000). These public interventions were unlawful because the Spanish authorities had not complied with the obligation of prior notification to the Commission. In the light of the information available, the Commission decided that the aids in question were incompatible with the common market.

In arriving at its decision, the Commission took particularly into account the fact that the aids had been granted to keep the companies in business artificially, without putting into place the restructuring measures which were necessary to guarantee their viability. Consequently, the Spanish Government was requested to obtain repayment of the aid element implicit in its subventions.

Machine tools

France

179. In December, following the procedure of Article 93(2) of the EEC Treaty, the Commission adopted a final negative decision regarding aid which had been granted to Brisard Machine-Outil and Berthiez Productics. These recently established enterprises had purchased the assets of the French machine tool manufacturer, MFL (Machines Françaises Lourdes), following its bankruptcy. In order to facilitate the initial operation of the companies, the French authorities had, in 1988, provided interest-free advances of FF 25 million and FF 17 million (ECU 3.6 and 2.5 million) respectively, with highly preferential repayment conditions. This particular public intervention is considered to be unlawful because the French authorities did not comply with the obligation of prior notification to the Commission.

In the light of the information available, the Commission decided that the aid element contained in these advances was incompatible with the common market. The Commission took into account in its decision, the disruptive effects resulting from *ad hoc* aids in the machine tool sector, which is characterized by strong competition among Community producers. The Commission furthermore, took into consideration the fact that the aid was not linked to a restructuring of the companies, involving specific capacity reductions; a circumstance which could have justified the granting of the aid. Consequently, the French Government was asked to remove the aid element in the advance of FF 25 million made to Brisard Machine Outil. The request for the recovery of the FF 17 million granted in aid to Berthiez Productics was not made, due to the fact that this company has been wound up.

Paper

Italy

180. In May, the Commission adopted a final negative decision in respect of aid for newsprint manufacturers in Italy. The procedure under Article 93(2) had been initiated in June 1988. [1] The Commission subsequently established that the Ente nazionale per la cellulosa e per la carta (ENCC), a body under public law, financed by a parafiscal charge on pulp and paper, assisted the Italian newsprint industry by including Italian newspaper publishers to purchase increasing quantities of domestic newsprint at artificially high prices in relation to the market price. The amount of aid in the period 1985-87 was estimated at LIT 34 000 million (ECU 22.4 million). In its decision, the Commission required that these operating aids be abolished from the date of notification of the decision.

Cement

Greece

181. In April, the Commission decided to open the Article 93(2) procedure against aid to the Greek cement manufacturer Halkis. [2] The Commission noted that the firm in question was on the verge of bankruptcy, that its debts amounted to DR 27 000 million (ECU 144 million) at the end of 1987 and that the Greek Government intended to convert part of the debt into capital. The Commission considered that the non-recovery of the debts and their conversion into capital constituted rescue aid aimed at keeping the firm in business and

---

[1] Eighteenth Competition Report, point 235.
[2] OJ C 156, 24.6.1989.

was not therefore covered by any of the exemptions provided for in Article 92(3).

Motor vehicles and related industries

Decisions preceding the adoption of the Community framework

182.   The following decisions taken by the Commission in 1989 were not covered by the Community framework on State aid to the motor-vehicle industry as they concerned aid cases notified or implemented prior to the entry into force of the framework on 1 January 1989.

Portugal

183.   In March 1989, the Commission decided not to object to an investment aid which the Portuguese Government planned to award to Ford Lusitana SA, a subsidiary of Ford Europe. The aid, totalling ESC 245 million (ECU 1.4 million), which corresponds to 30% of the investment costs, is to enable the plant to undergo a thorough rationalization.

Spain

184.   In May, the Commission closed two procedures initiated in 1987 and 1988 [1] by adopting a final conditional decision, authorizing the Spanish Government to award, through the building company INI, PTA 47 000 million (ECU 359 million) representing capital grants and extraordinary contributions to the 1987-91 restructuring plan of Enasa, a manufacturer of 'Pegaso' commercial vehicles.

The Commission concluded that because the plan provided for major production capacity cuts, it contributed to the overall restructuring of the commercial vehicles industry in the Community, a sector which has suffered from excess production capacity since the early 1980s. Although the restructuring enables the company to recover, the Commission nevertheless considered that the aid was excessive compared with restructuring costs of PTA 128.4 billion (ECU 980 million). Having analysed the financial resources of the company and consulted the Spanish authorities, it decided that the aid element of the

---

[1]   See OJ C 124, 11.5.1988; Eighteenth Competition Report, point 226; and OJ C 213, 11.8.1987; Seventeenth Competition Report, point 226.

measures corresponding to PTA 70 billion (ECU 534 million) should be reduced to PTA 23 billion (ECU 176 million). The aid intensity was thus reduced to 36% of restructuring costs and is therefore comparable with the 31% cut in vehicle production capacity provided for in the restructuring plan. The reduction in the aid, which will not jeopardize the economic and financial recovery of the company at the end of the restructuring plan, will thus prevent any market distortion due to excessive aid. The authorization is valid only on condition that the Spanish Government does not award further aid to Enasa during the restructuring and ensures that it is fully implemented.

Italy

185.   In May 1989, the Commission decided that the aid of LIT 615 000 million (ECU 405 million) awarded in 1985 and 1986 to the vehicle manufacturer Alfa Romeo was incompatible with Community law and should be refunded by Finmeccanica, the State-holding company which owned Alfa Romeo.[1] The Commission thus concluded the procedure opened in July 1987 and extended in May 1988.[2]

The Commission considered that the two capital injections carried out without prior notification by the Italian Government into Alfa Romeo and against which it had opened the Article 93(2) procedure, were not consistent with the actions of a shareholder operating under normal market conditions. Alfa Romeo had incurred continuous losses since 1975 and, after 1984, had deteriorated rapidly. The aid, which was to offset the losses and was awarded at a time when the European car industry was faced with serious overcapacity problems, was not tied to any rationalization measures which would have resolved the structural crisis within the firm. By keeping Alfa Romeo artificially afloat until it was sold, the aid seriously distorted competition and it cannot be justified from a regional standpoint since it was not used for proper restructuring enabling viable jobs to be kept in a less-favoured region such as the Mezzogiorno, where there are several Alfa Romeo plants. The Commission also concluded that the Fiat offer, accepted by Alfa Romeo at the end of 1986, did not contain any State aid elements, either in relation to the competing offer from Ford Motor Company, which was rejected, or as regards the price paid for the assets.

---

[1]   OJ L 394, 30.12.1989.
[2]   See OJ C 276, 15.10.1987; Seventeenth Competition Report, point 225; OJ C 213, 13.8.1988; Eighteenth Competition Report, point 232.

Netherlands

186. The Commission decided in July 1989 to open the Article 93(2) procedure against the modification by the Dutch Government of three aid schemes in favour of Volvo Car BV, agreed in 1977, 1979 and 1981 [1] between the Swedish company Volvo AB and the Dutch Government. Volvo Sweden has a 30% stake in Volvo Car BV, the remaining 70% being controlled by the Dutch public sector. The plan is to modify the repayment terms of the interest-free loans granted by the shareholders of Volvo Car between 1977 and 1987 and to re-utilize the loans to develop new generations of cars. Volvo Car would in future repay the loans to two Funds with a maximum capital of HFL 958 million (ECU 418 million) of which the Dutch Government will hold 73% or up to a maximum of HFL 698 million (ECU 305 million). In the opinion of the Dutch Government, the new scheme does not contain any new aid elements in relation to the first schemes approved by the Commission. However, although the private shareholder is involved in the two Funds, the Commission considers the proposed modification comprises new elements of aid.

France

187. On 15 November, the Commission decided that its decision of 29 March 1988 against aid granted to the Renault Group [2] had not been implemented correctly, the French Government having failed to comply with two essential conditions imposed by the Commission.

In its decision, the Commission had authorized the award by the French Government of FF 20 000 million (ECU 2 890 million) to Renault, of which FF 8 000 million (ECU 1 156 million) had already been granted as capital contributions in 1985 and 1986, and FF 12 000 million (ECU 734 million) in the form of a debt write-off. The award of FF 12 000 million was approved on condition that the French Government implemented its plan to change the status of Renault from a 'régie' to a legal entity subject to normal commercial law before the end of 1988. A further condition was that Renault carry out its restructuring plan. This provides, in particular, that an average reduction of 25% in vehicle production capacity should take place, between the date of the decision and the end of 1990. The Commission found that:

(i) the modification of Renault's status by means of a regulation was not sufficient to place it legally on completely the same footing as its competitors subject to all the obligations of national commercial law;

---

1   See Tenth Competition Report, point 209.
2   OJ C 220, 11.8.1988; Eighteenth Competition Report, point 227.

(ii) the Renault Group had abandoned its plan to reduce vehicle production capacity through closures or gradual reductions in assembly plants, contrary to the undertakings given by the French Government.

The authorization referred to above is therefore null and void.

The Commission requested the French Government to inform it within three months of the measures it proposed to take to comply with the decision. It noted the indications of the latest position of the French Government and expressed the hope that it would result in satisfactory proposals. In the absence of such proposals, however, the French Government will be required to recover FF 12 000 million from Renault. The Commission also decided that, failing a reply or in the case of an unsatisfactory reply within the time indicated, the matter would be referred to the Court of Justice.

Decisions under the framework

188.   The Commission took the following decisions under the Community framework on State aid to the motor vehicle industry:

Italy

189.   In September 1989, the Commission decided to approve a proposal from the Italian authorities to assist Ferrari's technological innovation programme. The programme covers approximately half of Ferrari's research and development expenditure in the period 1986-91. The aid will be paid pursuant to Law 46/82 (Technological Innovation Fund) in the form of a subsidized loan of LIT 41.6 billion (ECU 27.4 million), and will have an intensity of 20% net grant equivalent. The Commission took account of the special characteristics of the sports car market, the low production volume, high prices and high profit margins. It concluded that the innovation programme satisfies the criteria laid down in the framework for research and development aid and innovation aid, and that it enables new products and processes to be introduced in the relevant sector.

Portugal

190.   In September 1989, the Commission decided to approve an aid which the Portuguese Government planned to grant to the audio-electronics department of the Ford Motor Company to build a new manufacturing plant for car audio equipment at Pinhal Novo (Setubal). Ford's plan provides for a total investment

of some ESC 17 000 million (ECU 95.0 million) and the creation of 1 700 new jobs in the ailing region of Setubal. Aid totalling ESC 8 920 million (ECU 49.8 million) will be granted under the regional aid scheme, i.e. 58.3 % of eligible investment costs. The investment will have a considerable positive impact on this economically under-developed region and an appreciable overall effect on national economic and technological development, without any visible adverse effects on the Community motor vehicle industry.

Film industry

Greece

191. In December 1988, the Commission concluded the Article 93(2) procedure it had opened in December 1987 with a decision that the film industry aid scheme introduced by Law No 1597/86 is incompatible with the common market within the meaning of Article 92(1) of the EEC Treaty on the ground that the award of aid is subject to nationality conditions that are incompatible with Articles 7, 48, 52 and 59 of the EEC Treaty.

The Greek Government had until 15 May 1989 to remove the restrictions and inform the Commission of the measures taken to comply with the decision.

The law provides for such aids as automatic grants equal to the public entertainment tax on films shown in cinemas, which are no longer granted when they equal production costs, and a selective aid in the form of participation (50 %) in the costs of film production, or State financing consisting of advances (20 %) of production costs granted by the Greek Cinematography Centre.

The Commission has always considered that aid to the film industry should, in view of its combined economic and cultural functions, qualify for exemption under Article 92(3)(c) of the EEC Treaty provided, however, that it satisfies all the requirements of the Treaty, notably those concerning the free movement of persons and freedom to provide services. The Greek aid measures, however, discriminate against nationals of other Member States and do not therefore qualify for exemption under Article 92 of the EEC Treaty.

Denmark and France

192. In May, the Commission decided to close the procedures opened under Article 93(2) against aid to the film industry in France and Denmark. The French scheme consists of aids to producers based on receipts generated by a

film, and tax relief on investment in audiovisual productions. The budget for the scheme is fixed annually and in 1986 amounted to ECU 50 million. The Danish scheme provides for advances on receipts or guarantees for production loans and direct grants towards production costs. The Commission had not objected to the aid measures themselves but to the fact that the aid was linked to certain discriminatory practices based on nationality, which were detrimental to nationals of other Member States wishing to produce or take part in the production of an assisted film. The Commission having argued that no distinction should be made between Community nationals, the Danish authorities adopted a new Law No 218 on 5 April 1989 on aids awards to films made with other Community nationals and which therefore treat the latter in the same way as Danish nationals. The French authorities for their part published a Decree in the Official Journal of the French Republic on 3 March 1989 under which nationals of other Member States of the Community are treated in the same way as French nationals.

Italy

193.   The legislation on aid to film-making in Italy (Law No 1213 of 4 November 1965 and Law No 163/1985) contained restrictions based on nationality which limited participation by nationals of other Member States in films receiving aid. Two procedures under Article 93(2) of the EEC Treaty were therefore opened against the laws in question.

While it was not opposed in principle to aid for the film industry in view of its special nature, the Commission requested the Italian Government in the course of the procedure to remove the restrictions so as to bring the laws governing aid into line with the provisions of the Treaty on the free movement of persons and freedom to provide services.

The Italian Government having kept the Commission informed of the steps it was taking to bring these laws into line with the requirements of the Treaty, forwarded the text of an administrative measure which entered into force on 25 October 1988 and which abolishes all restrictions based on nationality in the laws in question. The Commission, having noted that the legislation complied with the EEC Treaty, decided to close the procedure in April.

Spain

194.   On 31 October 1989, the Commission decided pursuant to Article 92(3)(c) not to object to a scheme to assist the Spanish film industry which replaces a scheme in force since 1983, introduced by Royal Decree No 2304/1983.

Under the scheme, aid is awarded in the form of grants for film production, promotion, scriptwriting and participation in festivals and competitions. For the production of a film, producers will automatically be granted a general aid amounting to 15 % of the revenue generated in commercial cinemas in the two years following the release of the film. In addition, aid will be granted on a selective basis for their financing, subject to approval of the production plans. The Decree fixes specific ceilings for each type of aid. The initial budget is PTA 3 385 billion (ECU 25.8 million) for 1990, broken down as follows: production aid: 77 %, promotion aid: 18 %, other aid: 5 %.

The Decree also provides that nationals of other Member States are to be treated in the same way as Spanish nationals for the production of films and as regards film industry occupations. In the case of employees, the Decree establishes limitations, in line with Article 56 of the Act of Accession of Spain which provides that Articles 1 to 6 of Regulation (EEC) No 1612/68 on freedom of movement for persons are applicable in Spain to nationals of other Member States only from 1 January 1993. Until then, the Spanish authorities must notify a new version of the Decree which brings their provisions into line with the principle of free movement established by the Treaty.

Railway equipment

United Kingdom

195. In April, the Commission decided to approve a UKL 64 million (ECU 86.5 million) debt write-off by the British Government as part of the privatization of BREL-British Engineering Ltd, the railway equipment design, manufacture and repair subsidiary of the British Railways Board (BRB).

Following an open bid, a consortium made up of the firm's management, Trafalgar House and Asea Brown Boveri was selected by BRB to take over BREL. The consortium paid UKL 14 million (ECU 18.9 million) for the company and property relating to its operations and will carry out major restructuring, capacity and streamlining operations. The cost of the restructuring plan, estimated at UKL 75 million (ECU 101.4 million), will be borne entirely by the new owners without State assistance.

In reaching its decision on the basis of the exemption in Article 92(3)(c), the Commission took account of the fact that the market for railway equipment was largely closed because of national restrictions on public procurement and that, because of the privatization, the company will operate under normal market conditions without future aid which will allow the BRB to pursue a more open procurement policy. In addition, the restructuring plan will contribute to the reduction of overcapacity in this sector.

Spain

196.   In April, the Commission decided to approve, pursuant to Article 92(3)(c), a notified aid package of PTA 25 billion (ECU 191 million) to the Spanish railway equipment producers MTM and Ateinsa, two wholly-owned subsidiaries of the Spanish public holding company INI, which had made heavy losses in recent years.

These companies have for some time been involved in carrying out a restructuring programme involving extensive reductions in capacity, manpower levels and the elimination of a number of non-railway equipment engineering activities. The Spanish authorities decided, after inviting bids, to sell the companies to the French firm Alsthom in order to secure an adequate transfer of technology and thereby ensure their future viability. No further assistance will be given after privatization, and the new owners bear all the costs of the streamlining and restructuring programme, including new investment.

In reaching its decision, the Commission took account of the specific characteristics of the railway equipment sector where procedures operate in largely closed markets that are dependent on the national railways with low levels of capacity utilization. The proposed aid will contribute to a reduction of capacity in this sector and help it to adjust to open competition.

Aid to employment

Netherlands

197.   In 1986, the Commission had authorized the implementation of a Dutch draft law, the 'Vermeend-Moor' Law, which introduced a scheme of aid for the recruitment of the long-term unemployed, defined as those who had been out of work for three years or more. [1]

In March 1989, The Dutch Government notified a proposal to amend the Vermeerd-Moor Law in order to extend it to those who have been out of work for two years and to create 'work experience' jobs at the same time.

---

[1]   Sixteenth Competition Report, point 255.

In future, partial exemption from social security contributions (amounting to approximately 20 % of the wage) will be granted for four years when recruiting the long-term unemployed (out of work for at least two years).

Employers providing training will receive additional aid in the form of a grant of HFL 4 000 to 6 000 (ECU 1 750 to 2 625) depending on the length of unemployment of the person recruited. In addition, the creation by firms of work experience jobs for persons out of work for over three years which give them one year of employment and training will give entitlement to a grant of HFL 15 000 (ECU 6 563) and exemption from social security contributions as described above.

In view of the social problems posed by the large number of long-term unemployed in the Netherlands and the fact that the programme is in line with objectives Nos 3 and 4 assigned to the structural Funds in connection with the fight against long-term unemployment, the Commission decided to approve the implementation of the amended Vermeend-Moor Law. The Dutch authorities hope by this means to recruit some 18 000 unemployed persons in 1989 and again in 1990 and to create 5 500 work experience jobs in 1989 and 22 000 in 1990.

Environmental protection aid

France

198.   In June, the Commission opened the Article 93(2) procedure against a French State aids scheme introduced by the Agence pour la Qualité de L'Air (Air Quality Agency) for investments in desulphurization plant. The aid took the form of grants of up to 50 % of investment costs, its annual budget totalling FF 90 million (ECU 13 million). The Commission considered that the intensity of the aid and size of the budget were liable to distort competition and affect intra-Community trade since they reduce some of the running costs of the recipient firms which their competitors in other Member States have to bear in full.

Netherlands

199.   In January, the Commission opened the procedure provided for in Article 93(2) against tax measures for less-polluting cars notified by the Dutch Government. Reductions in the special consumer tax would be granted to

persons buying cars which anticipated Community standards (a reduction of HFL 850 − ECU 371) or complied with even stricter standards (a reduction of HFL 1 700 − ECU 42). Having obtained further information in the course of the procedure, the Commission decided to close it in March on the ground that it did not constitute aid within the meaning of Article 92(1). The Commission took account of the fact that the tax reduction covered only part of the extra cost of the depolluting equipment, that it was granted irrespective of the origin of the less-polluting cars and that all manufacturers are technically capable of producing this type of vehicle. It concluded that the measure did not threaten to distort competiton by favouring certain undertakings or certain products.

Tax measures

200.   In August, the Commission decided to initiate the Article 93(2) procedure in respect of the tax measures provided for by Decree Law No 174 published in the Gazzetta Ufficiale of the Italian Republic of 15 May 1989 under the heading 'Urgent tax measures to promote the reorganization of the manufacturing industry'. The Commission considered that the Italian measures in question were not general measures which consistently applied a general taxation system and were applicable automatically and indiscriminately to the economy as a whole, but were aids intended for a very small number of firms or even exclusively for the Enimont operation. The Commission considered that the financial advantage resulting from the tax exemption could amount to LIT 774 000 million (ECU 509 million) and would be likely to strengthen the position of the chemicals manufacturer Montedison in relation to other competitors as regards intra-Community trade. The Commission therefore concluded that the aid was likely to distort competition and effect trade between Member States.

In November, the Commission decided to extend the Article 93(2) procedure opened in August 1989 [1] against the tax measures provided for in Decree Law No 174 of May 1989, to the measures contained in a draft law of October aimed at confirming the legal position created by the abovementioned Decree Law, which had ceased to apply in the meantime. The Commission considered that the unnotified draft law was intended to make definitive the award of tax advantages to Montedison for the Enimont operation, which was the only one to have been carried out under the Decree Law objected to by the Commission.

---

[1]   OJ C 291, 7.11.1989.

Aid in the energy sector

201. In April, the Commission decided not to object to the continuation of the second programme of the German Government which comprises aid for energy research which the Commission had approved until the end of 1985. The German authorities had continued to apply the programme without notifying it. It includes projects in the fields of fossil energy (about 23% of the total budget), renewable energy (about 34% of the total budget) and nuclear energy (about 43% of the total budget). Industrial undertakings benefit from a budget of some DM 350 million (ECU 173 million), the remainder being allocated to research centres. The intensity of the aid varies according to the type of project. It can reach 50% and exceed this limit in exceptional cases.

An analysis of the programme and the detailed project reports showed that the awards constituted aid within the meaning of Article 92(1) of the Treaty. The Commission nevertheless authorized an extension of the programme until the end of 1989 under the derogation provided for in Article 92(3)(c) in view of the objectives of the programme, the nature of the projects and the recipients.

Export aid

202. In May 1987, the Commission decided to adopt a final negative decision under Article 93(2) of the EEC Treaty in respect of aid to Greek exporting firms taking the form of exemption from the single special tax established by Ministerial Decision No E 3789/128 of 15 March 1988.

The Commission considered that the tax, calculated on the basis of net profits of the firms, minus the share of profits corresponding to gross export earnings, should be regarded as aid to exports to other Member States and was incompatible with the common market.

It therefore decided that the Greek Government should immediately modify the single special tax scheme in question, abolishing the incompatible aid and recovering from the recipients the aid enjoyed by the firms under the Ministerial Decision by requiring them to pay the part of the tax not collected.

§ 5 — Regional aids

Spain

203. In June, the Commission decided to approve a proposal for the region of Castilla y Leon establishing a regional aid scheme to regulate the various financial aids to investment in the region. The total aid granted for one investment may not exceed 75% net grant equivalent in the provinces of Avilla, Leon, Salamanca, Soria, Zamora, and 45% net grant equivalent in the provinces of Burgos, Palencia, Segovia and Valladolid. The scheme will have a budget in 1989 of PTA 5 373.48 million (ECU 41.0). The Commission took account of the fact that Castilla y Leon is eligible for regional aid under Article 92(3)(a), that the aid intensity ceilings will not exceed the 75% net grant equivalent ceiling authorized by the Commission for the regions covered by this provision of the Treaty and that the regional differences in the ceilings are the same as those authorized by the Commission as part of the national regional aids scheme, taking account of the varying severity of regional problems.

In July, the Commission approved a proposal to raise the regional aid ceilings in certain areas of the Basque country from 30% net grant equivalent to 40% net grant equivalent on the left bank of the Nervion valley and from 20% to 30% net grand equivalent in the industrial areas around San Sebastian and the Bajo Deba. The scheme will be financed from the budget of the national regional aids scheme which, in 1989, totalled PTA 12 000 million (ECU 91.6 million). The Commission took particular account of the unfavourable social and economic situation of the regions in question from both the Community and the national standpoint; especially as regards unemployment, and of the huge impact on the regional economy of the industrial problems and of Community policies on the steel and shipping industries. It also considered that the project does not increase the size of Spanish assisted areas and does not modify the budget of the national regional aids scheme. The 40% ceiling was authorized for a period of three years, taking account of Protocol No 12 to the Act of Accession of Spain to the European Communities; the Commission will review the question of renewal at the end of that period.

In October, the Commission decided to approve an investment aid scheme in a mining area of the Spanish province of Huelva (Andalusia), and aids granted in Andalusia by the Andalusian Development Institute (IFA). All these aids are awarded by the Andalusian government, either directly in the case of Huelva or indirectly through the IFA which allocates the Andalusian government's investment aids. Aid to the mining area of Huelva consists of grants, the total budget for which was ECU 2.3 million in 1989. Aid from the IFA in 1989 took the form of grants (ECU 3.6 million), interest subsidies (ECU 18 million), guarantees (ECU 1.7 million), loans (ECU 14.6 million) and shareholdings (ECU 5.6 million). The Commission took account of the fact that the whole of Andalusia is eligible for aid under Article 92(3)(a) and that the amount of aid in question is relatively small. As regards the cumulation of aids for different purposes, the Spanish and Andalusian Governments agreed that the total aid awarded for a single investment in Andalusia would not exceed a net grant equivalent of 75%.

France

204. The Commission undertook a review of all regional aids granted in France. The French authorities were therefore requested in March 1989 to provide certain recent socio-economic data on areas eligible for regional aid and on several aid schemes.

The aim was to analyse the compatibility of existing aid measures with the common market in the light of structural changes which had taken place since earlier Commission decisions. In accordance with Article 93(1) of the EEC Treaty, the Commission will in due course propose the appropriate measures necessitated by any such changes.

In May, the Commission decide to authorize a number of reconversion measures implemented by the French authorities in declining mining areas. The measures are applied through the conversion companies Sofirem and Finorpa whose task is to award loans, acquire minority holdings in SMEs and provide them with advice. There are also Industrialization Funds (FIBM) whose main task is to create infrastructures.

In its decision, the Commission took account of the low intensity of the aids, the fact that they are essentially intended for SMEs and the difficult socio-economic circumstances of the mining areas which are, moreover, virtually all eligible for regional aid. It also ensured that the regional aid ceilings it had fixed would not be exceeded under any circumstances. Lastly, in order to improve its control, it approved only the refinancing for 1989 and requested the French authorities to submit regular reports.

In June, the Commission approved the creation of a conversion company by the group Compagnie Generale Maritime (Atlantique-Developpement). The company's task is to promote the reindustrialization of the areas of La Rochelle and Saintonge-Maritime (department of Charante-Maritime) to offset the negative impact caused by the closure of shipyards in those regions.

Atlantique-Developement will contribute in the form of loans on special terms and minority shareholdings.

The Commission took account in its decision of the difficult socio-economic situation in the areas in question all of which are eligible for regional aid. It also verified that the regional aid ceilings it had fixed would not be exceeded under any circumstances. It took account of the fact that the aids, whose intensity is limited, would be granted essentially to SMEs. It approved only the 1989 refinancing and requested the French authorities to submit annual and six-monthly reports regularly.

In December, the Commission took a decision in respect of the French enterprise zones whose creation it had approved in January 1987,[1] subject to certain undertakings given by the French authorities and the forwarding of quarterly reports. In the areas affected by the closure of shipyards, new firms are exempt from corporation tax for 10 years.

It emerged from an examination of the reports that the clause allowing 'economically marginal' aids only to be cumulated with the tax relief in the enterprise areas had been misused. The Commission decided to propose appropriate measures to the French authorities under Article 93(1) whereby, as from 1 March 1990, no more aids may be cumulated in enterprise areas with the tax aids concerned.

In December, the Commission also took a final decision concerning 24 PAT grants for investment projects outside the assisted areas. The 24 PAT grants had been the subject of an Article 93(2) procedure opened in April 1988[2] as they had not been notified to the Commission before they were awarded.

It decided to close the procedure in question in view of the fact that 12 awards were in fact compatible with the common market and the other 12 qualified for exemption under Article 92(3)(c) because of the high level of unemployment in the regions concerned at the time of the awards in question.

Ireland

205.   In April, the Commission decided not to object to the Irish Government's plan to remove the legislative provisions which limit the unrestricted availability of the 10% corporation tax scheme to service companies at Shannon Airport

---

[1]   Seventeenth Competition Report, point 245.
[2]   Seventeenth Competition Report, point 254.

employing fewer than 50 persons.[1] A number of firms had developed to an extent that they now employed over 50 persons.

In its decision, the Commission took account of the serious economic and social situation in the Mid-West Planning Region, the importance of the recipient firms to the developments of that region and also of the Commission's policy of approving operating aid under certain conditions in regions exempted under Article 92(3)(a). The Irish authorities were requested to submit detailed annual reports.

Italy

206.   In July 1989, the Commission initiated the Article 93(2) procedure against a number of regional aids awarded in the Friuli-Venezia-Giulia region under several regional laws and one national law.

The Commission examined the aids in the light of Article 92(3)(c) of the EEC Treaty.

Whilst the socio-economic situation in the four provinces of the region justifies maintaining certain regional aids in the provinces of Gorizia and Trieste, the same cannot be said of the provinces of Udine and Pordenone.

The Article 93(2) procedure was therefore opened against both the regional aid measures applicable in Udine and Pordenone and certain aid measures in the provinces of Gorizia and Trieste which were considered to be ill-suited to the nature and severity of the regional problems in question.

In October 1989, the Commission also opened the Article 93(2) procedure against a number of State aid measures adopted by the Italian authorities to supplement the industrial development project established by Law No 219/81 for the Mezzogiorno areas affected by the earthquake in 1980. The procedure was opened chiefly because the level of the aids, notably the investment aid awarded to the enterprise areas set up under Article 32 of Law No 219/81, is higher than the aid ceilings agreed by the Commission in its decision on Law No 64/86 establishing a new aid scheme for the Mezzogiorno.[2]

---

[1]   Seventeenth Competition Report, point 249.
[2]   Decision of 2 March 1988, OJ L 143, 10.6.1988.

Netherlands

207.   In June, the Commission initiated the Article 93(2)[1] procedure against a Dutch aid scheme for regional programmes.

Partly for demonstration purposes, the Dutch Government assists small and medium-sized firms in certain regions to carry out projects in industry, tourism, agriculture and services. The activities benefiting from aid are chiefly infrastructure and education projects and research projects. The aid is awarded in the form of grants and has been allocated a budget of HFL 137.5 million (ECU 60 million).

The aid instrument in question, known as 'regioprogramma's' (regional programmes) was not notified to the Commission in accordance with Article 93(3). The aid in question is therefore illegal under Community law. In addition, on the basis of the information it has obtained to date, the Commission considers that the aid in question distorts or threatens to distort competition, affects trade between the Member States pursuant to Article 92(2) of the Treaty and does not qualify for exemption under paragraphs 2 or 3 of that Article.

Federal Republic of Germany

208.   In August, the Commission opened the Article 93(2) procedure on the grounds that nine German labour market regions were not eligible for regional aid under the joint Federal Government/*Länder* programme for improving regional economic structures.

The decision is in line with previous Commission decisions on German regional aid.[2] In December 1987, the Commission had approved amendments to the German regional aid system which had resulted in a reduction, from 1 January 1988, in the percentage of persons living in assisted areas from 45% to 38% and in reduced aid levels. A further reduction in the population percentage to take effect on 1 January 1991 is being considered. The aim was to maintain the percentage of persons living in assisted areas at a constant 38% between 1 January 1988 and 31 December 1990. The Commission decision also contained a flexibility clause, permitting Germany to propose additional programmes in response to structural adjustments which might occur before the end of 1990 and which created unforeseen and substantial regional imbalances. The clause

---

[1]   OJ C 309, 8.12.1989.
[2]   OJ C 266, 18.10.1989.

at the same time allowed the Commission, shoudd the Federal Republic take advantage of this possibility, to remove regions where the socio-economic situation had improved significantly since 1986.

In 1988, the Commission approved the implementation by the German authorities, in accordance with the flexibility clause, of additional special programmes in Aachen, Jülich, Wezel-Moers and Hamm-Beckum which increased the aided population to over 40%. At the same time, the Commission proposed to the German authorities that nine regions be withdrawn from the list of aided regions as from 1 July 1989. These regions represented 1.70 % of the German population, which enabled the aided population to be reduced to some 38 %. The German authorities having rejected this recommendation on the grounds that the data used by the Commission did not adequately demonstrate the need to abolish the aids, the Commission decided to open the Article 93(2) procedure.

In November, the Commission decided to close the procedure. After examining six regions (Straubing, Nördlingen, Bamberg, Alsfeld-Ziegenhain, Soltau and Coesfeld) representing 0.7 % of the German population, it considered that the socio-economic situation had not improved sufficiently since 1986 to justify removing the six regions immediately from the list of assisted areas. It also noted that the German Government had itself decided not to award to the three labour market areas of Fallingbostel, Bocholt and Regensburg (areas not forming part of the frontier zone of the Resider programme area) which represent 1 % of the German population.

In November, the Commission approved the 18th general plan of the project of common interest entitled 'Improvement of regional economic structures'. The plan covers a four-year period up to 31 December 1992 and has a budget of DM 4 100 million (ECU 2 000 million) for 1989 which will be paid in the form of direct grants, loans, guarantees, etc. The 18th general plan is largely an updating of the 17th general plan. The Commission nevertheless informed the German authorities that its decision would not prejudice eligibility for regional aid after 1 January 1991.

In February, the Commission decided to open the Article 93(2) procedure in respect of an aid with a gross intensity of 6 % which North Rhine-Westphalia intends to award for an investment of ECU 28.8 million to Strepp GmbH & Co. KG Papierfabrik in the commune of Kreuzau, i.e. outside the areas eligible for regional aid.

In November, the Commission took a final negative decision against the aid in question. It considered that the award of individual, discretionary and selective aids outside eligible regions is not generally compatible with the principle of regional specificity defined in the 'principles of coordination'. [1] Furthermore, after examining the socio-economic situation in the labour market region of Düren in accordance with the method published by the Commission in its communication of 12 August 1988, [2] it concluded that the award of regional aid for an investment scheme in that region was not compatible with the common market and did not qualify for exemption under Article 92(3)(a) and (c).

United Kingdom

209.   In March, the Commission decided to approve the designation of a new enterprise zone in Sunderland in the north-east of England. In its decision, it took account in particular of the high level of unemployment and the fact that it is likely to deteriorate still further owing to the projected closure of North East Shipbuilders Limited. The Sunderland Enterprise Zone will enjoy the same advantages as other such zones in the United Kingdom, including rates exemption and accelerated depreciation on industrial buildings.

In 1988, the Commission reviewed the compatibility of all national regional aids in the United Kingdom in accordance with Article 93(1). The review forms part of the Commission's current policy of re-examining existing aid measures already approved by the Commission.

More specifically, the compatibility of existing aid measures with the common market is examined in the light of structural changes which have occurred since the adoption of the Commission decisions. In accordance with Article 93(1) of the EEC Treaty, it will in due course propose the appropriate measures which such changes may require.

---

[1]   OJ C 31, 3.2.1979.
[2]   OJ C 212, 12.8.1988.

§ 6 — Aid in the transport sector

Land transport

210. The Commission has continued its efforts to get the Council to adopt the proposals still pending on the carriage of persons and goods by road and by inland waterway and on combined transport. The bulk of the aid awarded in the land transport sector is still that paid to national railways, either in compensation for public service obligations under Regulations (EEC) No 1191/ 69 and No 1192/69, or as aid within the limits laid down by Regulation No 1107/70. The Commission informs the Council of the scale of such aid in the two-yearly reports provided for in Council Decision 75/327/EEC. The Commission also informed the Council of the aid granted in the combined transport sector on the basis of Regulation No 1107/70.

On 27 April 1989, the Council adopted Regulation (EEC) No 1100/89 [1] amending Regulation (EEC) No 1107/70 and extending such aid temporarily until 31 December 1992, where such aid is granted temporarily and is aimed at facilitating the development of combined transport. The aid must be intended either for investments in infrastructure of fixed and moveable facilities necessary for transshipment or the operating costs of combined transport in so far as intra-Community transit traffic through the territory of third countries is involved.

In the inland waterway sector, the Council adopted Regulation (EEC) No 1101/ 89 on 27 April 1989 on structural improvements in the sector, [1] the Regulation aims at reducing existing excess capacity by coordinating scrapping at Community level. Pursuant to Article 2(3) of the Regulation, the French Government communicated to the Commission a national improvement plan for French vessels with a deadweight of under 450 tonnes. The plan will be implemented between 1990 and 1992. The Commission approved the plan in December 1989.

Sea transport

211. The Commission continued the study started in 1988 on State aids awarded to Community shipowners. In order to clarify the exact conditions under which, on the basis of Articles 92 and 93 of the EEC Treaty, such aid may be deemed compatible with the common market, the Commission adopted

---

[1] OJ L 116, 28.4.1989.

'Guidelines for the examination of State aids to Community shipping companies' on 3 August 1989. The document was forwarded to the Council for information together with the new proposals aimed at improving the conditions in which Community fleets operate.

The Commission has already applied the guidelines to new State aid cases. On 11 October, it decided not to object to a 'Viability plan for the Merchant Navy' presented by the Spanish authorities.

Having carried out a financial study of certain Community ports, the Commission undertook a 'General study of State aid in the port sector'. The study reviews available financial data for the examination of State aids and presents general conclusions on the application of State aid provisions to ports; it also specifies the position of the Commission on the question of public investment in port infrastructures. The study was sent to the Member States for comments. Once they have been examined, the study will be forwarded to the Council.

Air transport

212.   In the course of 1989 the Commission's services terminated a comprehensive scrutiny covering all Member States, of existing aid measures in favour of Community air carriers.

As a result of this work, the Commission is considering the possibility of taking appropriate measures on the basis of Article 93(1) of the EEC Treaty with a view both to terminating or modifying aid measures with distortive effects and to creating more transparency.

The Commission will continue and reinforce its efforts in this area in order to ensure that the basic objectives of the liberalization process are not undermined by distortive subsidies.

§ 7 — Aid in the agriculture sector (Table 4)

213. The Commission pursued its policy on State aids to agriculture in accordance with a process of gradual development, the guidelines for which are described in the two preceding reports [1] and, in greater detail, in one of the *Green Europe* newsletters on the common agricultural policy. [2] The provisions of the Treaty which relate to the rules on competition, apply to production of and trade in agricultural products only to the extent determined by the Council (Article 42 of the EEC Treaty), account being taken of the objectives set out in Article 39.

Many State aids to agriculture are accordingly governed by Council regulations in accordance with the provisions of, and the procedure laid down in Article 43(2) and (3) of the EEC Treaty; under such regulations the granting of national aid may be prohibited or limited to certain measures.

The market intervention machinery applicable under EEC market organizations is fully comprehensive and precludes national intervention by Member States. Any such measures introduced by Member States are accordingly not compatible with the common market and can be authorized only by way of a Council decision adopted pursuant to Article 42 of the EEC Treaty or, if such a decision is justified by exceptional circumstances, pursuant to the third subparagraph of Article 93(2).

For its part, Regulation (EEC) No 797/85 on improving the efficiency of agricultural structures [3] contains provisions which govern much of national investment aid in agricultural production and the granting of annual compensatory allowances in less-favoured areas within the meaning of Directive 75/268/EEC. [4] Such aids are scrutinized in accordance with the procedures laid down in Article 24 of that Regulation.

In 1989 the Council adopted a Regulation establishing a system of transitional aids to agricultural income. [5] The system, which in some cases is eligible for Community financing, was introduced in order to contribute in particular to:

(i)   safeguarding agricultural income at fair levels during a process of adaptation which may affect the structure, organization or management of agricultural holdings;

---

1   Seventeenth Competition Report, point 259 *et seq.*; Eighteenth Competition Report, point 270 *et seq.*
2   *Green Europe* newsletter No 221 on competition policy in agriculture.
3   As last amended by Regulation (EEC) No 3808/89: OJ L 371, 20.12.1989.
4   OJ L 128, 19.5.1975.
5   Council Regulation (EEC) No 768/89 of 21 March 1989: OJ L 84, 29.3.1989.

(ii)   alleviating the impact, in terms of income, of the financial obligations of agricultural holdings;

(iii)   supporting the level of income during efforts to diversify the farmer's activity outside agriculture.

The level of the aid is determined on the basis of the injury arising for potential recipients from the adjustment of the markets in the context of the reform of the common agricultural policy and the adjustment of EEC market organizations. The detailed implementing rules are laid down in a Commission detailed implementing rules are laid down in a Commission regulation, [1] which defines 'agricultural income aid' as 'any public financial contribution granted exclusively to farmers, or to farmers and members of their families working on the holding, which supplements the overall family income ... and is not subject to any conditions relating to its use'.

Notwithstanding the foregoing and without prejudice to Articles 92 and 93 of the Treaty, public financial contributions granted through the taxation and social security systems, provided they are justified on the basis of criteria inherent in these systems, shall not be deemed agricultural income aid. The procedures for scrutiny of the measures concerned are laid down in Article 13 of Regulation (EEC) No 768/89.

Some years ago the Council began adopting *ad hoc* provisions in order to authorize the granting of national aids to producers whose prices expressed in national currency had fallen as a result of a change in the green rate. Such aids are currently granted in Germany, for instance, by way of the VAT mechanism. In 1987, however, the Council decided that compensation for such falls should in future be granted solely in respect of sociostructural measures. [2] The Commission has sent the Council a proposal for a Regulation laying down the implementing rules concerned. [3]

214.   Competition policy is being pursued, on the basis of Articles 92 and 93 of the Treaty, in all the other fields which are not covered by the regulations referred to above, the main ones being:

(i)   investments in the processing and marketing of products listed in Annex II to the Treaty, and

(ii)   measures to improve the quality of agricultural products.

---

[1]   Regulation (EEC) No 3813/89: OJ L 371, 20.12.1989.
[2]   Council Regulation (EEC) No 1889/87 of 2 July 1987 amending Regulation (EEC) No 1677/85 on monetary compensatory amounts in agriculture.
[3]   COM(89) 382 final, 1.8.1989.

The Commission has, for the purposes of Article 93 of the EEC Treaty, set guidelines for assessing aids to the processing and marketing of agricultural products. Those guidelines, which are sectoral or horizontal, as the case may be, were used as a basis for or were chosen, by the Commission by analogy with the development criteria laid down for common measures under Council Regulation (EEC) No 355/77 on common measures to improve the conditions under which agricultural and fishery products are processed and marketed. [1]

The objectives of those measures were recently reworked in the light of the changes in the CAP. The Commission intends in future to contribute to the financing of investment projects which:

(i)   help to guide production in keeping with foreseeable market trends or which encourage the development of new outlets for agricultural products, in particular through the production and marketing of new products, including organically grown products;

(ii) relieve the intervention mechanisms of the market organizations by furthering long-term structural improvement where this is needed;

(iii) are located in regions encountering special problems in adapting to the economic consequences of developments in the agricultural markets, or will benefit such regions;

(iv) help to improve or rationalize the marketing or processing of agricultural products;

(v)   help to improve the quality, preparation and presentation of products or encourage a better use of by-products, particularly by recycling waste.

The guidelines adopted by the Commission for assessing exclusively national aid schemes will have to be adjusted in the light of the criteria set out above.

The Commission has, moreover, given sympathetic consideration to measures likely to assist: (i) the development of rural areas in line with environmental-protection requirements; and (ii) the development of a policy which puts the emphasis on the quality of agricultural products.

The following schemes were thus adjudged by the Commission to be compatible with the common market: aid granted for the purpose of safeguarding, in the Member States, speciality foods and agri-foodstuffs qualifying for a special label (namely aid for quality control, for information campaigns aimed at producers or consumers and for advertising); and aid for investment or for the

---

[1]   OJ L 51, 23.2.1977.

launching of producers' groups with a view to encouraging the production and marketing of organically grown products and the marketing of foodstuffs.

The Commission has, on the other hand, endeavoured to phase out all forms of aid which visibly were producing the same effects as customs barriers or other forms of protection.

To this end it began a study of taxation in agriculture, aimed in particular at formulating (a) an integrated approach for determining the differences between, on the one hand, the various systems of taxation in agriculture and, on the other, general micro- or macroeconomic systems and (b) a framework for comparing the situation as between Member States.

215.   On the basis of the criteria described above a number of decisions were adopted by the Commission (or, in some cases, by the Council), the statistical breakdown of which is set out in previous years.

TABLE 4

Year	Aid cases notified	Number of aid cases scrutinized which had not been notified	No objection	Article 93(2) procedure initiated	Article 93(2) procedure terminated	Final negative decision	Decision by the Council pursuant to Article 93(2)
1985	112	—	87	13	20	4	3
1986	108	21	95	15	11	2	4
1987	118	14	98	20	19	3	3
1988	133	34	124	9	15	6	3
1989	130	21	113	14	9	6	3

As the table shows, the Commission took a favourable decision in respect of 113 aid cases (about 74 % of the total scrutinized), concerning in particular: environmental protection; measures to improve the quality of agricultural products; research; investment in processing and marketing facilities; and training.

216.   On the other hand the Commission had to initiate the procedure provided for in Article 93(2) of the EEC Treaty against seven operating aids designed to lower production costs or the prices of products. The Commission felt that such aids could have no lasting effect on the development of the sector concerned, since their impact would cease to be felt as soon as the scheme itself expired. Such schemes may well, moreover, adversely affect Community pricing

arrangements and CAP markets. They constitute unilateral measures by the Member States in areas covered by EEC market organizations where they no longer have the power to take decisions of their own.

The infringement inherent in that type of aid is a further major reason for not granting an exemption under Article 92(3) of the Treaty. The aid schemes concerned are as follows:

(i)   aid for the export of agricu`lutural products (breeding cattle and vegetative propagating material) to third countries, in the Netherlands, [1]

(ii)   subsidies for the spreading of insecticide by helicopter in Luxembourg, [2]

(iii)   reimbursement of contributions (0.04 % of the export value) in the case of exports of pigs (Belgium), [3]

(iv)   aid to farms and agricultural cooperatives in the Abruzzi in Italy [4] if the maximum subsidy equivalent of the aid to absorb onerous debts exceeds 35 % of the chargeable expenditure in the case of recipients in areas which are not less-favoured areas within the meaning of Directive 75/268/EEC and if the aid for recapitalization or an increase in capital is not conditional on the implementation of an investment plan,

(v)   aid in the form of equity investments and subsidized loans to absorb the losses of processing and marketing cooperatives and undertakings in the olive sector in Spain, [5]

(vi)   storage aid for ewe's milk cheese in Italy, [1]

(vii)   payment of a compensatory allowance in certain areas of the municipality of Lorca (Murcia).

217.   The Commission also had to decide on aids funded by central governments from the proceeds of financial charges (parafiscal charges or compulsory contributions) allocated to certain specific areas of expenditure; the levies concerned are made compulsory by law or by ministerial order.

The funds concerned are not transferred via the general budget: they are set directly against expenditure incurred in the sectors in which the levies are charged or in other sectors, as the case may be.

---

[1]   OJ C 24, 1.2.1990.
[2]   OJ C 302, 1.12.1989.
[3]   OJ C 22, 30.1.1990.
[4]   OJ C 108, 28.4.1989.
[5]   OJ C 313, 15.12.1989.

According to the case-law of the Court of Justice of the European Communities,[1] the funding of a State aid by a compulsory set-purpose charge is an essential component of that aid; the scrutiny of such schemes for the purpose of establishing whether they comply with the Community's rules should therefore cover both the aid itself and its funding.

Accordingly, even if an aid is compatible as regards both its form and its purpose, the fact that it is funded by parafiscal charges which apply also to imported products produced in the Community results in a protectionist effect which goes beyond the scope of the aid as such and makes it incompatible with the common market.

The Commission accordingly decided to initiate the procedure provided for in Article 93(2) of the EEC Treaty in respect of the following aid measures:

(i)   compulsory contributions for the promotion of pigmeat, beef/veal, sheepmeat, goatmeat and horsemeat products, where they are payable also on animals imported from the other Member States at the slaughter stage (Belgium),[2]

(ii)   compulsory contributions for the promotion of products in the poultry and small animals sectors, where they apply also to animals imported from the other Member States at the slaughter stage and compound feedingstuffs imported from the other Member States by specialized importers (Belgium),[3]

(iii) compulsory contributions which are payable also in respect of livestock (beef cattle, calves and swine) imported from the other Member States which are used to fund aid schemes in these sectors, namely measures to control animal diseases and improve animal health and hygiene and the quality of livestock and livestock products (Belgium),[3]

(iv)   parafiscal charges on production, processing and import of fresh and dried cultivated mushrooms and preserved mushrooms, where such charges apply also to imports from the other Member States, and are used to fund measures designed to support the development of the industry (France).[4]

---

[1]   In particular Case 47/69 *France* v *Commission* (1970) ECR 487.
[2]   OJ C 22, 30.1.1990.
[3]   OJ C 24, 1.2.1990.
[4]   OJ C 302, 1.12.1989.

218. The Commission initiated the procedure provided for in Article 93(2) of the Treaty against two Spanish and one Belgian investment-aid schemes. The Spanish schemes concerned:

(i) the setting up of a new centre for the manufacture and processing of cheeses and pasteurized milk (Lácteos de Galicia SA) — subsidy of PTA 586 425 140, or approximately ECU 5 million, [1]

(ii) the extension and modernization of a cheese-manufacturing centre (Mantequerías Arias SA) subsidy of PTA 45 301 250, or approximately ECU 346 000. [1]

In sectors where supply tends to exceed demand (e.g. the milk sector) that type of aid is authorized only where the increase in capacity to use cow's milk is offset by the abandonment of equivalent capacities in the same or in other undertakings.

The third investment-aid scheme was designed to equip an existing sugar refinery in Belgium with a 'pearl' sugar production plant. [2] In view of the structural situation of sugar production in the Community the Commission now regards all aid for sugarbeet, sugar cane and sugar as incompatible with the common market.

Moreover, investment in sugar undertakings which is intended for the production of sugar (irrespective of its presentation) must normally be funded by the sugar undertakings themselves, out of the standard processing margin which all sugar manufacturers in the Community are allowed when the annual common prices are fixed, and taking into account consumer prices for the various types of sugar.

Under the procedure provised for in Article 93(2) of the EEC Treaty the Commission also decided that the following were not compatible with the common market:

(i) aid to investment for the execution of primary irrigation structures for work of general interest to holdings (Spain); [3]

(ii) aid to investment for improving irrigated land (Spain), provided that work of general interest to holdings is concerned. [3]

The level of the aids (capital subsidy plus interest-rate subsidy) is too high compared with that normally authorized by the Commission for investment in

---

[1] OJ C 302, 1.12.1989.
[2] OJ C 297, 25.11.1989.
[3] OJ C 1, 4.1.1990.

primary production (75% in less-favoured areas within the meaning of Directive 75/268/EEC and 35% elsewhere).

219.   The Commission terminated the procedure provided for in Article 93(2) of the Treaty in the following cases in which Member States had complied with Commission requests by discontinuing or amending certain aid schemes which were incompatible with the common market;

(i)   operating aid and investment aid which exceeded the rates normally authorized by the Commission. The schemes in question, which were provided for in draft Sicilian Regional Law No 730 of 1984 on measures to assist cooperatives, trade, craft industries and fishing, were not put into effect;

(ii)   *una tantum* subsidy (equivalent to 70% of the ordinary interest payable over a four-year period) paid by the Region of Sicily to the 'Mugnai e Pastai della valle dei Platani' cooperative, the undertaking having gone bankrupt and ceased trading in 1986;

(iii)   the following aid schemes of the Region of Trento in Italy:

   (a) interest-rate subsidy over a 20-year period — or the capital-subsidy equivalent thereof (approximately 50%) for the purchase, construction or extension of facilities for transporting and storing milk (Article 3 of Law No 5 of 1986 amending Article 42 of Regional Law No 17 of 1981), since the provisions in question were repealed;

   (b) allowance for the use of Alpine pastures (see Article 3 of draft Law No 101 amending Article 35 of Regional Law No 17 of 1981); with a view to achieving an improvement in livestock quality and encouraging the use of Alpine pastures, the Article provided for an Alpine pasture allowance in respect of cattle aged 30 months or more. The allowance payable is LIT 100 000 (ECU 65.8) per beast, rising to LIT 300 000 (ECU 197.4) in the case of livestock entered in a herd-book. The measure in question was repealed;

   (c) the granting of 12-month subsidized loans (approximately 14%) for the purchase of cattle for fattening (see Article 3 of Law No 5 of 1986 amending Article 41 of Regional Law No 17 of 1981). The aid in question was repealed;

   (d) the granting of subsidies of up to 70% of eligible expenditure to dairies in respect of their milk-transport costs. The aid was calculated on the basis of the distance between the milk-collection points and the dairy (Article 3 of Law No 5 of 1986 amending Article 42 of Regional Law No 17 of 1981). The subsidy was abolished;

(e) the granting of five-year interest-rate subsidies or, alternatively, capital subsidies ranging from 35% to 70%, for the purchase of agricultural machinery and facilities for processing agricultural products (Article 3 of Law No 5 of 1986 amending Article 43 of Regional Law No 17 of 1981), the Italian authorities having undertaken to bring the subsidies down to the levels advocated by the Commission;

(iv) aid schemes provided for in Italy's multiannual Law No 752 of 1986 on a series of measures to assist agriculture:

(a) aid granted by the Italian Government for yield and quality testing under Article 4(2)(b) of Law No 752 of 1986, in conjunction with Annex C/1(b) to the Decision of the CIPE of 23 April 1987, the Italian authorities having undertaken to bring the rates of aid down to the levels normally authorized by the Commission;

(b) Italian State aid under Article 4(3)(b) of Law No 752 of 1986 (aid to encourage agricultural producers' groups), in conjunction with Annex C/2(b) to the Decision of the CIPE of 23 April 1987 defraying, for a limited period, the cost of insuring against non-payment for products taken over by processing undertakings, the Italian authorities having discontinued the scheme;

(c) Article 8 of Law No 752 of 1986 (amending Law No 674 of 1978 on agricultural producers' associations), the Italian authorities having pointed out that, in Italy, intervention on the market in fruit and vegetables is carried out solely by first-tier producers' groups for the purposes of and in accordance with Regulation (EEC) No 1035/72 i.e. in accordance with Community rules;

(d) Italian State aid under Article 4(2)(f) of Law No 752 of 1986 (advertising and commercial promotion schemes), in conjunction with Annex C/1(f) to the Decision of the CIPE of 23 April 1987, which provides in particular for future commercial promotion campaigns covering the domestic market, the Italian authorities having stated that they will in future notify the Commission, pursuant to Article 93(3) of the Treaty, of all new contracts which they are considering signing with the trade interests concerned;

(e) schemes to encourage the setting-up and operation of national associations of recognized producers' groups under Article 4(3)(b) of Law

No 752 of 1986, in conjunction with Annex C/2(b) to the Decision of the CIPE of 23 April 1987;

(f) launching aid for national agencies and syndicates of agricultural cooperatives and producers' groups Article 4(3)(c) of Law No 752 of 1986, in conjunction with Annex C/2(c) of the Decision of the CIPE of 23 April 1987, the Italian authorities having notified the Commission that the aid granted would comply with Regulation (EEC) No 1360/78;

(v) Italian aid schemes provided for in two AIMA circulars of 25 May 1989 repealing earlier circulars on detection and testing programmes and projects for improving stockfarming hygiene, since the aid schemes applicable under the new circulars refer only to detection and testing required under national and Community law;

(vi) Italian aid schemes in the Abruzzi for agricultural cooperatives and undertakings, following a decision by the Italian authorities:

(a) to reduce the maximum capital-subsidy equivalent of the aid to absorb non-interest-free debts to 35% of eligible expenditure where the recipient is not located in a less-favoured area within the meaning of Directive 75/268/EEC;

(b) to authorize the granting of aid for recapitalization or an increase in capital only in cases where the measures concerned are linked to investment aimed at structural improvement or the introduction of technological innovation, while undertaking to comply with the criteria and limits set by the Commission, in particular in the case of the sugar and isoglucose sectors and the framework system established by the Commission as regards the manufacture and marketing of dairy products and of substitute products;

(vii) storage aid for hemp seed in France, the Commission having taken note of the fact that the production of and trade in the product concerned was negligible and could not, therefore, restrict competition or adversely affect trade between Member States;

(viii) aid granted in France to stockfarmers specializing in the fattening of bovine animals, the French authorities having notified the Commission of their decision that the aid should be granted only to farmers who had previously invested in the fattening of bovine animals and should be used to reduce the financial costs of loans relating to that investment;

(ix) the grant, in Denmark, of aid funded by the income from parafiscal charges on imports in the poultry-farming sector, following a declaration by the Danish Government that the parafiscal charges were no longer payable in respect of eggs in shell (other than eggs for hatching).

220. The Commission adopted negative final decisions against the following schemes:

(i) the granting, by the Italian Government, of monthly aid of LIT 5 000 (ECU 3.3)/quintal in January and February 1988 for the storage and marketing of olive oil. The aid is a form of operating aid and infringes the rules of the market organization for oils and fats; [1]

(ii) aid in the form of a supplement to the Community premium per ewe/she-goat in 1987 (France). This constitutes operating aid and infringes the market organization for sheepmeat and goatmeat; [2]

(iii) aid granted by the Belgian Government in the pigmeat, beef/veal, sheep-meat, goatmeat and horsemeat sectors and funded by means of compulsory contributions. Since, on the basis of the information available, no distinction could be made between aid funded by the said contributions, which contravened Article 12 of the Treaty, and aids funded by way of other contributions and the State's capital grant, all aids funded by the Ondah pursuant to Article 1 of the Law of 11 April 1983 in the pigmeat, sheepmeat, goatmeat and horsemeat sectors (other than horses for slaughter or horse-meat) must be regarded as incompatible with the common market;

(iv) a scheme in France whereby stockfarmers/cereal growers are refunded special fiscal and parafiscal charges levied in respect of deliveries of grain to approved collectors. Such refunds constitute operating aid and infringe the rules of several market organizations;

(v) aid schemes funded via the 'Produktschap voor Veevoerder' (Cattlefeed Association) in the Netherlands and intended for studies and research into: the nutrition and health of calves intended for slaughter; the fodder-equivalent value of cattlefeed and products used in the preparation thereof; the undesirable substances which such products may contain; the welfare of domestic animals; and organic waste surpluses in relation to the feeding-stuffs used. Such aids cannot be regarded as compatible with the common market, since the parafiscal charges designed to fund them apply also to products imported from the other Member States;

---

[1]   OJ 172, 30.9.1966.
[2]   OJ L 110, 29.4.1988.

(vi) aid schemes financed by the 'Produktschap voor Landbouwzaaizaden' (Seed Association) and intended for research into cultural and performance values and selection trials designed to develop new types of seeds. The aids cannot be regarded as compatible with the common market, since the parafiscal charges used to fund them are also applicable to products imported from the other Member States.

221. For its part the Council authorized three national aids in 1989 on the basis of the third subparagraph of Article 93(2) of the EEC Treaty. The schemes concerned were as follows:

(i) distillation aid of DM 33 (ECU 16) per hl granted by the *Land* of Rheinland-Pfalz in respect of up to 150 000 hl of wine suitable for yielding quality wine psr produced in 1989/90; [1]

(ii) national aid in the form of an advance on the premium per ewe/she-goat in France; [1]

(iii) national schemes whereby short-term private storage aid is granted, until 15 December, for table wines and musts in France and Italy in respect of the marketing year 1989/90. [2]

---

[1] Decision of 23 October 1989.
[2] Decision of 3 May 1989.

§ 8 — Aid in the fisheries sector (Table 5)

222.   In 1989, the Commission examined 13 new cases of notified aids and two cases of unnotified aids or aids notified late in the fisheries sector. It decided:

(i)   not to object to the implementation of the aids in question in 11 cases;

(ii)   to initiate the procedure provided for in Article 93(2) of the EEC Treaty in 18 cases, three of which concerned Spain, three Italy and 12 France;

(iii)   to terminate the procedure provided for in Article 93(2) in nine cases, one of which concerned Denmark, three the Federal Republic of Germany and six France.

223.   The following table summarizes progress on a number of aid cases with regard to fisheries and the Commission's work on these aids. The figures in question are based on the data on which the decisions were taken and do not, therefore, necessarily tally with the number of cases scrutinized.

TABLE 5

Decisions adopted

Year	Cases examined	No objection	Article 93(2) procedure initiated	Article 93(2) procedure terminated	Final decision under Article 93(2)
1982	23	16	7	—	—
1983	15	10	5	3	5
1984	18	13	5	3	—
1985	12	8	4	2	2
1986	9	6	—	2	2
1987	43	24	3	2	1
1988	44	25	10	2	—
1989	45	11	18	9	1

224.   The Commission adopted a negative final decision against certain aids granted by the 'Produktschap voor Vis en Visprodukten' (sectoral agency for fishing and fisheries products) in The Netherlands and funded by parafiscal charges. The arrangements in question are designed to stabilize market prices for mussels and to provide aid for the advertising of mussels and herring.

225.   In order not to jeopardize the attainment of common fisheries policy objectives, in particular as regards the problem of overcapacity of fleets, the Commission decided not to authorize national aids in 1988 under the Sixth Directive on shipbuilding for fishing vessels intended for the Community fleet. [1] In the light of that decision the Commission adopted a negative decision in respect of aid projects in Germany and The Netherlands concerning the construction of a fishing vessel intended for the Irish fleet.

---

[1]   Eighteenth Competition Report, points 194 and 306.

Chapter II

Public undertakings

§ 1 — Telecommunications

226. The Commission undertook a review of the measures adopted by Member States pursuant to its Directive 88/301/EEC of 16 May 1988 [1] on competition in the market for telecommunications terminal equipment. The Directive provides for the abolition of exclusive rights granted in this field by Member States. At the time of its adoption, there were some 35 such rights throughout the Community. By the end of 1989, about 20 had been abolished under the Directive. The abolition of the remaining exclusive or special rights has either already been or is about to be embodied in Member States' legislation. Four Member States have as yet to adopt the appropriate measures.

In Belgium, Germany and Ireland, exclusive rights still apply to the purchase of the first telephone set which accounts for the largest share of the terminals market. In Denmark, the exclusive rights cover PABXs. This situation does not comply with the Directive. The Commission decided on 12 July to initiate against those Member States the infringement procedure provided for in Article 169 of the EEC Treaty.

The Commission plans to initiate the same procedure should the Directive also be incorrectly applied in other Member States.

As a general rule, the Commission plans to use Article 90 of the Treaty where preventive measures are necessary to avoid infringements of the Treaty or where accompanying measures are require over and above simply noting that there has been a failure to comply within the meaning of Article 169. Furthermore, although the Commission is solely empowered to apply Article 90, subject to review by the Court of Justice of the legality of its acts, it may be wise, as

---

[1] OJ L 131, 27.5.1988, p. 73; Eighteenth Competition Report, point 307.

Sir Leon Brittan stated to the European Parliament on 11 October [1] 'to structure better consultation of Parliament for any future draft directives based on Article 90 of the Treaty'.

The Commission also adopted a new Directive on 28 June based on Article 90 of the EEC Treaty on competition in the markets for telecommunications services. [2] The salient points of the Directive are:

(i) the abolition of exclusive rights for all services to the general public except voice telephony, although Member States may make such services subject to objective and non-discriminatory trade regulations;

(ii) special transitional arrangements up to 31 December 1992, allowing a prohibition on the simple resale of leased line capacity which could then be used to compete with the public data-transmission service before tariff structures have been revised;

(iii) mandatory publication by Member States of technical interfaces by 31 December 1990 at the latest, thus providing the information necessary for private operators;

(iv) abolition of all restrictions on the processing of signals before and after their transmission via the public network;

(v) separation of regulatory powers from the activities of telecommunications organizations;

(vi) measures to allow long-term contracts to be terminated.

It should be noted that the Directive does not affect exclusive or special rights to set up and provide public networks. For this reason, the Commission Directive is tied to the adoption of the Council Directive on open network provision which harmonizes the conditions for access to such networks. The plan, therefore, was to notify the two Directives simultaneously to the Member States.

Belgium and Italy did not wait for the notification before instituting proceedings for the annulment of the Directive on the basis of Article 173 of the EEC Treaty. [3]

At the meeting of the Council of Ministers for Telecommunications on 7 December, the Commission undertook to clarify certain points in the Services Directive so that overall agreement could be reached on the two Directives.

---

[1] Verbatim report of proceedings of the European Parliament, 11.10.1989, p. 151.
[2] See point 31 of this Report.
[3] Cases 319/89 and 331/89, OJ C 309, 8.12.1989.

The Council was thus able to adopt a common position on the ONP Directive on 21 December.

Under that agreement, the Commission will stipulate in the Services Directive that Member States may include in the licensing or declaration procedures for the supply of packet or circuit switched data services, conditions aimed at compliance not only with the essential requirements but also with the trade regulations relating to the conditions of permanence, availability and quality of the services, or with measures to safeguard the task of general economic interest entrusted to a telecommunications organization if the performance of that task is likely to be obstructed by the activities of private service providers.

§ 2 — Energy

227.   In accordance with the priorities it laid down in 1988 for the internal energy market, [1] the Commission, with the cooperation of the Member States, began a review of the problems connected with electricity distribution monopolies, exclusive rights for the utilization of interconnected distribution and transmission systems and exclusive rights for the utilization of high-voltage interconnections. It has drawn up a report describing the legal situation in the different Member States.

---

[1]   See *Energy in Europe,* Commission of the European Communities, ISBN 92-825-8507-7.

§ 3 — Individual cases

Italy

228. Following action by the Commission under Article 90 in conjunction with Article 86 of the Treaty, the Italian Government, by circular dated 4 March,[1] lifted certain restrictions on private international express couriers which could have favoured the public undertaking 'Corriere Accelerato Internazionale delle Poste'.

In future, private international express couriers will be able to operate freely in the international messenger service sector. Other Member States[2] had already accepted this solution following intervention by the Commission.

Netherlands

229. On 29 December, the Commission adopted a decision based on Article 90(3) of the Treaty concerning the adoption in the Netherlands at the end of 1988, despite the reservations of the Commission, of a new postal law[3] which extends the Post Office monopoly to part of the express courier service, until then in competition with private couriers. The law also imposes stricter conditions on express courier services than on those of the PTT.

The Commission considers that this discrimination, and the extension of the Post Office monopoly to an adjacent but separate market is incompatible with Article 90(1) in conjunction with Article 86. Furthermore, The Netherlands have not shown that the extension is necessary to the continued provision of a service of general economic interest.

Greece

230. As regards the Greek scheme of insurance for public property and loans granted by State-owned banks,[4] the Commission decided to follow up the infringement procedure initiated on 20 March by sending Greece, on 11 October,

---

1 Official Journal of the Italian Republic, Special series No 99, 29.4.1989, p. 41.
2 Fifteenth Competition Report, point 259.
3 Articles 2 and 12(2) of Law of 26.10.1988 (Stb. 1988, 522), and implementing Decrees of 19.12.1988 (Stb. 1988, 605) and 12.5.1989.
4 Established by Article 13 of Law No 1256/82.

a reasoned opinion under Article 169 of the EEC Treaty for failure to fulfil an obligation under Article 171 of the Treaty.

Greece has still not complied with the judgment of the Court of Justice of 30 June 1988 in Case 226/87.[1] The Court had ruled that in failing to adopt within the prescribed time the necessary measures to comply with Commission Decision No 85/276,[2] the 'Hellenic Republic has failed to fulfil its obligations under the EEC Treaty'.

Federal Republic of Germany

231.   The Commission requested the German Government to adopt a position on certain instructions it is alleged to have given to its departments requiring their officials and agents to make use exclusively of the national airline Lufthansa for their flights. In its reply to the Commission, the Government communicated a circular from the Ministry of the Interior dated 2 March 1990 which confirmed the existence of such instructions. These constitute State measures pursuant to Article 90(1) of the Treaty and are likely to be contrary to the provisions of Article 59 which require the abolition of restrictions on the freedom to provide services.

The German Government, however, has already announced that it plans to abolish the disputed circular.

---

[1]   Seventeenth Competition Report, point 281.
[2]   Eighteenth Competition Report, point 308; OJ L 152, 11.6.1985, p. 25.

Chapter III

Adjustment of State monopolies of a commercial character

Greece

232.   With regard to the oil monopoly, the Commission considered it necessary to pursue the infringement proceedings instituted on 16 August 1988 against the Greek rules on compulsory storage [1] by sending the Greek Government on 18 October a reasoned opinion pursuant to Article 169 of the EEC Treaty.

The Commission considers that the obligation, which does not apply when petroleum products are purchased from local refineries by the refiners and/or distributors, discriminates against imported products and is therefore contrary to Community law, in particular Articles 30 and 37 of the EEC Treaty.

Spain

233.   Taking account of the undertakings given by the Spanish Government concerning the adjustment of its oil monopoly, the Commission decided to pursue negotiations with the Spanish authorities and to ensure that the political agreement concluded with them, [2] in particular as regards quotas, prices, access to major consumers, abolition of exclusive rights and the development of the parallel service-station network, is strictly complied with.

In view of the time that has elapsed since accession, however, the Commission informed the Spanish Government on 6 November that, on the basis of results at 1 January 1990, it reserved the right to assess the situation and decide whether to resume the infringement proceedings in abeyance for failure to

---

[1]   Article 3(3) of Law No 176/88; OJ of the Hellenic Republic A 66/7.4.1988; Eighteenth Competition Report, point 311.
[2]   Eighteenth Competition Report, point 312.

comply with Article 48 of the Act of Accession and Articles 30 and 37 of the EEC Treaty by placing the matter before the Court of Justice.

234. On 29 November, the Commission decided however to close the infringement proceedings it had initiated on 28 December 1988 against Spain for failing progressively to adjust its manufactured tobacco monopoly, [1] as provided for in Article 48 of the Act of Accession.

The Commission concluded from the comments submitted by the Spanish Government on 10 April 1989 that the basic provisions promulgated to date, to which the Commission had not objected, already constituted an adequate legal framework allowing manufactured tobacco to be freely marketed, and that the Spanish Government did not need to adopt any further measures.

The Commission also checked that the draft ministerial decree it had received in July 1987 had not finally been promulgated by Spain. The draft, which imposed restrictions on non-monopoly wholesalers, had resulted in strong objections from the Commission.

Portugal

235. From the comments submitted by the Portuguese Government under an infringement procedure initiated on 21 February 1989 against its oil monopoly, [2] the Commission concluded that Portugal had put an end to certain infringements, the chief one being the abolition of prior authorization for eight petroleum products not subject to the monopoly. A favourable solution was also found for the volume and publishing of the opening of quotas and the redistribution of unused quotas among the operators concerned. In respect of these specific aspects, Portugal has complied with Article 208 of the Act of Accession.

Portugal has not, however, complied as yet with the provisions of Article 208(2) of the Act of Accession as regards the adjustment of marketing quotas allocated to companies other than Petrogal prior to accession.

Nor were the Commission's doubts dispelled that the rules governing prices and taxation of petroleum products in Portugal favour domestic products to the detriment of those from other Member States, which is contrary to the provisions of Articles 30 and 95 of the EEC Treaty.

---

[1] Eighteenth Competition Report, point 312.
[2] Eighteenth Competition Report, point 313.

The Commission therefore decided on 13 May to pursue the infringement procedure by sending the Portuguese Government a reasoned opinion under Article 169 of the EEC Treaty.

236. As regards the alcohol monopoly — which concerns ethyl alcohols of agricultural and non-agricultural origins and wine spirits for use in the making of port wine [1] — the comments presented by the Portuguese Government in reply to the letter of formal notice dated 27 December 1988 allowed the Commission to conclude that Portugal has not to date adopted any specific adjustment measures in accordance with Article 208 of the Act of Accession.

Once again the Commission decided on 29 November that it was necessary to resume the infringement procedure by delivering a reasoned opinion to the Portuguese Government. The Commission is currently examining the two cases.

France

237. On 31 May, the Commission decided to close the infringement procedure it had initiated in July 1988 against France for failing to comply with the requirement for an adjustment of its monopoly in potassic fertilizers [2] in relation to Spain and Portugal, as provided for in Articles 208 of the Act of Accession.

France responded to the procedure by deciding, at the beginning of 1989, [3] progressively to open and increase quota volumes, which will lead to the total abolition of exclusive rights to import and market the products in question by the end of the transitional periods laid down in the abovementioned Articles of the Act of Accession.

The Commission also requested the French Government to ensure that the opened quotas were fixed without discrimination.

This resulted from the fact that, on receiving a complaint at a later date, the Commission discovered that the criterion used by the French authorities, namely, the examination of export licence applications on a 'first come first served' basis, discriminates against the last to apply.

---

[1] Eighteenth Competition Report, point 313.
[2] Eighteenth Competition Report, point 314.
[3] Notice to operators published in the Official Journal of the French Republic, 29.12.1988, p. 16605.

Chapter IV

Main decisions of the Court of Justice

238.   In 1989 the Court of Justice delivered one judgment in a State aid case, and its President made one interim order. [1]

§ 1 — Recovery of aid unlawfully granted — legitimate expectation

239.   The judgment of the Court of Justice in Case 94/87 (*Commission* v *Germany*), confirms and develops the precedent set in the Court's 1986 judgment in Case 52/84 (*Commission* v *Belgium*). [2] The Commission was seeking here a finding that by failing to comply with Commission Decision 86/60/EEC of 14 December 1985, which required the Federal Republic of Germany to recover aid paid to an aluminium producer, the Federal Republic had failed to fulfil its obligation under the EEC Treaty. [3]

Neither the German Government nor the recipient firm had brought any action for annulment of the Decision at the time, but the German Government now maintained that the definitive and binding character of the Decision did not extend to the obligation to recover the aid. Unlawful aid had to be recovered, but subject to the principles of national law, which was the law applicable to the recovery. If the Decision did impose an obligation to recover the aid, the principle of legitimate expectations would make it legally impossible to comply with that obligation. The Court rejected these contentions at the outset. It held that the obligation to recover the aid, which had been imposed unconditionally and unambiguously, was a definitive one.

Recalling its judgment in Case 52/84 *Commission* v *Belgium*, the Court said that the only defence left would be to plead that it was absolutely impossible

---

1   Judgment in Case 94/87 *Commission* v *Germany;* Order in Case 303/88R *Italy* v *Commission.*
2   Sixteenth Competition Report, point 315.
3   Point 169 of this Report.

to implement the decision properly. A Member State which encountered unforeseen or unforeseeable difficulties, or perceived consequences overlooked by the Commission, was free to submit those problems for consideration by the Commission, so that they could work together in good faith with a view to overcoming the difficulties, in the spirit of genuine cooperation required by Article 5 of the Treaty.

But in this case the German Government had taken no steps whatever to recover the aid from the firm, and had not made any suggestions to the Commission regarding ways of overcoming the difficulties; the Court concluded that the defendant government was not entitled to allege that it was absolutely impossible to implement the Commission's Decision. The Federal Republic of Germany had accordingly failed to fulfil its obligations under the EEC Treaty.

The Court took the opportunity to state that in so far as national law did govern the procedure for the recovery of unlawful aid, it could not be applied in such a way as to render practically impossible the recovery required by Community law. The Community's interests had also to be taken fully into account in the application of a national rule under which the withdrawal of an irregular administrative act depended on an assessment of the various interests involved.

§ 2 — Interim measure suspending the operation of a decision

240.   The Order made by the President of the Court in Case 303/88R *Italy* v *Commission* followed the Court's settled case-law in holding that the urgency of an application for interim measures had to be assessed in the light of the extent to which an interlocutory order was necessary to avoid serious and irreparable damage to the party seeking the interim measure. It was for the applicant to show that he could not await the conclusion of the main action without personally suffering damage which would have serious and irreparable effects for him.

In the case in point the President dismissed an application by the Italian Government, on the grounds that the government had not given any indication either of the present financial situation of the firms involved, which had since been privatized, nor of the number of people they employed; this information might have allowed an assessment to be made of the firms' importance to the national economy, and thus of any damage which might have been caused to the Italian Republic, which was making the application.

The President added that even if the firms concerned had themselves claimed that recovery of the disputed aid might cause them serious and irreparable damage, they would have had to show that the danger derived from recovery measures actually taken by the Italian authorities, and that domestic remedies could not prevent it.

Part Four

The development of concentration, competition and competitiveness

Chapter I

Mergers and acquisitions involving Community-scale firms in 1988/89

241.   The present part of the competition report first describes major changes in the competitive environment based on an analysis of the financial transactions of 1 000 leading industrial firms in the Community and 500 of the largest firms worldwide, as well as operations in distribution, banking and insurance.

The aim of the Commission is thus to produce realistic data, chiefly on mergers and acquisitions of firms, that are of considerable importance to the competition policy of the Community.

The following analysis is aimed at determining the effects of mergers, acquisitions and joint ventures in industry, distribution, banking and insurance. It seeks to identify the reasons for these operations and studies their effects on competition. The analysis is based on data published in the specialist press regarding operations involving at least one of the largest enterprises in the Community.

The following operations are examined:

(i)   acquisitions of majority holdings, including mergers;

(ii)   acquisitions of minority holdings;

(iii) industrial and commercial joint ventures.

The reference period is June 1988 to June 1989.

§ 1 — Overview (Tables 6 and 7)

242. The total number of financial operations in all the sectors concerned reached a record level of 1 122 representing an increase of 9% compared with the preceding period. A large majority of operations again took place in industry, where mergers rose by 28%, a rate which is considerably higher than the average. On the other hand, the total number of such operations fell in the banking sector and on the whole stayed at the same level in the other sectors.

TABLE 6

National, Community and international mergers (a), acquisitions of minority holdings (b)
and joint ventures (c) in the Community in 1988/89

Sector	National[1]			Community[2]			International[3]			Total			Grand Total
	(a)	(b)	(c)	(a)	(b)	(c)	(a)	(b)	(c)	(a)	(b)	(c)	
Industry	233	102	56	197	37	36	62	20	37	492	159	129	780
Distribution	53	8	7	4	6	4	1	8	3	58	22	14	94
Banking	51	32	11	16	20	6	16	11	7	83	63	24	170
Insurance	15	9	8	8	13	5	10	7	3	33	29	16	78
Total	352	151	82	225	76	51	89	46	50	666	273	183	1 122

Source: Data gathered by the Commission from the specialist press.
[1] Operations of firms from the same Member State.
[2] Operations of firms from different Member States.
[3] Operations of firms Member States and third countries with effects on the Community market.

TABLE 7

Breakdown of national, Community and international majority acquisitions (including mergers) in industry, distribution, banking and insurance (combined turnover > 1 000 > 2 000 > 5 000 > 10 000 million ecus)

Sector	Year	National[1]				Community[2]				International[3]				Total			
		> 1	> 2	> 5	> 10	> 1	> 2	> 5	> 10	> 1	> 2	> 5	> 10	> 1	> 2	> 5	> 10
Industry	1986/1987	111	73	42	18	52	42	24	13	8	3	2	—	171	118	67	31
	1987/1988	135	84	48	24	86	61	34	22	47	40	28	15	268	185	110	61
	1988/1989	163	118	60	29	148	110	72	53	62	60	38	24	373	288	170	106
Distribution	1986/1987	19	12	6	1	2	2	2	—	—	—	—	—	21	14	8	1
	1987/1988	15	11	6	2	5	3	1	—	2	2	2	—	22	16	9	2
	1988/1989	21	17	8	—	1	1	1	—	1	1	1	—	23	19	10	—
Banking	1986/1987	9	6	5	3	2	2	1	1	9	7	5	3	20	15	11	7
	1987/1988	19	14	7	4	10	10	8	4	7	5	4	2	36	29	19	10
	1988/1989	22	15	3	1	11	9	4	2	8	8	5	4	41	32	12	7
Insurance	1986/1987	5	3	2	2	1	—	—	—	2	1	—	—	8	4	2	2
	1987/1988	1	1	—	—	7	6	1	—	8	3	1	—	16	10	2	—
	1988/1989	5	5	3	—	3	3	2	—	4	3	2	—	12	11	7	—
Total	1986/1987	144	94	55	24	57	46	27	14	19	11	7	3	220	151	88	41
	1987/1988	170	110	61	30	108	80	44	26	64	50	35	17	342	240	140	73
	1988/1989	211	155	74	30	163	123	79	55	75	72	46	28	449	350	199	113

Source: See Table 6.
[1] Operations of firms from the same Member State.
[2] Operations of firms from different Member States.
[3] Operations of firms from Member States and third countries with effects on the Community market.

As regards the nationality of the firms concerned, whilst the number of purely national operations continued to predominate, there was a significant shift towards operations between firms from different Member States. The number of transactions involving third country firms fell in absolute terms. The influence of Japan, at least in this respect, is not as strong as generally believed. By far the most frequent partners were, first, US firms, followed by Swiss, Swedish and Japanese companies. Firms from other third countries are generally isolated cases. Japanese firms wishing to enter the Community tended to opt primarily for the creation of undertakings (including joint ventures with Community firms), whereas US firms had a marked preference for direct acquisitions.

The preferred form of operation continued to be through majority acquisitions or mergers, although a large number of minority holdings were acquired in banking and insurance.

§ 2 — Mergers, acquisitions and joint ventures in industry

Mergers (Tables 8 and 9)

243. In industry, majority acquisitions (including takeovers and mergers) were once again the chief mode of operation, strengthening their position in relation to minority acquisitions. There was a sharp rise in majority acquisitions among Community firms.

TABLE 8

National, Community and international mergers (including acquisitions of majority holdings) in the Community

Sector[1]	National				Community				International				Total			
	1985/ 1986	1986/ 1987	1987/ 1988	1988/ 1989	1985/ 1986	1986/ 1987	1987/ 1988	1988/ 1989	1985/ 1986	1986/ 1987	1987/ 1988	1988/ 1989	1985/ 1986	1986/ 1987	1987/ 1988	1988/ 1989
1. Food	25	39	25	35	7	11	18	27	2	2	8	14	34	52	51	76
2 Chem.	23	38	32	37	28	27	38	56	6	6	15	14	57	71	85	107
3 Elec.	10	33	25	23	—	6	4	18	3	2	7	8	13	41	36	49
4 Mech.	19	21	24	31	3	8	5	17	7	2	9	7	29	31	38	55
5 Comp.	1	2	2	3	—	—	1	—	—	—	—	1	1	2	3	4
6 Meta.	14	15	28	16	1	4	9	13	2	—	3	6	17	19	40	35
7 Trans.	6	15	3	7	—	6	9	6	4	—	3	1	10	21	15	14
8 Pap.	18	17	24	32	4	7	6	26	5	1	4	3	27	25	34	61
9 Extra.	7	8	9	11	3	1	2	5	—	—	1	3	10	9	12	19
10 Text.	7	4	11	11	1	2	2	7	1	—	1	2	9	6	14	20
11 Cons.	12	13	21	20	2	3	12	19	—	3	—	—	14	19	33	39
12 Other	3	6	10	7	3	—	5	3	—	1	7	3	6	7	22	13
Total	145	211	214	233	52	75	111	197	30	17	58	62	227	303	383	492

Source: See Table 6.
[1] Key:
    Food: Food and drink.
    Chem.: Chemicals, fibres, glass, ceramic wares, rubber.
    Elec.:   Electrical and electronic engineering, office machinery.
    Mech.: Mechanical and instrument engineering, machine tools.
    Comp.: Computers and data-processing equipment.
    Meta.: Production and preliminary processing of metals, metal goods.
    Trans.: Vehicles and transport equipment.
    Pap.:   Wood, furniture and paper.
    Extra.: Extractive industries.
    Text.:   Textiles, clothing, leather and footwear.
    Cons.: Construction.
    Other: Other manufacturing industry.

TABLE 9

Breakdown of national, Community and international acquisitions of majority holdings
by sector and combined turnover of firms
involved >1 000, >5 000, >10 000 millions ecus

Sector[1]	National[2]				Community[3]				International[4]				Total			
	>1	>2	>5	>10	>1	>2	>5	>10	>1	>2	>5	>10	>1	>2	>5	>10
1. Food.	30	23	5	—	21	16	9	7	12	12	8	7	63	51	22	14
2. Chem.	31	25	15	8	45	40	31	20	14	13	11	7	90	78	57	35
3. Elec.	17	9	3	3	15	13	11	9	9	9	8	7	41	31	22	19
4. Mech.	20	16	12	3	12	8	3	2	7	7	2	—	39	31	17	5
5. Comp.	3	2	1	—	—	—	—	—	1	1	1	1	4	3	2	1
6. Meta.	10	7	4	—	10	3	2	2	6	5	2	—	26	15	8	2
7. Trans.	7	6	4	4	5	4	4	3	1	1	1	1	13	11	9	8
8. Pap.	20	12	2	—	19	11	2	2	3	3	—	—	42	26	4	2
9. Extra.	10	6	6	5	4	4	3	3	4	4	2	1	18	14	11	9
10. Text.	5	3	3	2	4	1	1	—	2	2	1	—	11	6	5	2
11. Cons.	5	4	1	1	11	8	4	3	—	—	—	—	16	12	5	4
12. Other	5	5	4	3	2	2	2	2	3	3	2	—	10	10	8	5
Total	163	118	60	29	148	110	72	53	62	60	38	24	373	288	170	106

Source: See Table 6.
[1] Key: See Table 8, note 1.
[2] Mergers of firms from the same Member State.
[3] Mergers of firms from different Member States.
[4] Mergers of firms from Member States and third countries with effects on the Community market.

Once again, most operations occurred in the chemical sector, followed by the food and drink industry. The trend in the paper industry was up, with a 12% share of total operations.

In the chemicals sector, majority acquisitions concerned a large number of firms: in virtually all cases, a relatively small firm was acquired by a large one. Almost every one of the 25 largest firms in the sector was involved in this type of operation, although only three were involved im more than three. The aim of the large chemicals undertakings was thus to strengthen their position on the Community market.

On the other hand, only half of the 25 largest food and drink firms took part in this type of operation, and in most cases acquired relatively large companies. Given a comparable degree of concentration in both sectors, the structure of competition in the food industry appears to have deteriorated.

There appears to be a greater degree of differentiation in the paper industry. Only a few major paper manufacturers took part in such operations, whereas in publishing, the concentration probably increased owing to the fact that the large firms in this area were often involved in operations with major companies.

The largest number of operations occurred in France, the United Kingdom and Germany, owing to their economic importance. A number of mergers took place in Spain. An atypical trend is the large number of majority acquisitions in the mechanical engineering sector in Germany, which could however be explained by the size of this sector which comprises a considerable number of medium-sized firms. Nevertheless, 70% of operations involving firms with a combined turnover in excess of ECU 1 000 million were national. This result is indicative of major restructuring in the German mechanical engineering industry.

A country-by-country analysis reveals other trends. Whilst acquisitions by foreign companies clearly predominate in the smaller Member States, the situation is more balanced in the larger Member States, with the exception of Italy where foreign investments are dominant. In France, however, national mergers were prominent, as were large-scale operations, in The Netherlands. As a rule, operations in Ireland, Spain and Portugal almost exclusively involved partners of different nationalities, which indicates major restructuring in these industries using foreign capital.

The breakdown by combined turnover of the firms concerned (Table 9) reveals a continuing trend towards large-scale majority acquisitions involving combined turnovers in excess of ECU 1 000 million. In 35% of such cases, the combined turnover of participants exceeded ECU 5 000 million, whereas in 22% of operations, the firms had a combined turnover of over ECU 10 000 million. This category notably includes the major chemicals, electrical engineering and food and drink companies, which accounted for almost more than two-thirds of the operations.

Detailed analysis of two industrial sectors

244. The following sectors were chosen because of the sharp rise in the number of cases.

Food

245. The food and drink industry experienced 76 majority acquisitions, i.e. 15% of all such operations. This represents an increase of almost 50%. Two-thirds of the acquisitions involved firms with a combined turnover of over

ECU 2 000 million, the largest transactions consisting solely of crossfrontier operations.

Everything points to the fact that this industry is engaged in intensive preparations for the completion of the internal market and for competition from multinational undertakings, chiefly in the USA. As these acquisitions mainly involved large firms, there is undeniably some concentration taking place, in view of the very modest growth in the market overall. Since barriers to trade persist, the degree of concentration in this industry is generally higher nationally than at Community level. In most Member States, there is a decline in the number, but an increase in the size, of firms. This is why a close watch should be kept on restructuring which, whilst certainly necessary for the completion of the internal market and to cope with strong competition from third countries, can nevertheless lead to restrictions of competition.

Paper

246. This sector, which apart from wood and paper also includes printing and publishing, has experienced the most dynamic growth from the standpoint of the number of majority acquisitions which increased by almost 80%. Aggregate turnover in this sector is far lower than in other industries: only two takeovers concerned firms in the highest turnover category, i.e. in excess of ECU 10 000 million. This can, however, be explained by the structure of many of the subsectors, chiefly made up of medium-sized firms in the processing, printing and publishing sectors in particular. It is probable that with the increase in competition, essentially from third countries, further mergers will occur.

Acquisitions of minority holdings (Table 10)

247. In industry as a whole, minority acquisitions decreased overall compared with other forms of operation.

Most minority acquisitions involved paper and electrical engineering firms, which experienced a noticeable upswing in activity, although only at national level. It is possible, in view of this development and on the basis of past experience, that majority acquisitions will increase in these sectors in future. The outward-looking strategy in the mining industry should also be noted.

TABLE 10

National, Community and international acquisitions of minority holdings
in the Community

Sector[1]	National				Community				International				Total			
	1985/1986	1986/1987	1987/1988	1988/1989	1985/1986	1986/1987	1987/1988	1988/1989	1985/1986	1986/1987	1987/1988	1988/1989	1985/1986	1986/1987	1987/1988	1988/1989
1. Food.	7	13	17	15	3	7	9	4	1	1	9	2	11	21	35	21
2. Chem.	16	16	9	10	5	6	6	5	6	1	2	3	27	23	17	18
3. Elec.	10	9	8	18	1	2	4	5	2	—	3	2	13	11	15	25
4. Mech.	13	10	10	7	3	2	—	1	1	1	3	—	17	13	13	8
5. Comp.	1	1	1	—	1	—	—	1	—	—	—	1	2	1	1	2
6. Meta.	18	9	11	6	1	2	2	7	4	1	2	3	23	12	15	16
7. Trans.	4	4	8	4	3	1	1	1	3	—	—	3	10	5	9	8
8. Pap.	5	7	19	15	1	—	7	9	1	4	3	1	7	11	29	25
9. Extra.	4	5	5	11	—	—	2	2	—	2	5	1	4	7	12	14
10. Text.	1	2	5	5	—	1	1	—	1	1	—	1	2	4	6	6
11. Cons.	7	8	15	6	2	—	5	2	1	1	1	2	10	9	21	10
12. Other	2	—	7	5	—	—	—	—	2	—	1	1	4	—	8	6
Total	88	84	115	102	20	21	37	37	22	12	29	20	130	117	181	159

Source: See Table 6.
[1] Key: See Table 8, note 1.

Joint ventures (Table 11)

248. The number of joint ventures remained virtually unchanged. This form
of operation is fairly common in sectors with extensive research activities, such
as the chemicals and electrical engineering industries, and also the metals
industry.

A strong trend in cross-frontier cooperation has emerged in the first two sectors,
reflected in the lively interest shown by third countries, notably the USA and
also Japan and Switzerland.

TABLE 11

Joint ventures in the Community

Sector [1]	National				Community				International				Total			
	1985/ 1986	1986/ 1987	1987/ 1988	1988/ 1989	1985/ 1986	1986/ 1987	1987/ 1988	1988/ 1989	1985/ 1986	1986/ 1987	1987/ 1988	1988/ 1989	1985/ 1986	1986/ 1987	1987/ 1988	1988/ 1989
1. Food	2	—	6	4	1	1	3	2	1	4	1	3	4	5	10	9
2. Chem.	7	3	7	8	7	1	5	9	9	10	12	11	23	14	24	28
3. Elec.	10	4	8	8	4	3	5	7	5	14	7	14	19	21	20	29
4. Mech.	5	9	4	6	1	—	—	2	4	8	3	2	10	17	7	10
5. Comp.	—	1	2	—	1	1	1	2	1	3	2	3	2	5	5	5
6. Meta.	5	1	2	9	1	1	6	3	4	1	2	3	10	3	10	15
7. Trans.	—	1	1	4	3	3	4	2	1	—	1	1	4	4	6	7
8. Pap.	—	3	7	4	—	1	1	5	—	2	1	—	—	6	9	9
9. Extra.	2	—	3	2	—	1	1	—	—	—	1	—	2	1	5	2
10. Text.	—	—	—	3	—	—	2	—	—	—	1	—	—	—	3	3
11. Cons.	3	3	1	4	2	2	2	3	—	—	3	—	5	5	6	7
12. Other	—	4	4	4	—	2	1	1	2	3	1	—	2	9	6	5
Total	34	29	45	56	20	16	31	36	27	45	35	37	81	90	111	129

Source: See Table 6.
[1] Key: See Table 8, note 1.

Main motives for mergers and joint ventures (Table 12)

Mergers

249. Whilst it is not easy to identify the different motives for mergers, it is useful to identify the reasons most frequently given in the Press. Reinforcement of market position and expansion of commercial activities continued to be among the most important; these motives are given in three out of four cases (as against 45% last year).

TABLE 12

**Main motives for mergers
and joint ventures in 1988/89**

Motive	Mergers (including acquisitions of majority holdings)	Joint ventures
Strengthening of market position	155	22
Expansion	115	17
Complementarity	39	11
Diversification	26	4
Restructuring (including rationalization)	14	5
R&D and production and marketing	—	12
Cooperation	—	10
Other	18	6
Not specified	125	42
Total	492	129

While it would not be true to attribute this phenomenon solely to the prospect of a single European Market, there is nevertheless a general increase in measures to prepare for the resulting intensification of competition and larger markets in various sectors.

Joint ventures

250.   A frequent motive for joint ventures is to strengthen market position or develop the commercial activities of firms, but this form of operation is also to a large extent explained, as would be expected, by the pooling of research and development. In many cases, large firms share certain activities in a new company so as to acquire a larger joint share of the market in a Member State, or to maintain competitiveness in traditional areas.

§ 3 — Mergers, acquisitions and joint ventures in services

251.   There were fewer acquisitions in services (limited here to distribution, banking and insurance) than in industry; there was a rather surprising decline in this respect in the banking sector. The number of banks in third countries acquiring minority holdings in banks in Member States has dropped. On the other hand, the insurance sector has increased its efforts to expand in other Member States. Distribution, however, has experienced a strong move back towards national operations through increased majority acquisitions.

The breakdown by size of firm is based on turnover in distribution and industry, and on one-tenth of assets in the case of banks and gross premium income in the case of insurance companies. These are the same criteria as those adopted for the Regulation on the control of concentrations between undertakings (merger control).

The breakdown by size shows that, with two exceptions, large-scale operations in distribution were at national level. In banking, however, there was a strong move towards cross-frontier operations, which have risen sharply in keeping with the size of the banks concerned. This tendency was less defined in the insurance sector.

Acquisitions of majority holdings (including mergers) (Table 13)

252.   Banks again led the field in majority acquisitions in the services industry; for the most part they involved international operations. Insurance companies, however, acquired fewer holdings in companies in other Member States. Distribution accounted for only five cross-frontier operations (compared with 17 in the previous year).

TABLE 13

National, Community and international mergers (including acquisitions of majority holdings) in the Community

Services

Sector	National				Community				International				Total			
	1985/ 1986	1986/ 1987	1987/ 1988	1988/ 1989	1985/ 1986	1986/ 1987	1987/ 1988	1988/ 1989	1985/ 1986	1986/ 1987	1987/ 1988	1988/ 1989	1985/ 1986	1986/ 1987	1987/ 1988	1988/ 1989
Distribution	27	40	40	53	6	5	8	4	—	4	9	1	33	49	57	58
Banking	12	22	53	51	4	3	12	16	9	10	13	16	25	35	78	83
Insurance	5	17	14	15	3	7	14	8	4	4	12	10	12	28	40	33
Total	44	79	107	119	13	15	34	28	13	18	34	27	70	112	175	174

Source: See Table 6.

Acquisitions of minority holdings (Table 14)

253. There were far more minority than majority acquisitions at the Community and international levels in the distribution sector, a trend also observed in insurance. On the other hand, banks were more inward-looking than the previous year and focused on national operations.

Joint ventures (Table 15)

254. The only area in which the number of joint ventures increased was distribution. This development took place not only on the national level, but also in the area of Community and international operations. The latter confirms a trend first identified two years ago.

TABLE 14

National, Community and international acquisitions of minority holdings in the Community

Services

Sector	National				Community				International				Total			
	1985/ 1986	1986/ 1987	1987/ 1988	1988/ 1989	1985/ 1986	1986/ 1987	1987/ 1988	1988/ 1989	1985/ 1986	1986/ 1987	1987/ 1988	1988/ 1989	1985/ 1986	1986/ 1987	1987/ 1988	1988/ 1989
Distribution	7	7	13	8	1	3	4	6	—	1	5	8	8	11	22	22
Banking	10	11	38	32	3	9	15	19	8	13	28	11	21	33	81	62
Insurance	4	5	8	9	—	1	4	13	—	5	7[1]	7	4	11	19[1]	29
Total	21	23	59	49	4	13	23	38	8	19	40[1]	26	33	55	122[1]	113

Source: See Table 6.
[1] Figures in Eighteenth Competition Report amended.

TABLE 15

Joint ventures in the Community

Services

Sector	National				Community				International				Total			
	1985/1986	1986/1987	1987/1988	1988/1989	1985/1986	1986/1987	1987/1988	1988/1989	1985/1986	1986/1987	1987/1988	1988/1989	1985/1986	1986/1987	1987/1988	1988/1989
Distribution	3	3	4	7	1	1	3	4	1	1	—	3	5	5	7	14
Banking	10	18	16	11	6	5	7	6	—	1	7	7	16	24	30	24
Insurance	—	1	10	8	—	1	3	5	—	—	3	3	—	2	16	16
Total	13	22	30	26	7	7	13	15	1	2	10	13	21	31	53	54

Source: See Table 6.

§ 4 — Conclusions

255.   The analysis of mergers, acquisitions and joint ventures reported in the Press and involving at least one of the sample firms prompts the following conclusions for the period 1988/89:

(i)   the number of operations has continued to increase: 70% concerned industry, of which 63% were majority acquisitions. There was also an increase in cross-frontier cooperation;

(ii)   majority acquisitions in the chemicals, food and drink, paper, electrical engineering and mechanical engineering sectors account overall for 71% of all operations (against 64% the previous year); their share of minority acquisitions was 61%. Furthermore, two-thirds of large-scale operations (combined turnover in excess of ECU 2 000 million took place in these sectors;

(iii)   majority acquisitions resulted in a general increase in the combined turnover of the firms concerned; whereas in the previous year one operation in six represented more than ECU 10 000 million, the proportion was one in five in the period studied. Mechanical engineering and metals experienced a relative decline in 'large-scale' operations;

(iv)   the overall increase in mergers, acquisitions and joint ventures and the rise in the number of majority acquisitions and cross-frontier operations involving major industrial firms all indicate that the degree of concentration will generally continue to strengthen. Whilst this can improve the competitiveness of Community firms in both Community and national markets, it must not lead to restrictions of competition within the Community. The Regulation on merger control adopted by the Council therefore constitutes an essential means of preventing the damage that such mergers could inflict on competition.

Chapter II

The programme of studies and its results

§ 1 — Objectives of the 1989 programme of studies

256.   The studies published in 1989 fell within two broad subject areas: the modification of market structures from the standpoint of competition policy and government support for enterprises.

The studies were commissioned from universities and independent consultants who are responsible for the data and views set out therein. They are published as documents.

§ 2 — Studies concerning the modification of market structures from the point of view of competition policy

European conglomerate firms

257.   Recent annual reports have highlighted a constant increase in merger activity in the Community. The Commission has already published a study on competitive trends following certain merger operations in the motor vehicle and telecommunications sectors. This year, research was carried out into conglomerate mergers and their effects on competition.

The data suggest that conglomerate structures are less prevalent in Europe than in the USA and that, in the Community, they are most prevalent in the United Kingdom. The authors focused in particular on two situations in which such structures can have anti-competitive effects: predatory strategies and mutual forbearance.

Conglomerates can, more readily than other enterprises, adopt predatory strategies by using their financial reserves to eliminate competitors from some of their sectors of activity. Even if a firm does not utilize such a strategy, the fact that it has the necessary means can be enough to discipline smaller competitors. More important, however, is the anti-competitive effect arising from mutual forbearance: when conglomerate firms have an overlapping presence in a range of markets, they may be reluctant to compete against each other.

The main comparative advantage of a conglomerate is financial: they benefit from a lower cost of capital than other firms, chiefly because of the smaller risk inherent in diversification.

In short, the study reveals that conglomerate mergers may have negative effects on the intensity of competition. A selective monitoring of mergers in accordance with the new Regulation is thus necessary. The Commission may use the results of the study in implementing Community control of concentrations.

The effects of joint ventures upon competition

258.   The study drew distinctions between different types of joint ventures on the basis of their characteristics, the reasons they were set up and their effects.

The impact of joint ventures on competition was studied in particular in the chemicals and petrochemicals industry. A sharp rise in the number of joint ventures was identified in this sector. The impact of a joint venture on competition depends on a variety of factors.

The creation of joint ventures with horizontal links between the parent companies is more likely to produce anti-competitive effects than in the case of conglomerate or vertical relationships. The reasons underlying the agreement, for example the sharing of risks connected with research and development or production rationalization, should also be taken into account in this analysis. Sectoral factors also play a part; a rapid rise in demand would make a decrease in competition less likely following the creation of a joint venture. The existence of over-capacities, the technology used and economies of scale are also important criteria. The study thus concludes with a check-list of the factors to be considered when analysing specific cases.

Hostile takeover bids from the standpoint of competition policy

219. Hostile takeover bids are currently a topic of discussion from the theoretical point of view and with regard to their control. Particular attention is focused on the consequences of takeover bids for the financing of enterprises, the capital markets and the markets for corporate control.

As far as competition is concerned, the important factors are the links between takeovers, the behaviour of management and the goods and services markets.

The authors of the study drew the following conclusions:

(1) The capital markets of Western economies do not operate with perfect efficiency; consequently, the corporate control market can only imperfectly fulfil its selection functions.

(2) A number of empirical studies have pointed to the limited profitability of external growth operations; it may be inferred that these operations have other motives, e.g. prestige for management and their desire to increase their remuneration.

The effect which the market for corporate control has for optimizing resource allocation, and disciplining and penalizing management must not be overestimated; the competitive processes in the markets for capital, goods and services are complementary rather than substitutable. The analysis of the corporate control market does not, therefore, rule out the need for merger control.

The study also advocates some limitation of the defence methods of management used by target companies, which can have anti-competitive effects, together with various measures to increase the transparency and efficacy of the corporate control market, for example by regulating the content of the information given to shareholders and limiting the power of banks in the Federal Republic of Germany.

§ 3 — Studies relating to government support for enterprises

The effect of State aids on intra-Community competition; the example of the automobile sector

260.   Owing to the economic importance of the automotive industry, a number of Member States awarded huge sums of aid during the crisis years in the 1970s and in the following period of restructuring.

The study takes stock of the current position of the industry in the Community, now faced with the increased production capacity of Japanese manufacturers and their growing penetration of the upper segment of the market. There is some justification for the award of subsidies to the motor vehicle industry, notably the positive external effects of investment in less-favoured regions, the high risk attached to certain investments and the maintenance of competition by preventing the disappearance of certain manufacturers.

On the other hand, this aid has caused extensive distortions and could have contributed to the misallocation of resources owing to the absence of motivation they can cause. The theoretical analysis reveals cases where aid is liable to alter the relative market shares of manufacturers and diminish general well-being even more acutely if other Member States also step up their own contributions.

It is precisely with the aim of avoiding such escalation that the Commission adopted a framework for State aid to this sector aimed at increasing transparency and subjecting the award of aid to more stringent tests.

Assessment of catchment areas

261.   Several Member States have created 'employment areas' in order to provide fresh opportunities in areas of high unemployment and to make regions experiencing extensive restructuring problems more attractive. There are, however, substantial differences in the aid schemes developed in the three Member States covered by the study (the United Kingdom, Belgium and France) and in the impact of the schemes.

In Belgium and France, the main benefit is a 10-year exemption from corporation tax; the efficacy of this incentive thus depends on the ability of the newly established enterprises to achieve profitability in the first years of operation. In the United Kingdom, the effect of the advantages granted is more complex, the consequences of exemption from property tax being reflected in land prices in the employment areas.

The impact of the employment areas varies considerably from contry to country: in Belgium, they have led to the creation of only a few jobs and firms, chiefly because many other aid schemes are in existence. In France, the system is still developing but a rapid rise in the number of jobs is expected in the areas where the programme is under way. The employment areas have had the greatest success in the UK: according to official reports, the programme has resulted in some 35 000 new jobs. New enterprises are generally small and aimed at local and regional markets, which tends to limit the impact of the aid policy on intra-Community trade.

Repercussions of subsidies for exports to non-member countries, on intra-Community competition

262.   After the last war, reductions in customs tariffs under the GATT and the establishment of the common market substantially lowered the barriers to trade.

International constraints, however, and especially the consensus between the OECD countries, leave considerable room for manoeuvre as regards the award of export subsidies. Member States have used these as one of several means of maintaining or increasing their market shares. Susbsidies for intra-Community exports are generally prohibited; the Commission nevertheless considered it appropriate to examine what effects subsidies for exports to non-member countries had on intra-Community trade. Subsidies can be granted, either in the form of loans on more favourable terms than those of the market, or through public export insurance systems where the premiums paid do not cover losses and operating costs. Elements of aid for firms may also be included in development aid and in loans to developing countries where they are tied to purchases to be made in the awarding country.

The results of the empirical study show the extent of subsidies tied to export credits; however, the subsidies included in the insurance schemes have recently developed more rapidly.

Sectorally, subsidies are distributed very unevenly in some countries and represent over 10% of the value of exports to non-OECD countries, The industries most affected were mechanical engineering, metals, electrical equipment, means of transport and construction. Some data also show that subsidies are specifically directed towards exports to certain countries.

These data point to the conclusion that export subsidies can increase the export market shares of some Member States at the expense of others and can therefore affect competition in the common market. The effect is even greater in cases where the cost difference between exporting firms is small, demand is elastic, competition in the sector is intense, product differentiation is low and economies of scale considerable.

Annex

European Parliament:

Resolution on the Eighteenth Report of the Commission of the European Communities on Competition Policy

Economic and Social Commitee:

Opinion on the Eighteenth Report of the Commission of the European Communities on Competition Policy

Council Regulation (EEC) No 4064/89 of 21 December 1989 on the control of concentrations between undertakings:

Notes

I — Competition policy towards enterprises — List of Decisions, communications and rulings
1. Decisions pursuant to Articles 85 and 86 of the EEC Treaty
2. Notices pursuant to Articles 85 and 86 of the EEC Treaty
    (a) Pursuant to Article 19(3) of Council Regulation No 17
    (b) Pursuant to Article 5(2) of Council Regulation (EEC) No 3975/87
    (c) Pursuant to Article 12(2) of Council Regulation No 4056/86
3. Decisions pursuant to Articles 65 and 66 of the ECSC Treaty
4. Rulings of the Court of Justice

II — Competition policy and government assistance to enterprises
1. Final negative decisions adopted by the Commission following the Article 93(2) EEC procedure
2. A. Conditional Decision adopted by the Commission following the Article 93(2) EEC procedure
    B. Review of Conditional Decision adopted by the Commission following the Article 93(2) EEC procedure
3. Decision relating to Article 95 of the ECSC Treaty
4. Judgments delivered by the Court of Justice
5. Aid cases in which the Commission raised no objection
6. Aid cases in which the Commission decided to open the Article 93(2) EEC procedure
7. Aid cases in which the Commission decided to close the Article 93(2) EEC procedure
8. Aid case in which the procedure provided for in Article 93(1) of the EEC Treaty was initiated to examine existing aid schemes

III — Competition policy and government assistance in the agricultural sector
1. Aid cases in which the Commission raised no objection
2. Aid cases in which the procedure provided for in Article 93(2) of the EEC Treaty was initiated
3. Aid cases in which the procedure provided for in Article 93(2) of the EEC Treaty was closed
4. Aid cases in which the Commission adopted negative opinions under Article 92(3)(a) of the EEC Treaty
5. Council Decisions under Article 93(2) of the EEC Treaty

IV — List of studies published in 1989 and to be published

European Parliament

Resolution on the Eighteenth Report of the Commission of the European Communities on Competition Policy

The European Parliament,

— having regard to the Eighteenth Report of the Commission of the European Communities on Competition Policy (SEC(89) 873 — Doc. C3-123/89),

— having regard to its earlier resolutions on competition policy,

— having regard to the report of the Committee on Economic and Monetary Affairs and Industrial Policy and the opinions of the Committee on Legal Affairs and Citizens Rights and the Committee on Agriculture, Fisheries and Rural Development (Doc. A3-108/89),

A — General remarks

1. Emphasizes again the crucial importance of the European Community having an effective competition policy

(i) as the basic prerequisite for a genuine European internal market in which even small and medium-sized enterprises will be able to develop freely across frontiers without suffering the effects of concentration processes and State aids that distort competition,

(ii) as a necessary and indispensable part of a coherent, effective Community-wide legal framework providing clear and reliable ground rules for Member States, third countries and all parties involved in the common market;

2. Welcomes the Commission's decision to produce for the first time in 1989 a complete and autonomous report on State aid in the European Community and expects this report to be formally submitted to Parliament;

3. Notes with approval that in the period covered by the report the Commission once again took a series of individual decisions on the basis of Articles 85 and 86 of the EEC Treaty and with reference to the application of Articles 65 and 66 of the ECSC Treaty, to obviate — partly by fixing heavy fines — any prevention, restriction or distortion of competition;

4. Considers, however, that competition policy cannot be pursued in an economic and social vacuum and that the reduction in State aids for certain sectors should be accompanied by the development of a European industrial policy to avert the collapse of key industiral sectors in the Community;

notes, however, that there is no mention whatsoever of such a much needed parallel approach:

5. Welcomes the Commission's approach in discussing at length procedures planned by undertakings or groups of undertakings which could lead to the prevention or distortion of competition with a view to reaching a balanced decision which would promote competition;

6. Reiterates the view it expressed in its motion for a resolution on the 17th Report, that, in view of the increasing importance of world markets, close cooperation between the European Community, OECD, EFTA and the United Nations is even more urgently required than ever, without neglecting the need for sustained efforts to intensify solidarity within the Community area;

B — Application of Community competition policy to undertakings

7. Notes the increasing number of mergers in the Community in the run-up to the single market and considers that the reorganization of the European market must be monitored continuously by the Commission and Parliament to prevent the distortion of competition and abuses of a dominant position that might otherwise arise;

8. Considers that the legal basis cited by the Commission in the case of the two contested takeover proposals involving Irish Distillers and British Airways/British Caledonian is not reliable and permanent enough to permit effective control of takeovers;

9. Warmly welcomes, therefore, with reference to its resolution of 26 October 1988, the Commission's efforts to obtain a Council decision by the end of 1989 on a regulation to control takeovers in the EEC, to promote competition in the Community and prevent market domination;

10. Assumes that the agreed intervention thresholds will ultimately be reduced, to bring within the scope of the European law on cartels not only large-scale mergers but all mergers with a Community dimension;

11. Calls, however, for the Commission to submit a proposal on the basis of Article 236 of the EEC Treaty, once the intervention threshold has been lowered, to transfer the power to examine proposed mergers to a European cartel office responsible to the European Parliament;

12. Calls for the Commission to include considerations of the regional and social implications of mergers and also to recognize the necessity for consultation with workers affected by mergers and takeovers;

13. Welcomes the drafting of two block exemption regulations (on franchising and know-how) as instruments providing effective assistance for small and medium-sized undertakings in the common market;

14. Notes that on 28 June 1989 the Commission enacted a regulation on the basis of Article 90(3) of the EEC Treaty on competition in the telecommunication services market; recognizes the Commission's right to take swift and effective action under Article 90(3) to protect or restore the rules of competition for public undertakings or those having the character of a monopoly; believes, however, that Article 100a of the EEC Treaty is a more appropriate legal basis for adopting directives relating to such enterprises; also calls on the Commission to give Parliament sufficient opportunity to deliver an opinion before deciding, where necessary, to take specific measures on the basis of Article 90(3) of the EEC Treaty;

15. Regards the achievement of adequate competition in the field of computer programs as a particularly topical and important taks for the Community; argues in addition that all non-protectable components of system and applications software, including interfaces, should be freely accessible so as to prevent hardware manufacturers from dominating the software market;

16. Recognizes the role played by national, regional and local public agencies in assisting economic development, particularly in the most deprived areas of the Community, and recalls Article 92 of the EEC Treaty, which recognizes the legitimacy of State aid;

C — Application of competition policy in the Member States

17. Notes with concern the ever-increasing proportion of the gross national product accounted for by national and Community aids; notes that in Italy, according to the figures given by the Commission (but contested by the Italian Court of Auditors), four times more State aids were provided than in France and eight times more than in the United Kingdom; urges the Commission, therefore, to complete its data, particularly the missing statistics concerning Spain, Portugal and Greece, and, if necessary, to make use of the scope for intervention offered by Article 93 of the EEC Treaty;

18. Is concerned at the estimation that State aids amount to 3% of the Community's GDP per annum, but welcomes the Commission's obvious efforts in monitoring State aids and would welcome a review of the procedures currently in force;

19. Reiterates its proposal that the Commission adopt a regulation on the basis of Articles 93 and 94 of the EEC Treaty in connection with the granting of inadmissible State aids, in accordance with which any aid granted illegally would be paid back not to the Member State responsible but to the Community budget;

20. Takes the view that even those Member States whose economic strength exceeds the Community average must retain a legally safeguarded and adequate freedom to pursue an autonomous, effective regional economic policy, provided the resources deployed do not exceed present limits;

21. Calls on the Commission in future to extend the report on State aids to cover those national and Community aids granted in the following fields:

— fiscal benefits,

— resources for public institutions, research projects and to finance university and other contracted-out research including that in the military domain,

— payments from the European Regional Development Fund and the EAGGF, Guidance Section,

— subsidies in the energy sector and the transport sector,

— subsidies to banks, to the construction industry and public utilities;

22. Asks the Commission in future to express trends in the national subsidies in both ecus and the relevant national currency;

23. Proposes that the Commission should send to Parliament, on its completion, the inventory of all aids in the Community it is drawing up in addition to the report on State aids;

24. Warmly supports the Commission's efforts to assist the transformation of the State monopolies in Spain, Portugal, Greece and France;

D — Problems in specific sectors

25. Recognizes, like the Commission, that the competition in the Community's air transport sector leaves much to be desired; welcomes, accordingly, the Commission's initiative in submitting six proposals for regulations on 8 September 1989 with a view to generating more competition in air transport both on intra-Community and domestic routes;

26. Considers that limited and temporary aids to individual undertakings in the maritime sector are justified only where the competitive position of European shipbuilders in relation to third countries is thereby enhanced; considers that it is necessary to publish clear directives for granting such aids in that sector;

27. Reiterates the view it expressed in connection with the 17th Report on competition that more competition in the banking and insurance sector continues to be necessary and regrets that the Commission has not taken any measures in that field or referred to any in its 18th Report on competition;

28. Also considers that insufficient progress has been made in achieving competition in the media and calls on the Commission, as it did in the resolution on its previous report, to pay more attention to that sector;

29. Calls on the Commission to inform Parliament to what extent in future it intends to preserve competition in the field of telecommunications and the market in telecommunications terminal equipment;

30. Regrets again that in the 18th Report on competition the Commission does not give wide enough coverage to the competition problems in the service sector and that no mention is made of further consideration of studies in response to Parliament's demand in the resolution on its previous report;

31. Continues to regard with concern, despite the adjustments made in the intervening period, the situation in agriculture and its continued dependence on the price-supported market;

32. Points out that under Article 42 of the EEC Treaty, first sentence, the chapter relating to rules on competition applies to production of and trade in agricultural products only to the extent determined by the Council, account being taken of the objectives set out in Article 39;

33. Points out in addition that, under subparagraph(a) of the second paragraph of Article 42 of the EEC Treaty, the Council may in particular authorize the granting of aid for the protection of enterprises handicapped by structural or natural conditions;

34. Notes that there are regional differences in the requirements imposed on European agriculture with a view to protecting the environment and nature;

35. Takes the view that the diversity of Europe's countryside is part of the European identity and that it is agriculture in particular which has shaped the countryside; considers, accordingly, that aids which are likely to preserve Europe's diversity are desirable and compatible with the Treaty;

36. Calls upon the Commission to take greater account of this aspect than it has done when examining State aids;

37. Believes that, although public aid granted by certain Member States to the coal industry is justified by the need to guarantee the security of supplies and the social stability of certain areas and although such aid cannot be considered to affect competition policy since there is practically no internal trade in coal in the Community, the increase in the overall volume of such aid is a cause for concern;

38. Calls on the Commission to exercise more effective control over State aids, to speed up its procedures by avoiding excessive bureaucracy and above all to ensure that substantial aids which create lasting distortions of competition are not granted;

39. Calls on the Commission to report to Parliament annually on compliancy by the Member States with Article 223(1)(b) of the EEC Treaty and on the action taken in respect of infringements thereof;

E — Implementation of Community competition law by the Commission

40. Expects that the 19th Report on competition will be submitted to Parliament by 30 April 1990 at the latest, in view of the fact that earlier reports, including the 18th Report, have each year been submitted later despite repeated requests by Parliament;

41. Stands by its view that the Directorate-General for Competition (DG IV) urgently needs a permanent increase in its staff in view of its increasing importance and work-load;

42. Suggests that in view of the ever increasing scope of the report on competition policy, which has now been extended to include a separate report on aid, it should include an index to enable individual sections to be found more quickly;

43. Asks the Commission:

(i)   to ensure that adequate publicity is given to settlements reached by the Commission with undertakings so that greater transparency in the Commission's procedures and thinking be achieved to the benefit of legal practitioners and of any complainant undertakings concerned;

(ii)   to state clearly the authority within the Commission that may decide on a settlement in a given case; and

(iii) to inform Parliament of the priorities to be applied in clearing the backlog of 3 451 files outstanding at year end 1988;

44. Asks the Commission to ensure that the Hearings Officer is permitted to exploit to the full the powers attributed to him under the Terms of Reference published in the 13th Report on competition policy and that the Commission's DG IV be structured in such a way that there is a separation of its functions as investigator, prosecutor and judge within its internal administrative procedures (in this regard it will be interesting to observe the experience now to be acquired by the Court of First Instance on the application of the rules on competition);

45. Instructs its President to forward this resolution to the Commission, Council, the competition authorities in the Member States and the governments and parliaments of the Member States.

Economic and Social Committee

Opinion on the Eighteenth Report of the Commission of the European Communities on Competition Policy

On 1 December 1989 the Commission decided, under Article 198 of the Treaty setting up the European Economic Community, to consult the Economic and Social Committee on the Eighteenth Report on Competition Policy.

The Section for Industry, Commerce, Crafts and Services, which was responsible for preparing the Committee's work on the matter, adopted its Opinion on 29 November 1989. The rapporteur was Mr Mourgues.

At its 272nd Plenary Session (sitting of 19 December 1989) the Economic and Social Committee adopted the following Opinion unanimously (apart from one abstention):

1. Introduction

1.1. The introduction to the Eighteenth Report on Competition Policy states that Community competition policy is at a crossroads. The favourable short-term economic situation has led economic operators to incorporate increasingly in their planning the need to adapt to the new market conditions expected for 1993. The strategic planning implemented by firms leads them to overcome the Community's internal economic barriers by conducting a variety of transnational operations.

1.2. On these general grounds, the Committee has thought it best to divide the Opinion into two specific parts.

1.2.1. Part I will be a critical view — both positive and negative — of the 18th Report.

1.2.2. Part II will formulate suggestions for certain guidelines for Community competition policy in the run-up to the single market.

1.3. These suggestions will take account not only of competition conditions within the EEC but also of those associated with commercial transactions with third countries.

2. Opinion on the Eighteenth Report on Competition Policy proper

2.1. General comments

2.1.1. The long wait for a Regulation on the control of mergers, acquisitions and joint ventures

2.1.1.1. Chapter I of the fourth part of the Eighteenth Report makes an instructive assessment of the progress in links between firms. These data are not exhaustive, and are not based on official, systematic statistics, but on general information.

2.1.1.2. However, the data enable the Commission to distinguish operations which foster the harmonious development of competition from those which produce distorsions in practice and structure. In this connection the Committee would point out that, in the absence of a specific provision under Article 86 of the Treaty, the Commission has no legal power to grant exemptions approving or encouraging concentrations which favour competitions.

2.1.1.3. Moreover, if due account is taken of the *Continental-Can* judgement of 21 February 1973, the abuse of a dominant position in the Common Market or in a substantial part thereof jeopardizes an effective competition structure.

2.1.1.4. Accordingly the Committee proposes that, at the next amendment of the Treaty, an additional provision should be incorporated into Article 86, similar in spirit to Article 85(3), enabling the Commission to grant exemptions for concentration operations regarded as compatible with the aims of improving production or distribution, or likely to promote technical or economic progress, and to the extent that they are ultimately beneficial to consumers.

2.1.2. The major disadvantages of this situation

2.1.2.1. The Commission states that 'the impact of mergers and majority acquisitions on competition is likely to be more severe in already highly concentrated industries, such as chemicals' and particularly 'downstream' for pharmaceutical products and certain food products (point 327). Price-fixing in these sectors shows that the degree of concentration has reached a critical point.

2.1.2.2. This tendency appears to be accelerated by:

(a) the imminent prospect of the single market;

(b) but also probably by the delay in introducing Community rules in this field, or by the temporary retention of sometimes illegally imposed prices;

(c) the promotion of research and development agreements which establish links between enterprises.

2.1.2.3. The juxtaposition of these reasons may prompt the belief that there is a combination of circumstances favourable to the development of capital movement operations (takeover bids etc.) within the Community.

2.1.2.4. At the same time there is a blatant slowness in the development of social provisions and in regulating public tenders; these are other factors influencing the market and competition.

2.1.2.5. This discord in the factors contributing to competition policy threatens to cause serious difficulties, and the Committee, which is deeply concerned about this, feels duty bound to warn the Commission.

2.1.3. The direct and indirect causes of inequality of treatment of enterprises and holdings

2.1.3.1. The inequality results primarily from the 'notification' conditions required sometimes in advance and sometimes retrospectively.

2.1.3.2. In addition, some factors of inequality result from the fact that the Commission exercises control retrospectively by defining the Community dimension of a concentration operation mainly on the basis of a threshold based on a high turnover figure,[1] but also because

(i) the only enterprises concerned are those engaged in trade between Member States or with third countries;

(ii) Community case-law has introduced the concept of 'collective dominant position' (see point 2.1.4. below).

2.1.3.3. On the other hand, in those sectors exempted from Article 85 for which rules have been drawn up, prior notifications are controlled without a lower limit. This applies to know-how licensing, franchising and research and development agreements.

---

[1]   The draft rules currently before the Council seek to diversify notification conditions on the basis of geographical criteria, competition external to and within the Community and market shares held by a firm outside the country where it is based.

2.1.3.4. In this connection, attention is drawn to the Commission's positive stance in the following cases:

Research and development

In three interesting cases, the Commission proved that it favoured technical progress and innovation in the Community. The first of these cases concerns the development by the Continental and Michelin companies of a tyre of entirely new design requiring considerable investment and involving an economic risk which is difficult to assess.

In this context reference should also be made to the Commission decision in the case of Brown-Boveri AG, a company which had concluded agreements with the Japanese company NGK Insulators Ltd. This decision authorizes intensive cooperation between these two firms for the purpose of developing, manufacturing and marketing high-performance batteries, intended primarily for use in electrically powered vehicles.

Franchising

In a decision on franchising, the Commission also showed that it is prepared in certain cases to waive the conditions laid down by the block exemption regulation concerned where the structure of competition on the market in question so allows (ServiceMaster).

2.1.3.5. The same applies to subsidies policy: in particular, CAP subsidies are precisely assessed irrespective of the size of holdings, whereas in other sectors the severity of the checks is a function of their impact on intra-Community trade.

2.1.4. The 'activism' of case-law

2.1.4.1. There is a hallowed tradition that, when the Community legislator is marking time, the Courts move things along through case-law, which emphasizes the spirit of Community law.

2.1.4.2. This is true of:

(a) the *Pascal van Eycke* v *Aspa* judgment, which confirms that Member States are prohibited from enacting or maintaining in force measures likely to render Articles 85 and 86 inoperative (point 98).

Attention should be drawn to the Court of Justice ruling in the *Pascal van Eycke* v *Aspa* case by which it confirmed and extended its critical case-law in respect of national measures which prejudice competition. The Court ruled that Member States must not enact or maintain in force measures likely to render Articles 85 and 86 of the EEC Treaty inoperative. This judgment confirms earlier case-law (e.g. Vereniging van Vlaamse reisbureaus — Association of Flemish Travel Agents, 1 October 1987) in that it maintains that the effective benefit of the competition rules is limited: when a Member State imposes or encourages the conclusion of agreements contrary to Article 85; or when by adopting certain rules, it reinforces the impact of such agreements; or when it undermines its own rules by delegating to private operators responsibility for taking decisions on economic intervention (paragraph No 16 of the judgment).

The need for this approach to competition law is seen (for instance) in the efforts made by cooperatives, faced with global competition, to set up an integrated cooperative network.

(b) judgments relating to the concept of delegated monopolies (point 106 *et seq.*) which hinge on 'whether the unconnected parallel conduct of several economically independent firms might be caught by Article 86 as constituting abuse of a collective dominant position' and confirm the Commission's conclusions in this respect;

(c) particular attention should be given to judgments made by certain national courts (e.g. in the Federal Republic of Germany) which 'directly apply European competition law' (point 127).

2.1.5. The inadequacy of DG IV resources

2.1.5.1. The comments in 2.2. and 2.3. illustrate that insufficient manpower, equipment and legal resources frequently prevent the Directorate-General for Competition from fully exploiting its high-quality work on analysing the markets and implementing competition policy in the Community — a policy which has the hallmarks of common sense and realism.

2.1.5.2. The Committee therefore notes that:

(a) the Annual Report appears much too late;

(b) there is a significant delay in decision-making on issues subject to the decision procedure (see point 45).

2.1.5.3. In these circumstances, the question arises whether 'an instrument to monitor concentrations with a Community dimension' (Introduction to the Report, penultimate paragraph) will have the resources necessary for its operation.

2.1.5.4. This leads the Committee to recommend continuing 'public relations' measures in order to ensure that all economic operators in whatever sector, and all consumers, are always kept informed of their rights and duties with regard to competition policy. Along these lines, the Commission has announced the publication of an additional White Paper on the single market. This White Paper will give particular attention to setting out the economic and social significance of competition as a basis for a democratic society.

2.1.6. Coordination with anti-dumping policy

2.1.6.1. In consultation with the other Commission departments, the Directorate-General for Competition needs to take account of the safeguard measures in Community trade policy authorized by the Treaty of Rome. Moreover, consideration should be given to reopening the debate in the Community on the implementation of anti-dumping policy.

2.1.6.2. The Community, and especially Member States which joined recently, are sometimes threatened by uncontrolled competition from certain third countries — either from those at an advanced stage of technological development or from those with a large, low-paid workforce.

2.1.6.3. It is not unusual for some countries or their firms to engage in dumping in particular sectors, either to provide an outlet for their goods or to discourage incipient competitive initiatives in the Community.

2.1.6.4. While guarding against the risk of a market imbalance which would impair fair pricing, the Commission needs an effective bulwark against certain unfair trading practices employed by third countries— practices which are often forms of protectionism contradicting and indeed violating international agreements such as GATT. In this context, the state of the Community market must be assessed not only in relation to world trade but also by production sector.

2.2. Sectors of activity deserving special attention

2.2.1. Maritime traffic is the subject of a Committee Opinion on positive maritime measures. [1] This involves certain competition policy aspects. These are:

(i) maritime conferences and exemptions by category, already referred to in 1986 (in this connection the 17th Report mentioned the formal complaints about the Regulation which came into force on 1 July 1987; the 18th Report provides little information on the follow-up to these cases);

(ii) intra-European maritime traffic competing with land and air links, raising the problem of taxation planned in principle but whose application to Community flags should be extended to the flags of third countries to avoid distortions of competition (legal difficulties to be overcome);

(iii) in connection with maritime traffic, subsidies to European shipyards: investments have considerable effects on freight charges, and difficulties are exacerbated by the disparity between subsidies;

(iv) similarly, the taxes and social security contributions paid by ships' crews give rise to distortions which also have an effect on these disparities.

---

[1] CES 1257/89, 16.11.1989.

2.2.2. Competition rules and copyright

2.2.2.1. Throughout the twentieth century, the participation of 'authors' in economic activities has been increasing. Going beyond the traditional arts, the development of cinema and audio-visual productions calls for new talents. In addition, a new type of 'author' now exists, producing computer software.

2.2.2.2. Sometimes misguided protection of intellectual property rights, either by certain national provisions (e.g. a single price), or by exercising a dominant position with regard to software and refusing information, whether subject to copyright or not, prompts the statement that 'the exercise of exclusive copyrights will not prejudice the application of the competition rules and the imposition of effective remedies in appropriate cases...'.

2.2.2.3. Such unfair protection is incompatible with the abolition of internal frontiers. It is essential for Community law to develop in such a way as to prohibit certain 'perverse' forms of discrimination which hamper free competition and create new non-tariff barriers.

2.2.2.4. In this connection, the Committee has reservations about the *Tetra Pak* decision. In this case the Commission took the view that an enterprise may exploit its dominant position by acquiring another enterprise which holds exclusive licence rights. The Commission did not oppose this concentration, but in order to avoid competitive disadvantage for one of Tetra Pak's competitors, the Commission threatened to withdraw Tetra Pak's exemption from the patent licensing agreements. Tetra Pak had to relinquish its exclusive licence rights, whilst its competitor benefited from a non-exclusive licence. By doing this the Commission interfered with a contractual relationship which was in existence before the merger and had no connection with that merger. This case leads the Committee (a) to stress the sometimes arbitrary attitude adopted by the Commission for a particular purpose, and (b) to oppose its attitude strongly in order to stop this becoming a trend.

2.2.3. Competition policy and intervention by public authorities in favour of enterprises

2.2.3.1. In its first report on State aid in the European Community, published at the beginning of 1989, the Commission seeks to shed some light on the jungle of European subsidies, and ultimately to exercise tighter control on national aid granted by Member States.

2.2.3.2. The concept of aid distinct from capital input, on which this study is based, covers the widest possible field. Thus subsidies to public enterprises (particularly national concerns) are included. Taking its cue from Articles 92 and 93 of the EEC Treaty, the report regards measures to encourage certain enterprises or forms of production as subsidies which distort or threaten to distort competition and which affect trade among Member States.

2.2.3.3. An overall survey of all Member States shows that the bulk of the aid goes to railways, agriculture, coal and regional development. In France and Ireland, however, the emphasis is more on promoting trade and exports. In the Federal Republic of Germany regional aid frequently has a higher priority, arising partly from the federal structure. The importance of regional aid is further enhanced by the special situation of Berlin and the economic position of the regions bordering on the German Democratic Republic.

2.2.3.4. The first report on subsidies in the Community has some gaps, mainly due to the inadequacy of the data:

(a) important areas of the taxation and social security systems have not been taken into account;

(b) the survey does not include funds granted to public establishments' research projects, or the funding of university research and research assignments (including the military field), although these budget headings constitute subsidies under the very broad basic definition of aid;

(c) because so-called general measures are excluded, some subsidies whose importance has been proved by experience (e.g. the European Regional Development Fund or the EAGGF Guarantee Section) have not been taken into account;

(d) there is great uncertainty about subsidies granted in a wide variety of forms by local and regional authorities, especially in federal structures;

(e) some sectors are omitted, e.g. defence, energy (except coal), transport (except rail and inland waterway transport), press and media, banking, building and public utilities services;

(f) the data compiled in some Member States (Greece and Italy) are insufficient.

2.2.4. Other comments on the Eighteenth Report

2.2.4.1. The programme of studies

Studies commissioned from bodies independent of the Community enable it better to analyse the positive and negative impact of competition in the various sectors of activity.

These studies follow on from the proposal made in the Committee Opinion on the 12th Report, and their continuance is to be welcomed.

In connection with the Eighteenth Report, it is interesting to note that the border posts, whose abolition is envisaged by the 1984 White Paper, are not the only 'barrier to entry' and that advertising expenditure within or beyond an internal frontier can also be regarded as a brake on free competition.

It must also be noted that the idea of a merger analysis grid could be used in implementing the expected Directive.

Moreover, in the case of many enterprises, and particularly in countries which have recently joined the Community (as well as in developing countries), technology transfer contracts include leonine clauses preventing these enterprises from exporting or obtaining supplies where they wish and from having free access to the market. This delicate issue should be the subject of a research project, to be included in the study programme, to decide whether adequate competition-law procedures should be established.

The Committee hopes that the annual competition report will assess the results of the independently completed studies and the benefits reaped from them by the Commission.

2.2.4.2. Regional policies and the agricultural sector

In practice, these mean above all subsidies for regional purposes; the ESC Opinion on the Seventeenth Report mentioned these. Subsidies for agriculture are closely linked with CAP subsidies. Some general measures may lead to distortions of competition (EAGGF Guarantee Section). The result is that the level of agricultural subsidies is sometimes significantly underestimated. It was also asked whether instituting the incomes subsidy had had beneficial effects. The Eighteenth Report confines its treatment of these issues to analysing the subsidies granted by Member States, and refers to a publication in the 'Green Europe' series; it gives no answer to the question raised by the Committee.

The Committee feels it is very important for the Community and its trading partners to work in GATT for trade relations which lead to more balanced terms of competition in the agricultural sector.

2.2.4.3. Comparison of prices

For the consumer, whose freedom to choose his purchases is essential, 'domestic' competition policy holds out the possibility of comparing quality/price ratios. For the time being, prices, and especially large price disparities within the EC Member States, are important indicators for the consumer as to whether competition is working.

The ESC's Opinion on the Seventeenth Report sets great store by this and the segmentation of national markets, separated by the abovementioned non-tariff barriers. The Committee confirms its wish that this aspect be taken into consideration and that everything possible be done to ensure that the Community's competition policy accords with the above (see point 3 below).

3. Proposals for a necessary development of the Community's competition policy

3.1. In its successive Opinions, and latterly in examining the economic situation of the Community in mid-1989, the Committee mentioned certain conditions in the development of competition policy.

3.1.1. Genuine competition needs to be preserved in the Community in order to secure the advantages of the single market. All citizens will undoubtedly gain from its cost benefits. Thus the expected intensification of competition and improvement in firms' productivity and ability to innovate will come about naturally. On the other hand, the European Community must be given legal powers to vet concentrations of importance to the Community as a whole. The powers to vet these mergers and the powers provided by national legislation must be clearly demarcated under the Commission's authority. The Committee would refer to its 1988 Opinion on this matter. [1] Once barriers to trade have been abolished, market structures and the changes brought about by mergers will also have to be assessed in a Community-wide context. This would appear necessary when markets are open in principle to the rest of the world, if Community industry is to be capable of competing with the USA, Japan and some highly efficient, newly industrialized countries.

3.2. Community and national authorities must pay particular attention to small and medium-sized enterprises which are worse off than large firms with regard to information and planning. Public information and advisory services can help to offset these disadvantages. The Committee welcomes the steps taken by the Commission in helping to set up EC information and advisory services in all Member States. In addition, support for cooperation between firms is important for the reduction of small and medium-sized enterprises' competitive disadvantages.

3.3. In the introduction to its Eighteenth Report, the Commission states that 'Community competition policy has reached a crossroads'. This observation is of fundamental importance.

3.3.1. It should be noted at this point that neither the White Paper on the single market nor the Single Act involve Treaty amendments or decisive new prospects in the development of competition policy, which now appears to have lost its initial 'institutional lead' over the other Community policies.

3.3.2. It must now take account not only of commercial transactions between Member States but also of those within each of the Member States and of those with third countries.

3.3.3. DG IV must remain the driving force, and continue its work with the help of the relevant Government departments of Member States (including that of the customs services for commercial transactions with third countries).

3.3.4. The approach must be a global one since, in the overall Community context, competition policy acts as a jack of all trades and represents the highest common denominator of the various policies which help to create an EC economic policy.

3.3.5. But the essential monitoring of compliance with the rules of competition and harmonization of subsidies policy are not enough. Account must also be taken of:

(a) protection of the environment (constraints of an environmental policy and duties imposed on producers should be identical and have an equal effect on cost prices within the single market);

(b) equality of consumers, who must reap the benefits of healthy competition and obtain equal advantages for comparable services;

(c) the workers who help to keep the EC economy going are entitled to improved remuneration and social security at levels such that their impact on costs of production or services is likely to improve the terms of competition even further and encourage fair competition;

(d) this statement refocuses attention on the risks attached to work carried out and paid illegally, already mentioned in the Opinion on the Seventeenth Report: this is a special case, similar to the practice of non-invoiced sales in the commercial sector;

(e) the introduction to the Eighteenth Report states: 'It would seem that economic operators are making increasing provision in their forward planning for the need to adapt to the new market conditions of 1993; accordingly, it should be ascertained whether, in the present state of legislation (directives and regulations) there is sufficient response to the need for such adaptation:

   (i) in the various fields of application of Community instruments;

---

[1] OJ C 208/11, 8.8.1988.

(ii) in the internal legislation of Member States;

(f) in this connection it should also be stressed that 'The prohibition principle is translated, under Articles 85 and 86 of the EEC Treaty, into prohibition decisions which can comprise heavy fines' (Introduction to the Report, p. 15). This raises the issue of whether the fairness of contracts and markets could perhaps be facilitated by more positive measures.

4. Conclusions

4.1. In the Committee's view, the abolition of barriers within the Community should lead the Commission to consider an amendment — now essential — of the Treaty provisions covering the implementation of a healthy competition policy within the common market.

4.2. In this context, the Committee would ask the Commission to take up and implement the suggestions and practical proposals contained in this Opinion.

4.3. It is therefore important for the Commission to ask the Council to give it the resources needed to ensure that its departments are in a position — both in terms of manpower and work organization — to achieve this objective.

4.4. The Committee takes the view that the maximum effort must be made to strengthen competition policy within the EEC, so that a state of competition may be perpetuated both within the Community and in relation to third countries which will contribute to the prosperity of all. The future growth of the Community's prosperity and that of its citizens will depend to some extent on the success of Community competition policy.

Council Regulation (EEC) No 4064/89 of 21 December 1989 on the control of concentrations between undertakings

THE COUNCIL OF THE EUROPEAN COMMUNITIES,

Having regard to the Treaty establishing the European Economic Community, and in particular Articles 87 and 235 thereof,

Having regard to the proposal from the Commission, [1]

Having regard to the opinion of the European Parliament, [2]

Having regard to the opinion of the Economic and Social Committee, [3]

Whereas, for the achievement of the aims of the Treaty establishing the European Economic Community, Article 3 (f) gives the Community the objective of instituting 'a system ensuring that competition in the common market is not distorted';

Whereas this system is essential for the achievement of the internal market by 1992 and its further development;

Whereas the dismantling of internal frontiers is resulting and will continue to result in major corporate reorganizations in the Community, particularly in the form of concentrations;

Whereas such a development must be welcomed as being in line with the requirements of dynamic competition and capable of increasing the competitiveness of European industry, improving the conditions of growth and raising the standard of living in the Community;

Whereas. however, it must be ensured that the process of reorganization does not result in lasting damage to competition; whereas Community law must therefore include provisions governing those concentrations which may significantly impede effective competition in the common market or in a substantial part of it;

Whereas Articles 85 and 86, while applicable, according to the case-law of the Court of Justice, to certain concentrations, are not, however, sufficient to cover all operations which may prove to be incompatible with the system of undistorted competition envisaged in the Treaty;

Whereas a new legal instrument should be created in the form of a Regulation to permit effective monitoring of all concentrations from the point of view of their effect on the structure of competition in the Community and to be the only instrument applicable to such concentrations;

Whereas this Regulation should therefore be based not only on Article 87 but, principally, on Article 235 of the Treaty, under which the Community may give itself the additional powers of action necessary for the attainment of its objectives, and also with regard to concentrations on the markets for agricultural products listed in Annex II to the Treaty;

Whereas the provisions to be adopted in this Regulation should apply to significant structural changes the impact of which on the market goes beyond the national borders of any one Member State;

Whereas the scope of application of this Regulation should therefore be defined according to the geographical area of activity of the undertakings concerned and be limited by quantitative thresholds in order to cover

[1]   OJ C 130, 19.5.1988, p. 4.
[2]   OJ C 309, 5.12.1988, p. 55.
[3]   OJ C 208, 8.8.1988, p. 11.

those concentrations which have a Community dimension; whereas, at the end of an initial phase of the implementation of this Regulation, these thresholds should be reviewed in the light of the experience gained;

Whereas a concentration with a Community dimension exists where the aggregate turnover of the undertakings concerned exceeds given levels worldwide and throughout the Community and where at least two of the undertakings concerned have their sole or main fields of activities in different Member States or where, although the undertakings in question act mainly in one and the same Member State, at least one of them has substantial operations in at least one other Member State; whereas that is also the case where the concentrations are effected by undertakings which do not have their principal fields of activities in the Community but which have substantial operations there;

Whereas the arrangements to be introduced for the control of concentrations should, without prejudice to Article 90(2) of the Treaty, respect the principle of non-discrimination between the public and the private sectors; whereas, in the public sector, calculation of the turnover of an undertaking concerned in a concentration needs, therefore, to take account of undertakings making up an economic unit with an independent power of decision, irrespective of the way in which their capital is held or of the rules of administrative supervision applicable to them;

Whereas it is necessary to establish whether concentrations with a Community dimension are compatible or not with the common market from the point of view of the need to preserve and develop effective competition in the common market; whereas, in so doing, the Commission must place its appraisal within the general framework of the achievement of the fundamental objectives referred to in Article 2 of the Treaty, including that of strengthening the Community's economic and social cohesion, referred to in Article 130a;

Whereas this Regulation should establish the principal that a concentration with a Community dimension which creates or strengthens a position as result of which effective competition in the common market or in a substantial part of it is significantly impeded is to be declared incompatible with the common market;

Whereas concentrations which, by reason of the limited market share of the undertakings concerned, are not liable to impede effective competition may be presumed to be compatible with the common market; whereas, without prejudice to Articles 85 and 86 of the Treaty, an indication to this effect exists, in particular, where the market share of the undertakings concerned does not exceed 25% either in the common market or in a substantial part of it;

Whereas the Commission should have the task of taking all the decisions necessary to establish whether or not concentrations of a Community dimension are compatible with the common market, as well as decisions designed to restore effective competition;

Whereas to ensure effective control undertakings should be obliged to give prior notification of concentrations with a Community dimension and provision should be made for the suspension of concentrations for a limited period, and for the possibility of extending or waiving a suspension where necessary; whereas in the interests of legal certainty the validity of transactions must nevertheless be protected as much as necessary;

Whereas a period within which the Commission must initiate a proceeding in respect of a notified concentration and a period within which it must give a final decision on the compatibility with the common market of a notified concentration should be laid down;

Whereas the undertakings concerned must be accorded the right to be heard by the Commission as soon as a proceeding has been initiated; whereas the members of management and supervisory organs and recognized workers' representatives in the undertakings concerned, together with third parties showing a legitimate interest, must also be given the opportunity to be heard;

Whereas the Commission should act in close and constant liaison with the competent authorities of the Member States from which it obtains comments and information;

Whereas, for the purposes of this Regulation, and in accordance with the case-law of the Court of Justice, the Commission must be afforded the assistance of the Member States and must also be empowered to require information to be given and to carry out the necessary investigations in order to appraise concentrations;

Whereas compliance with this Regulation must be enforceable by means of fines and periodic penalty payments; whereas the Court of Justice should be given unlimited jurisdiction in that regard pursuant to Article 172 of the Treaty;

Whereas it is appropriate to define the concept of concentration in such a manner as to cover only operations bringing about a durable change in the structure of the undertakings concerned; whereas it is therefore necessary to exclude from the scope of this Regulation those operations which have as their object or effect the coordination of the competitive behaviour of independent undertakings, since such operations fall to be examined under the appropriate provisions of Regulations implementing Article 85 or Article 86 of the Treaty; whereas it is appropriate to make this distinction specifically in the case of the creation of joint ventures;

Whereas there is no coordination of competitive behaviour within the meaning of this Regulation where two or more undertakings agree to acquire jointly control of one or more other undertakings with the object and effect of sharing amongst themselves such undertakings or their assets;

Whereas the application of this Regulation is not excluded where undertakings concerned accept restrictions directly related and necessary to the implementation of the concentration;

Whereas the Commission should be given exclusive competence to apply this Regulation, subject to review by the Court of Justice;

Whereas the Member States may not apply their national legislation on competition to concentrations with a Community dimension, unless the Regulation makes provision therefor; whereas the relevant powers of national authorities should be limited to cases where, failing intervention by the Commission, effective competition is likely to be significantly impeded within the territory of a Member State and where the competition interests of that Member State cannot be sufficiently protected otherwise than by this Regulation; whereas the Member States concerned must act promptly in such cases; whereas this Regulation cannot, because of the diversity of national law, fix a single deadline for the adoption of remedies;

Whereas, furthermore, the exclusive application of this Regulation to concentrations with a Community dimension is without prejudice to Article 223 of the Treaty, and does not prevent the Member States' taking appropriate measures to protect legitimate interests other than those pursued by this Regulation, provided that such measures are compatible with the principles and other provisions of Community law;

Whereas concentrations not referred to in this Regulation come, in principle, within the jurisdiction of the Member States; whereas, however, the Commission should have the power to act, at the request of a Member State concerned, in cases where effective competition would be significantly impeded within that Member State's territory;

Whereas the conditions in which concentrations involving Community undertakings are carried out in non-member countries should be observed, and provision should be made for the possibility of the Council's giving the Commission an appropriate mandate for negotiation with a view to obtaining non-discriminatory treatment for Community undertakings;

Whereas this Regulation in no way detracts from the collective rights of workers as recognized in the undertakings concerned,

HAS ADOPTED THIS REGULATION:

Article 1

Scope

1. Without prejudice to Article 22 this Regulation shall apply to all concentrations with a Community dimension as defined in paragraph 2.

2. For the purpose of this Regulation, a concentration has a Community dimension where:

(a) the aggregate worldwide turnover of all the undertakings concerned is more than ECU 5 000 million, and

(b) the aggregate Community-wide turnover of each of at least two of the undertakings concerned is more than ECU 250 million, unless each of the undertakings concerned achieves more than two-thirds of its aggregate Community-wide turnover within one and the same Member State.

3. The thresholds laid down in paragraph 2 will be reviewed before the end of the fourth year following that of the adoption of this Regulation by the Council acting by a qualified majority on a proposal from the Commission.

Article 2

Appraisal of concentrations

1. Concentrations within the scope of this Regulation shall be appraised in accordance with the following provisions with a view to establishing whether or not they are compatible with the common market.

In making this appraisal, the Commission shall take into account:

(a) the need to preserve and develop effective competition within the common market in view of, among other things, the structure of all the markets concerned and the actual or potential competition from undertakings located either within or without the Community;

(b) the market position of the undertakings concerned and their economic and financial power, the opportunities available to suppliers and users, their access to supplies or markets, any legal or other barriers to entry, supply and demand trends for the relevant goods and services, the interests of the intermediate and ultimate consumers, and the development of technical and economic progress provided that it is to consumers' advantage and does not form an obstacle to competition.

2. A concentration which does not create or strengthen a dominant position as a result of which effective competition would be significantly impeded in the common market or in a substantial part of it shall be declared compatible with the common market.

3. A concentration which creates or strengthens a dominant position as a result of which effective competition would be significantly impeded in the common market or in a substantial part of it shall be declared incompatible with the common market.

Article 3

Definition of concentration

1. A concentration shall be deemed to arise where:

(a) two or more previously independent undertakings merge, or

(b) one or more persons already controlling at least one undertaking, or

— one or more undertakings

acquire, whether by purchase of securities or assets, by contract or by any other means, direct or indirect control of the whole or parts of one or more other undertakings.

2. An operation, including the creation of a joint venture, which has as its object or effect the coordination of the competitive behaviour of undertakings which remain independent shall not constitute a concentration within the meaning of paragraph 1 (b).

The creation of a joint venture performing on a lasting basis all the functions of an autonomous economic entity, which does not give rise to coordination of the competitive behaviour of the parties amongst themselves or between them and the joint venture, shall constitute a concentration within the meaning of paragraph 1 (b).

3. For the purpose of this Regulation, control shall be constituted by rights, contracts or any other means which, either separately or jointly and having regard to the considerations of fact or law involved, confer the possibility of exercising decisive influence on an undertaking, in particular by:

(a) ownership or the right to use all or part of the assets of an undertaking;

(b) rights or contracts which confer decisive influence on the composition, voting or decisions of the organs of an undertaking.

4. Control is acquired by persons or undertakings which:

(a) are holders of the rights or entitled to rights under the contracts concerned, or

(b) while not being holders of such rights or entitled to rights under such contracts, have the power to exercise the rights deriving therefrom.

5. A concentration shall not be deemed to arise where:

(a) credit institutions or other financial institutions or insurance companies, the normal activities of which include transactions and dealing in securities for their own account or for the account of others, hold on a temporary basis securities which they have acquired in an undertaking with a view to reselling them, provided that they do not exercise voting rights in respect of those securities with a view to determining the competitive behaviour of that undertaking or provided that they exercise such voting rights only with a view to preparing the sale of all or part of that undertaking or of its assets or the sale of those securities and that any such sale takes place within one year of the date of acquisition; that period may be extended by the Commission on request where such institutions or companies justify the fact that the sale was not reasonably possible within the period set;

(b) control is acquired by an office holder according to the law of a Member State relating to liquidation, winding up, insolvency, cessation of payments, compositions or analogous proceedings;

(c) the operations referred to in paragraph 1 (b) are carried out by the financial holding companies referred to in Article 5 (3) of the Fourth Council Directive 78/660/EEC of 25 July 1978 on the annual accounts of certain types of companies,[1] as last amended by Directive 84/569/EEC,[2] provided however that the voting rights in respect of the holding are exercised, in particular in relation to the appointment of members of the management and supervisory bodies of the undertakings in which they have holdings, only to maintain the full value of those investments and not to determine directly or indirectly the competitive conduct of those undertakings.

Article 4

Prior notification of concentrations

1. Concentrations with a Community dimension as referred to by this Regulation shall be notified to the Commission not more than one week after the conclusion of the agreement, or the announcement of the public bid, or the acquisition of a controlling interest. That week shall begin when the first of those events occurs.

2. A concentration which consists of a merger within the meaning of Article 3 (1) (a) or in the acquisition of joint control within the meaning of Article 3 (1) (b) shall be notified jointly by the parties to the merger or by those acquiring joint control as the case may be. In all other cases, the notification shall be effected by the person or undertaking acquiring control of the whole or parts of one or more undertakings.

3. Where the Commission finds that a notified concentration falls within the scope of this Regulation, it shall publish the fact of the notification, at the same time indicating the names of the parties, the nature of

---

[1]   OJ L 222, 14.8.1978, p. 11.
[2]   OJ L 314, 4.12.1984, p. 28.

the concentration and the economic sectors involved. The Commission shall take account of the legitimate interest of undertakings in the protection of their business secrets.

Article 5

Calculation of turnover

1. Aggregate turnover within the meaning of Article 1 (2) shall comprise the amounts derived by the undertakings concerned in the preceding financial year from the sale of products and the provision of services falling within the undertakings' ordinary activities after deduction of sales rebates and of value-added tax and other taxes directly related to turnover of an undertaking concerned shall not include the sale of products or the provision of services between any of the undertakings referred to in paragraph 4.

Turnover, in the Community or in a Member State, shall comprise products sold and services provided to undertakings or consumers, in the Community or in that Member State as the case may be.

2. By way of derogation from paragraph 1, where the concentration consists in the acquisition of parts, whether or not constituted as legal entities, of one or more undertakings, only the turnover relating to the parts which are the subject of the transaction shall be taken into account with regard to the seller or sellers.

However, two or more transactions within the meaning of the first subparagraph which take place within a two-year period between the same persons or undertakings shall be treated as one and the same concentration arising on the date of the last transaction.

3. In place of turnover the following shall be used:

(a) for credit institutions and other financial institutions, as regards Article 1 (2) (a), one-tenth of their total assets.

As regards Article 1 (2) (b) and the final part of Article 1 (2), total Community-wide turnover shall be replaced by one-tenth of total assets multiplied by the ratio between loans and advances to credit institutions and customers in transactions with Community residents and the total sum of those loans and advances.

As regards the final part of Article 1 (2), total turnover within one Member State shall be replaced by one-tenth of total assets multiplied by the ratio between loans and advances to credit institutions and customers in transactions with residents of that Member State and the total sum of those loans and advances;

(b) for insurance undertakings, the value of gross premiums written which shall comprise all amounts received and receivable in respect of insurance contracts issued by or on behalf of the insurance undertakings, including also outgoing reinsurance premiums, and after deduction of taxes and parafiscal contributions or levies charged by reference to the amounts of individual premiums or the total volume of premiums; as regards Article 1 (2) (b) and the final part of Article 1 (2), gross premiums received from Community residents and from residents of one Member State respectively shall be taken into account.

4. Without prejudice to paragraph 2, the turnover of an undertaking concerned within the meaning of Article 1 (2) shall be calculated by adding together the respective turnover of the following:

(a) the undertaking concerned;

(b) those undertakings in which the undertaking concerned, directly or indirectly:

— owns more than half the capital or business assets, or

— has the power to exercise more than half the voting rights, or

— has the power to appoint more than half the members of the supervisory board, the administrative board or bodies legally representing the undertakings, or

— has the right to manage the undertakings' affairs;

(c) those undertakings which have in an undertaking concerned the rights or powers listed in (b);

(d) those undertakings in which an undertaking as referred to in (c) has the rights or powers listed in (b);

(e) those undertakings in which two or more undertakings as referred to in (a) to (d) jointly have the rights or powers listed in (b).

5. Where undertakings concerned by the concentration jointly have the rights or powers listed in paragraph 4 (b), in calculating the turnover of the undertakings concerned for the purposes of Article 1 (2);

(a) no account shall be taken of the turnover resulting from the sale of products or the provision of services between the joint undertaking and each of the undertakings concerned with any one of them, as set out in paragraph 4 (b) to (e);

(b) account shall be taken of the turnover resulting from the sale of products and the provision of services between the joint undertaking and any third undertakings. This turnover shall be apportioned equally amongst the undertakings concerned.

Article 6

Examination of the notification and initiation of proceedings

1. The Commission shall examine the notification as soon as it is received.

(a) Where it concludes that the concentration notified does not fall within the scope of this Regulation, it shall record that finding by means of a decision.

(b) Where it finds that the concentration notified, although falling within the scope of this Regulation, does not raise serious doubts as to its compatibility with the common market, it shall decide not to oppose it and shall declare that it is compatible with the common market.

(c) If, on the other hand, it finds that the concentration notified falls within the scope of this Regulation and raises serious doubts as to its compatibility with the common market, it shall decide to initiate proceedings.

2. The Commission shall notify its decision to the undertakings concerned and the competent authorities of the Member States without delay.

Article 7

Suspension of concentrations

1. For the purposes of paragraph 2 a concentration as defined in Article 1 shall not be put into effect either before its notification or within the first three weeks following its notification.

2. Where the Commission, following a preliminary examination of the notification within the period provided for in paragraph 1, finds it necessary in order to ensure the full effectiveness of any decision taken later pursuant to Article 8 (3) and (4), it may decide on its own initiative to continue the suspension of a concentration in whole or in part until it takes a final decision, or to take other interim measures to that effect.

3. Paragraphs 1 and 2 shall not impede the implementation of a public bid which has been notified to the Commission in accordance with Article 4 (1) by the date of its announcement, provided that the acquirer does not exercise the voting rights attached to the securities in question or does so only to maintain the full value of those investments and on the basis of a derogation granted by the Commission pursuant to paragraph 4.

4. The Commission may, on request, grant a derogation from the obligations imposed in paragraphs 1, 2 or 3 in order to prevent serious damage to one or more undertakings concerned by a concentration or to a

third party. That derogation may be made subject to conditions and obligations in order to ensure conditions of effective competition. A derogation may be applied for and granted at any time, even before notification or after the transaction.

5. The validity of any transaction carried out in contravention of paragraph 1 or 2 shall be dependent on a decision pursuant to Article 6 (1) (b) or 8 (2) or (3) or by virtue of the presumption established by Article 10 (6).

This Article shall, however, have no effect on the validity of transactions in securities including those convertible into other securities admitted to trading on a market which is regulated and supervised by authorities recognized by public bodies, operates regularly and is accessible directly or indirectly to the public, unless the buyer and seller knew or ought to have known that the transaction was carried out in contravention of paragraph 1 or 2.

Article 8

Powers of decision of the Commission

1. Without prejudice to Article 9, each proceeding initiated pursuant to Article 6 (1) (c) shall be closed by means of a decision as provided for in paragraphs 2 to 5.

2. Where the Commission finds that, following modification by the undertakings concerned if necessary, a notified concentration fulfils the criterion laid down in Article 2 (2), it shall issue a decision declaring the concentration compatible with the common market.

It may attach to its decision conditions and obligations intended to ensure that the undertakings concerned comply with the commitments they have entered into *vis-à-vis* the Commission with a view to modifiyng the original concentration plan. The decision declaring the concentration compatible shall also cover restrictions directly related and necessary to the implementation of the concentration.

3. Where the Commission finds that a concentration fulfils the criterion laid down in Article 2 (3), it shall issue a decision declaring that the concentration is incompatible with the common market.

4. Where a concentration has already been implemented, the Commission may, in a decision pursuant to paragraph 3 or by a separate decision, require the undertakings or assets brought together to be separated or the cessation of joint central or any other action that may be appropriate in order to restore conditions of effective competition.

5. The Commission may revoke the decision it has taken pursuant to paragraph 2 where:

(a) the declaration of compatibility is based on incorrect information for which one of the undertakings concerned is responsible or where it has been obtained by deceit, or

(b) the undertakings concerned commit a breach of an obligation attached to the decision.

6. In the case referred to in paragraph 5, the Commission may take a decision pursuant to paragraph 3, without being bound by the deadline referred to in Article 10 (3).

Article 9

Referral to the competent authorities of the Member States

1. The Commission may, by means of a decision notified without delay to the undertakings concerned and the competent authorities of the other Member States, refer a notified concentration to the competent authorities of the Member States concerned in the following circumstances.

2. Within weeks of the date of receipt of the copy of the notification a Member State may inform the Commission which shall inform the undertakings concerned that a concentration threatens to create or to strengthen a dominant position as a result of which effective competition would be significantly impeded on a market, within that Member State, which presents all the characteristics of a distinct market, be it a substantial part of the common market or not.

3. If the Commission considers that, having regard to the market for the products or services in question and the geographical reference market within the meaning of paragraph 7, there is such a distinct market and that such a threat exists either:

(a) it shall itself deal with the case in order to maintain or restore effective competition on the market concerned, or

(b) it shall refer the case to the competent authorities of the Member State concerned with a view to the application of that State's national competition law.

If, however, the Commission considers that such a distinct market or threat does not exist it shall adopt a decision to that effect which it shall address to the Member State concerned.

4. A decision to refer or not to refer pursuant to paragraph 3 shall be taken where:

(a) as a general rule within the six-week period provided for in Article 10 (1), second subparagraph, where the Commission has not initiated proceedings pursuant to Article 6 (1) (b), or

(b) within three months at most of the notification of the concentration concerned where the Commission has initiated proceedings under Article 6 (1) (c), without taking the preparatory steps in order to adopt the necessary measures pursuant to Article 8 (2), second subparagraph, (3) or (4) to maintain or restore effective competition on the market concerned.

5. If within the three months referred to in paragraph 4 (b) the Commission, despite a reminder from the Member State concerned, has taken no decision on referral in accordance with paragraph 3 or taken the preparatory steps referred to in paragraph 4 (b), it shall be deemed to have taken a decision to refer the case to the Member State concerned in accordance with paragraph 3 (b).

6. The publication of any report or the announcement of the findings of the examination of the concentration by the competent authority of the Member State concerned shall be effected not more than four months after the Commission's referral.

7. The geographical reference market shall consist of the area in which the undertakings concerned are involved in the supply of products or services, in which the conditions of competition are sufficiently homogeneous and which can be distinguished from neighbouring areas because, in particular, conditions of competition are appreciably different in those areas. This assessment should take account in particular of the nature and characteristics of the products or services concerned, of the existence of entry barriers or of consumer preferences, of appreciable differences of the undertakings' market shares between neighbouring areas or of substantial price differences.

8. In applying the provisions of this Article, the Member State concerned may take only the measures strictly necessary to safeguard or restore effective competition on the market concerned.

9. In accordance with the relevant provisions of the Treaty, any Member State may appeal to the Court of Justice, and in particular request the application of Article 186, for the purpose of applying its national competition law.

10. This Article will be reviewed before the end of the fourth year following that of the adoption of this Regulation.

Article 10

Time-limits for initiating proceedings and for decisions

1. The decisions referred to in Article 6 (1) must be taken within one month at most. That period shall begin on the day following the receipt of a notification or, if the information to be supplied with the notification is incomplete, on the day following the receipt of the complete information.

That period shall be increased to six weeks if the Commission receives a request from a Member State in accordance with Article 9 (2).

2. Decisions taken pursuant to Article 8 (2) concerning notified concentrations must be taken as soon as it appears that the serious doubts referred to in Article 6 (1) (c) have been removed, particularly as a result of modifications made by the undertakings concerned, and at the latest by the deadline laid down in paragraph 3.

3. Without prejudice to Article 8 (6), decisions taken pursuant to Article 8 (3) concerning notified concentrations must be taken within not more than four months of the date on which the proceeding is initiated.

4. The period set by paragraph 3 shall exceptionally be suspended where, owing to circumstances for which one of the undertakings involved in the concentration is responsible, the Commission has had to request information by decision pursuant to Article 11 or to order an investigation by decision pursuant to Article 13.

5. Where the Court of Justice gives a judgment which annuls the whole or part of a Commission decision taken under this Regulation, periods laid down in this Regulation shall start again from the date of the judgment.

6. Where the Commission has not taken a decision in accordance with Article 6 (1) (b) or (c) or Article 8 (2) or (3) within the deadlines set in paragraphs 1 and 3 respectively, the concentration shall be deemed declared compatible with the common market, without prejudice to Article 9.

Article 11

Requests for information

1. In carrying out the duties assigned to it by this Regulation, the Commission may obtain all necessary information from the Governments and competent authorities of the Member States, from the persons referred to in Article 3 (1) (b), and from undertakings and associations of undertakings.

2. When sending a request for information to a person, an undertaking or an association of undertakings, the Commission shall at the same time send a copy of the request to the competent authority of the Member State within the territory of which the residence of the person or the seat of the undertaking or association of undertakings is situated.

3. In its request the Commission shall state the legal basis and the purpose of the request and also the penalties provided for in Article 14 (1) (b) for supplying incorrect information.

4. The information requested shall be provided, in the case of undertakings, by their owners or their representatives and, in the case of legal persons, companies or firms, or of associations having no legal personality, by the persons authorized to represent them by law or by their statutes.

5. Where a person, an undertaking or an association of undertakings does not provide the information requested within the period fixed by the Commission or provides incomplete information, the Commission shall by decision require the information to be provided. The decision shall specify what information is required, fix an appropriate period within which it is to be supplied and state the penalties provided for in Articles 14 (1) (b) and 15 (1) (a) and the right to have the decision reviewed by the Court of Justice.

6. The Commission shall at the same time send a copy of its decision to the competent authority of the Member State within the territory of which the residence of the person or the seat of the undertaking or association of undertakings is situated.

Article 12

Investigations by the authorities of the Member States

1. At the request of the Commission, the competent authorities of the Member States shall undertake the investigations which the Commission considers to be necessary pursuant to Article 13 (1), or which it has ordered by decision pursuant to Article 13 (3). The officials of the competent authorities of the Member States responsible for conducting those investigations shall exercise their powers upon production of an authorization in writing issued by the competent authority of the Member State within the territory of which the investigation is to be carried out. Such authorization shall specify the subject matter and purpose of the investigation.

2. If so requested by the Commission or by the competent authority of the Member State within the territory of which the investigation is to be carried out, officials of the Commission may assist the officials of that authority in carrying out their duties.

Article 13

Investigative powers of the Commission

1. In carrying out the duties assigned to it by this Regulation, the Commission may undertake all necessary investigations into undertakings and associations of undertakings.

To that end the officials authorized by the Commission shall be empowered:

(a) to examine the books and other business records;

(b) to take or demand copies of or extracts from the books and business records;

(c) to ask for oral explanations on the spot;

(d) to enter any premises, land and means of transport of undertakings.

2. The officials of the Commission authorized to carry out the investigations shall exercise their powers on production of an authorization in writing specifying the subject matter and purpose of the investigation and the penalties provided for in Article 14 (1) (c) in cases where production of the required books or other business records is incomplete. In good time before the investigation, the Commission shall inform, in writing, the competent authority of the Member State within the territory of which the investigation is to be carried out of the investigation and of the identities of the authorized officials.

3. Undertakings and associations of undertakings shall submit to investigations ordered by decision of the Commission. The decision shall specify the subject matter and purpose of the investigation, appoint the date on which it shall begin and state the penalties provided for in Articles 14 (1) (c) and 15 (1) (b) and the right to have the decision reviewed by the Court of Justice.

4. The Commission shall in good time and in writing inform the competent authority of the Member State within the territory of which the investigation is to be carried out of its intention of taking a decision pursuant to paragraph 3. It shall hear the competent authority before taking its decision.

5. Officials of the competent authority of the Member State within the territory of which the investigation is to be carried out may, at the request of that authority or of the Commission, assist the officials of the Commission in carrying out their duties.

6. Where an undertaking or association of undertakings opposes an investigation ordered pursuant to this Article, the Member State concerned shall afford the necessary assistance to the officials authorized by the Commission to enable them to carry out their investigation. To this end the Member States shall, after consulting the Commission, take the necessary measures within one year of the entry into force of this Regulation.

Article 14

Fines

1. The Commission may by decision impose on the persons referred to in Article 3 (1) (b), undertakings or associations of undertakings fines of from ECU 1 000 to 50 000 where intentionally or negligently:

(a) they omit to notify a concentration in accordance with Article 4;

(b) they supply incorrect or misleading information in a notification pursuant to Article 4;

(c) they supply incorrect information in response to a request made pursuant to Article 11 or fail to supply information within the period fixed by a decision taken pursuant to Article 11;

(d) they produce the required books or other business records in incomplete form during investigations pursuant to Articles 12 or 13, or refuse to submit to an investigation ordered by decision taken pursuant to Article 13.

2. The Commission may by decision impose fines not exceeding 10% of the aggregate turnover of the undertakings concerned within the meaning of Article 5 on the persons or undertakings concerned where, either intentionally or negligently, they:

(a) fail to comply with an obligation imposed by decision pursuant to Article 7 (4) or 8 (2), second subparagraph;

(b) put into effect a concentration in breach of Article 7 (1) or disregard a decision taken pursuant to Article 7 (2);

(c) put into effect a concentration declared incompatible with the common market by decision pursuant to Article 8 (3) or do not take the measures ordered by decision pursuant to Article 8 (4).

3. In setting the amount of a fine, regard shall be had to the nature and gravity of the infringement.

4. Decisions taken pursuant to paragraphs 1 and 2 shall not be of a criminal law nature.

Article 15

Periodic penalty payments

1. The Commission may by decision impose on the persons referred to in Article 3 (1) (b), undertakings or associations of undertakings concerned periodic penalty payments of up to ECU 25 000 for each day of the delay calculated from the date set in the decision, in order to compel them:

(a) to supply complete and correct information which it has requested by decision pursuant to Article 11;

(b) to submit to an investigation which it has ordered by decision pursuant to Article 13.

2. The Commission may by decision impose on the persons referred to in Article 3 (1) (b) or on undertakings periodic penalty payments of up to ECU 100 000 for each day of the delay calculated from the date set in the decision, in order to compel them:

(a) to comply with an obligation imposed by decision pursuant to Article 7 (4) or 8 (2), second subparagraph, or

(b) to apply the measures ordered by decision pursuant to Article 8 (4).

3. Where the persons referred to in Article 3 (1) (b), undertakings or association of undertakings have satisfied the obligation which it was the purpose of the periodic penalty payment to enforce, the Commission may set the total amount of the periodic penalty payments at a lower figure than that which would arise under the original decision.

Article 16

Review by the Court of Justice

The Court of Justice shall have unlimited jurisdiction within the meaning of Article 172 of the Treaty to review decisions whereby the Commission has fixed a fine or periodic penalty payment; it may cancel, reduce or increase the fine or periodic penalty payment imposed.

Article 17

Professional secrecy

1. Information acquired as a result of the application of Articles 11, 12, 13 and 18 shall be used only for the purposes of the relevant request, investigation or hearing.

2. Without prejudice to Articles 4 (3), 18 and 20, the Commission and the competent authorities of the Member States, their officials and other servants shall not disclose information they have acquired through the application of this Regulation of the kind covered by the obligation of professional secrecy.

3. Paragraphs 1 and 2 shall not prevent publication of general information or of surveys which do not contain information relating to particular undertakings or associations of undertakings.

Article 18

Hearing of the parties and of third person

1. Before taking any decision provided for in Article 7 (2) and (4), 8 (2), second subparagraph, and (3) to (5), 14 and 15, the Commission shall give the persons, undertakings and associations of undertakings concerned the opportunity, at every stage of the procedure up to the consultation of the Advisory Committee, of making known their views of the objections against them.

2. By way of derogation from paragraph 1, a decision to continue the suspension of a concentration or to grant a derogation from suspension as referred to in Article 7 (2) or (4) may be taken provisionally, without the persons, undertakings or associations of undertakings concerned being given the opportunity to make known their views beforehand, provided that the Commission gives them that opportunity as soon as possible after having taken its decision.

3. The Commission shall base its decision only on objections on which the parties have been able to submit their observations. The rights of the defence shall be fully respected in the proceedings. Access to the file shall be open at least to the parties directly involved, subject to the legitimate interest of undertakings in the protection of their business secrets.

4. Insofar as the Commission and the competent authorities of the Member States deem it necessary, they may also hear other natural or legal persons. Natural or legal persons showing a legitimate interest and especially members of the administrative or management organs of the undertakings concerned or recognized workers' representatives of those undertakings shall be entitled, upon application, to be heard.

Article 19

Liaison with the authorities of the Member States

1. The Commission shall transmit to the competent authorities of the Member States copies of notifications within three working days and, as soon as possible, copies of the most important documents lodged with or issued by the Commission pursuant to this Regulation.

2. The Commission shall carry out the procedures set out in this Regulation in close and constant liaison with the competent authorities of the Member States, which may express their views upon those procedures. For the purposes of Article 9 it shall obtain information from the competent authority of the Member State as referred to in paragraph 2 of that Article and given in the opportunity to make known its views at every stage of the procedure up to the adoption of a decision pursuant to paragraph 3 of that Article; to that end it shall give it access to the file.

3. An Advisory Committee on concentrations shall be consulted before any decision is taken pursuant to Articles 8 (2) or (5), 14 or 15, or any provisions are adopted pursuant to Article 23.

4. The Advisory Committee shall consist of representatives of the authorities of the Member States. Each Member State shall appoint one or two representatives; if unable to attend, they may be replaced by other representatives. At least one of the representatives of a Member State shall be competent in matters of restrictive practices and dominant positions.

5. Consultation shall take place at a joint meeting convened at the invitation of and chaired by the Commission. A summary of the facts, together with the most important documents and a preliminary draft of the decision to be taken for each case considered, shall be sent with the invitation. The meeting shall take place not less than 14 days after the invitation has been sent. The Commission may in exceptional cases shorten that period as appropriate in order to avoid serious harm to one or more of the undertakings concerned by a concentration.

6. The Advisory Committee shall deliver an opinion on the Commission's draft decision, if necessary by taking a vote. The Advisory Committee may deliver an opinion even if some members are absent and unrepresented. The opinion shall be delivered in writing and appended to the draft decision. The Commission shall take the utmost account of the opinion delivered by the Committee. It shall inform the Committee of the manner in which its opinion has been taken into account.

7. The Advisory Committee may recommend publication of the opinion. The Commission may carry out such publication. The decision to publish shall take due account of the legitimate interest of undertakings in the protection of their secrets and of the interest of the undertakings concerned in such publication taking place.

Article 20

Publication of decisions

1. The Commission shall publish the decisions which it takes pursuant to Article 8 (2), where conditions and obligations are attached to them, and to Article 8 (2) to (5) in the Official Journal of the European Communities.

2. The publication shall state the names of the parties and the main content of the decision; it shall have regard to the legitimate interest of undertakings in the protection of their business secrets.

Article 21

Jurisdiction

1. Subject to review by the Court of Justice, the Commission shall have sole competence to take the decisions provided for in this Regulation.

2. No Member State shall apply its national legislation on competition to any concentration that has a Community dimension.

The first subparagraph shall be without prejudice to any Member State's power to carry out any enquiries necessary for the application of Article 9 (2) or after referral, pursuant to Article 9 (3), first subparagraph, indent (b), or (5), to take the measures strictly necessary for the application of Article 9 (8).

3. Notwithstanding paragraphs 1 and 2, Member States may take appropriate measures to protect legitimate interests other than those taken into consideration by this Regulation and compatible with the general principles and other provisions of Community law.

Public security, plurality of the media and prudential rules shall be regarded as legitimate interests within the meaning of the first subparagraph.

Any other public interest must be communicated to the Commission by the Member State concerned and shall be recognized by the Commission after an assessment of its compatibility with the general principles and other provisions of Community law before the measures referred to above may be taken. The Commission shall inform the Member State concerned of its decision within one month of that communication.

Article 22

Application of the Regulation

1. This Regulation alone shall apply to concentrations as defined in Article 3.

2. Regulations No 17,[1] (EEC) No 1017/68,[2] (EEC) No 4056/86[3] and (EEC) No 3975/87[4] shall not apply to concentrations as defined in Article 3.

3. If the Commission finds, at the request of a Member State, that a concentration as defined in Article 3 that has no Community dimension within the meaning of Article 1 creates or strengthens a dominant position as a result of which effective competition would be significantly impeded within the territory of the Member State concerned it may, insofar as the concentration affects trade between Member States, adopt the decisions provided for in Article 8 (2), second subparagraph, (3) and (4).

4. Articles 2 (1) (a) and (b), 5, 6, 8 and 10 to 20 shall apply. The period within which the proceedings defined in Article 10 (1) may be initiated shall begin on the date of the receipt of the request from the Member State. The request must be made within one month at most of the date on which the concentration was made known to the Member State or effected. This period shall begin on the date of the first of those events.

5. Pursuant to paragraph 3 the Commission shall take only the measures strictly necessary to maintain or restore effective competition within the territory of the Member State at the request of which it intervenes.

6. Paragraphs 3 to 5 shall continue to apply until the thresholds referred to in Article 1 (2) have been reviewed.

Article 23

Implementing provisions

The Commission shall have the power to adopt implementing provisions concerning the form, content and other details of notifications pursuant to Article 4, time-limits pursuant to Article 10, and hearings pursuant to Article 18.

---

[1]   OJ 13, 21.2.1962, p. 204/62.
[2]   OJ L 175, 23.7.1968, p. 1.
[3]   OJ L 378, 31.12.1986, p. 4.
[4]   OJ L 374, 31.12.1987, p. 1.

Article 24

Relations with non-member countries

1. The Member States shall inform the Commission of any general difficulties encountered by their undertakings with concentrations as defined in Article 3 in a non-member country.

2. Initially not more than one year after the entry into force of this Regulation and thereafter periodically the Commission shall draw up a report examining the treatment accorded to Community undertakings, in the terms referred to in paragraphs 3 and 4, as regards concentrations in non-member countries. The Commission shall submit those reports to the Council, together with any recommendations.

3. Whenever it appears to the Commission, either on the basis of the reports referred to in paragraph 2 or on the basis of other information, that a non-member country does not grant Community undertakings treatment comparable to that granted by the Community to undertakings from that non-member country, the Commission may submit proposals to the Council for the appropriate mandate for negotiation which a view to obtaining comparable treatment for Community undertakings.

4. Measures taken pursuant to this Article shall comply with the obligations of the Community or of the Member States, without prejudice to Article 234 of the Treaty, under international agreements, whether bilateral or multilateral.

Article 25

Entry into force

1. This Regulation shall enter into force on 21 September 1990.

2. This Regulation shall not apply to any concentration which was the subject of an agreement or announcement of where control was acquired within the meaning of Article 4 (1) before the date of this Regulation's entry into force and it shall not in any circumstances apply to any concentration in respect of which proceedings were initiated before that date by a Member State's authority with responsibility for competition.

This Regulation shall be binding in its entirely and directly applicable in all Member States.

Done at Brussels, 21 December 1989.

Notes

For all appropriate purposes and, in particular, with a view to clarifying the scope of certain articles of the Regulation, the following texts are drawn to the notice of interested parties:

re Article 1

(a) The Commission considers that the threshold for world turnover as set in Article 1(2)(a) of this Regulation for the initial stage of implementation must be lowered to ECU 2 000 million at the end of that period. The *de minimis* threshold as set out in (b) should also be revised in the light of experience and the trend of the main threshold. It therefore undertakes to submit a proposal to that effect to the Council in due course.

(b) The Council and the Commission state their readiness to consider taking other factors into account in addition to turnover when the thresholds are revised.

(c) The Council and the Commission consider that the review of the thresholds provided for in Article 1(3) will have to be combined with a special re-examination of the method of calculation of the turnover of joint undertakings as referred to in Article 5(5).

re Article 2

(a) The Commission states that among the factors to be taken into consideration for the purpose of establishing the compatibility or incompatibility of a concentration — factors as referred to in Article 2(1) and explained in recital 13 — account should be taken in particular of the competitiveness of undertakings located in regions which are greatly in need of restructuring owing *intra alia* to slow development.

(b) Under the first subparagraph of Article 2(1), the Commission has to establish in respect of each concentration covered by the Regulation whether that concentration is compatible or incompatible with the common market.

The appraisal necessary for this purpose will have to be made on the basis of the same factors as defined in Article 2(1)(a) and (b) and within the context of a single appraisal procedure.

If, at the end of the first stage of appraisal (within one month of notification), the Commission reaches the conclusion that the concentration is not likely to create or reinforce a dominant position within the meaning of Article 2(3), it will decide against initiating proceedings. Such a decision will then establish the concentration's compatibily with the common market. It will be presented in the form of a letter and will be notified to the undertakings concerned and to the competent authorities of the Member States.

If the Commission has decided to initiate proceedings because it concludes that there is prima facie a real risk of creating or reinforcing a dominant position, and if further investigation (within a maximum period of four months of the initiation of proceedings) confirms this suspicion it will declare the concentration incompatible with the common market. If, on the contrary, the initial assumption is proved to be unfounded in the light of the further investigation, possibly in view of the changes made by the undertakings concerned to their initial project, the Commission will adopt a final decision noting that the operation is compatible with operation of the common market.

The decision on compatibility is therefore only the counterpart to a decision on incompatibility or prohibition.

(c) The Commission considers that the concept of 'the structure of all the markets concerned' refers both to markets within the Community and to those outside it.

(d) The Commission considers that the concept of technical and economic progress must be understood in the light of the principles enshrined in Article 85(3) of the Treaty, as interpreted by the case-law of the Court of Justice.

re Article 3(2), first indent

The Commission considers that this rule also applies to consortia in the liner trades sector.

re Article 5(3)(a)

The Council and the Commission consider that the criterion defined as a proportion of assets should be replaced by a concept of banking income as referred to in Directive 86/635 on the annual accounts and consolidated accounts of banks and other financial institutions, either at the actual time of entry into force of the relevant provisions of that Directive or at the time of the review of thresholds referred to in Article 1 of this Regulation and in the light of experience acquired.

re Article 9

(a) The Council and the Commission consider that, when a specific market represents a substantial part of the common market, the referral procedure provided for in Article 9 should only be applied in exceptional cases. There are indeed grounds for taking as a basis the principle that a concentration which creates or reinforces a dominant position in a substantial part of the common market must be declared incompatible with the common market. The Council and the Commission consider that such an application of Article 9 should be confined to cases in which the interests in respect of competition of the Member States concerned could not be adequately protected in any other way.

They consider that the review of Article 9 referred to in paragraph 10 thereof should be carried out in the light of the experience gained in its application (which it is envisaged will be exceptional), having regard to the importance of the principle of exclusivity and the need to provide clarity and certainty for firms, with a view to considering whether it remains appropriate to include it in the Regulation.

(b) The Commission states that the preparatory steps within the meaning of Article 9(4)(b) which must be taken during the period of three monts are preliminary measures which should lead to a final decision within the remaining period of two-and-a-half months and normally take the form of the notification of objections within the meaning of Article 18(1).

re Article 9(5) and 10(5)

The Commission states that it intends, in all cases of concentrations which are duly notified, to take the decisions provided for in Article 6(1), Article 8(2) and (3) and Article 9(3). Any Member State or undertaking concerned may ask the Commission to give written confirmation of its position with regard to the concentration.

re Articles 12 and 13

The Commission states that, pursuant to the principle of proportionality, it will carry out investigations within the meaning of Articles 12 and 13 only where particular circumstances so require.

re Article 19

The Council and the Commission agree that the arrangements for publication referred to in Article 19(7) will be reviewed after four years in the light of the experience acquired.

re Article 21(3)

1. Application of the general clause on 'legitimate interests' must be subject to the following principles:

   (i)   It shall create no new rights for Member States and shall be restricted to sanctioning the recognition in Community law of their present reserved powers to intervene in certain aspects of concentrations affecting the territory coming within their jurisdiction on grounds other than those covered by this Regulation. The application of this clause therefore reaffirms Member States' ability on those grounds either to prohibit a concentration or to make it subject to additional conditions and requirements. It does not imply the attribution to them of any power to authorize concentrations which the Commission may have prohibited under this Regulation.

   (ii) Nor, by invoking the protection of the legitimate interests referred to, may a Member State justify itself on the basis of considerations which the Commission must take into account in assessing concentrations on a European scale. While mindful of the need to conserve and develop effective competition in the common market as required by the Treaty, the Commission must — in line with consistent decisions of the Court of Justice concerning the application of the rules of competition contained in the Treaty — place its assessment of the compatibility of a concentration in the overall context of the achievement of the fundamental objectives of the Treaty mentioned in Article 2, as well as that of strengthening the Community's economic and social cohesion referred to in Article 130a.

   (iii) In order that the Commission may recognize the compatibility of the public interest claimed by a Member State with the general principles and other provisions of Community law, it is essential that prohibitions or restrictions placed on the forming of concentrations should constitute neither a form of arbitrary discrimination nor a disguised restriction in trade between Member States.

   (iv) In application of the principle of necessity or efficacity and of the rule of proportionality, measures which may be taken by Member States must satisfy the criterion of appropriateness for the objective and must be limited to the minimum of action necessary to ensure protection of the legitimate interest in question. The Member States must therefore choose, where alternatives exist, the measure which is objectively the least restrictive to achieve the end pursued.

2. The Commission considers that the three specific categories of legitimate interests which any Member State may freely cite under this provision are to be interpreted as follows:

   (i)   The reference to 'public security' is made without prejudice to the provisions of Article 223 on national defence, which allow a Member State to intervene in respect of a concentration which would be contrary to the essential interests of its security and is connected with the production of or trade in arms, munitions and war material. The restriction set by that Article concerning products not intended for specifically military purposes should be complied with.

   There may be wider considerations of public security, both in the sense of Article 224 and in that of Article 36, in addition to defence interests in the strict sense. Thus the requirement for public security, as interpreted by the Court of Justice, could cover security of supplies to the country in question of a product or service considered of vital or essential interest for the protection of the population's health.

   (ii) The Member States' right to plead the 'plurality of the media' recognizes the legitimate concern to maintain diversified sources of information for the sake of plurality of opinion and multiplicity of views.

   (iii) Legitimate invocation may also be made of the prudential rules in Member States, which relate in particular to financial services; the application of these rules is normally confined to national bodies for the surveillance of banks, stockbroking firms and insurance companies. They concern, for exemple, the good repute of individuals, the honesty of transactions and the rules of solvency. These specific prudential criteria are also the subject of efforts aimed at a minimum degree of harmonization being made in order to ensure uniform 'rules of play' in the Community as a whole.

re Article 22

(a) The Commission states that it does not normally intend to apply Articles 85 and 86 of the Treaty establishing the European Economic Community to concentrations as defined in Article 3 other than by means of this Regulation.

However, it reserves the right to take action in accordance with the procedures laid down in Article 89 of the Treaty, for concentrations as defined in Article 3, but which do not have a Community dimension within the meaning of Article 1, in cases not provided for by Article 22.

In any event, it does intend to take action in respect of concentrations with a worldwide turnover of less than ECU 2 000 million or below a minimum Community turnover level of ECU 100 million or which are not covered by the threshold of two-thirds provided for in the last part of the sentence in Article 1(2), on the grounds that below such levels a concentration would not normally significantly affect trade between Member States.

(b) The Council and the Commission note that the Treaty establishing the European Economic Community contains no provisions making specific reference to the prior control of concentrations.

Action on a proposal from the Commission, the Council has therefore decided, in accordance with Article 235 of the Treaty, to set up a new mechanism for the control of concentrations.

The Council and the Commission consider, for pressing reasons of legal security, that this new Regulation will apply solely and exclusively to concentrations as defined in Article 3.

(c) The Council and the Commission state that the provisions of Article 22(3) to (5) in no way prejudice the power of Member States other than that at whose request the Commission intervenes to apply their national laws within their respective territories.

I — Competition policy towards enterprises — List of Decisions and Rulings

1. Decisions pursuant to Articles 85 and 86 of the EEC Treaty

Decision of 9 June 1989 on a proceeding under Article 85 of the EEC Treaty 'National Sulphuric Acid Association'	OJ L 190, 5.7.1989
Decision of 12 July 1989 on a proceeding under Article 85 of the EEC Treaty 'UIP'	OJ L 226, 3.8.1989 Bull. EC 7/8-1989, point 2.1.69
Decision of 19 July 1989 on a proceeding under Article 85 of the EEC Treaty 'Dutch banks'	OJ L 253, 30.8.1989 Bull. EC 7/8-1989, point 2.1.65
Decision of 2 August 1989 on a proceeding under Article 85 of the EEC Treaty 'Welded steel mesh'	OJ L 260, 6.9.1989 Bull. EC 7/8-1989, point 2.1.64
Decision of 15 September 1989 on a proceeding under Article 85 of the EEC Treaty 'Film purchases by German television stations'	OJ L 284, 3.10.1989 Bull. EC 9-1989, point 2.1.46
Decision of 13 December 1989 on a proceeding under Article 85 of the EEC Treaty 'Bayer AG'	OJ L 21, 26.1.1990 Bull. EC 12-1989, point 2.1.85
Decision of 14 December 1989 on a proceeding under Article 85 of the EEC Treaty 'Association Pharmaceutique Belge'	OJ L 18, 23.1.1990 Bull. EC 12-1989, point 2.1.82
Decision of 19 December 1989 on a proceeding under Article 85 of the EEC Treaty 'Sugar beet'	OJ L 31, 2.2.1990 Bull. EC 12-1989, point 2.1.80
Decision of 20 December 1989 on a proceeding under Article 85 of the EEC Treaty 'TEKO'	OJ L 13, 17.1.1990 Bull. EC 12-1989, point 2.1.83
Decision of 20 December 1989 on a proceeding under Article 85 of the EEC Treaty 'Concordato incendio'	OJ L 15, 19.1.1990 Bull. EC 12-1989, point 2.1.84

2. Notices pursuant to Articles 85 and 86 of the EEC Treaty

(a) Pursuant to Article 19(3) of Council Regulation No 17

Finnpap	OJ C 45, 24.2.1989
Film purchases by German television stations	OJ C 54, 3.3.1989
Bloemenveilingen Aalsmeer II and Cultra	OJ C 83, 4.4.1989
Métaleurop SA	OJ C 100, 21.4.1989
D'Ieteren — motor oils	OJ C 119, 13.5.1989
Alcatel espace — ANT Nachrichtentechnik	OJ C 179, 15.7.1989
Moosehead/Whitbread	OJ C 179, 15.7.1989
Fluke-Philips	OJ C 118, 25.7.1989
TEKO	OJ C 203, 8.8.1989
APB	OJ C 210, 16.8.1989
Aachener und Münchener Beteiligungs-AG/La Fondiaria Assicurazioni/Volksfürsorge	OJ C 210, 16.8.1989
Concordato Italiano Incendio	OJ C 259, 12.10.1989
KSB/Goulds/Lowara/ITT	OJ C 259, 12.10.1989
Cekacan	OJ C 293, 21.11.1989
Konsortium ECR 900	OJ C 308, 7.12.1989

(b) Pursuant to Article 5(2) of Council Regulation (EEC) No 3975/87

Cross-chartered flights Air France-Air Inter	OJ C 190, 27.7.1989
Joint operation Air France/NFD Luftverkehrs AG on the Nuremberg-Paris, Munich-Lyon and Munich-Marseilles routes	OJ C 204, 9.8.1989
Joint operation by Air France/Iberia of the Paris-Bilbao-Santiago de Compostella routes	OJ C 204, 9.8.1989
Joint operation by Air France/Alitalia of the Paris-Milan and Paris-Turin routes	OJ C 204, 9.8.1989
Joint operation by Air France/Brymon of the Paris-London City Airport routes	OJ C 204, 9.8.1989
Joint operation by Air France/Sabena of the Paris-Brussels route	OJ C 204, 9.8.1989

Joint operation by Air France/Sabena of the Bordeaux/Brussels and Toulouse/Brussels routes	OJ C 204, 9.8.1989
Joint operation by Air France/Sabena of the Brussels-Lyon-Marseilles routes	OJ C 204, 9.8.1989
Joint operation by Aer Lingus/Sabena of the Brussels-Dublin route	OJ C 204, 9.8.1989
Joint operation by London City Airways/Sabena of the London City Airport-Brussels route	OJ C 204, 9.8.1989
Coordination of IATA freight rates	OJ C 228, 5.9.1989

(c) Pursuant to Article 12(2) of Council Regulation (EEC) No 4056/86

Sealink-SNCF	OJ C 17, 21.1.1989
Sealink-SMZ	OJ C 17, 21.1.1989

3. Decisions pursuant to Articles 65 and 66 of the ECSC Treaty

Decision of 20 January 1989 on a proceeding under Article 66 of the ECSC Treaty authorizing Raab Karcher Ltd (UK), a wholly-owned subsidiary of Raab Karcher AG, Essen to acquire the entire share capital of Cory Coal Trading Ltd, London

Bull. EC 1-1989, point 2.1.31

Decision of 30 March 1989 on a proceeding under Article 65 of the ECSC Treaty authorizing Ruhrkohle AG, Essen and six other German steel undertakings to implement from 1 January 1989 to 31 December 1997, a collective agreement (*Hüttenverträge*), under which most of their solid fuel requirements will be supplied by Ruhrkohle AG

Bull. EC 3-1989, point 2.1.60
OJ L 101, 13.4.1989

Decision of 3 April 1989 on a proceeding under Article 66 of the ECSC Treaty authorizing Usinor-Sacilor SA, Paris to acquire 24.5 % of the capital of Lutrix srl, Brescia

Bull. EC 4-1989, point 2.1.71

Decision of 24 April 1989 on a proceeding under Article 66 of the ECSC Treaty authorizing ASD plc of Leeds to acquire the entire share capital of Welbeck International Ltd, Barking

Bull. EC 5-1989, point 2.1.84

Decision of 6 June 1989 on a proceeding under Article 66 of the ECSC Treaty authorizing British Steel plc, London to acquire the entire share capital of Bore Steel Group Ltd, Walsall (UK)

Bull. EC 6-1989, point 2.1.75

Decision of 19 June 1989 on a proceeding under Article 66 of the ECSC Treaty authorizing United Engineering Steels Ltd, Rotherham and Bird Group of Companies Ltd, to create a new company 'Hyfrag Ltd'

Bull. EC 6-1989, point 2.1.72

Decision of 27 June 1989 on a proceeding under Article 66 of the ECSC Treaty authorizing Mannesmannröhrenwerke AG, Klocker Stahl GmbH, Krupp Stahl AG, Lech Stahlwerke GmbH, Thyssen AG, Thyssen Edelstahlwerke AG and the *Land* of Bavaria to create a new undertaking 'Neue Maxhütte Stahlwerke GmbH'

Bull. EC 6-1989, point 2.1.74

Decision of 27 June 1989 on a proceeding under Article 66 of the ECSC Treaty authorizing Mannesmannröhrenwerke AG and Krupp Stahl AG to create a joint venture 'Hüttenwerke Krupp-Mannesmann GmbH'

Bull. EC 6-1989, point 2.1.73

Decision of 24 July 1989 on a proceeding under Article 66 of the ECSC Treaty authorizing United Engineering Steels Ltd, Rotherham and Lemforder Metallwaren AG to create a new company 'Special Products Lemforder Ltd'

Bull. EC 7/8-1989, point 2.1.68

Decision of 24 July 1989 on a proceeding under Article 66 of the ECSC Treaty authorizing Anglo United plc to acquire the entire share capital of Coalite Group plc

Bull. EC 7/8-1989, point 2.1.70

Decision of 11 September 1989 on a proceeding under Article 66 of the ECSC Treaty authorizing Usinor-Sacilor SA to acquire a 70% majority interest in the capital of the new holding company Dillinger Hütte-Saarstahl AG which will control Saarstahl and Diilinger Hütte

Bull. EC 9-1989, point 2.1.48

4. Rulings of the Court of Justice

Ruling of 11 April 1989 in Case 66/86 *Ahmed Saeed Flugreisen and Silverline*
OJ C 122, 17.5.1989

Ruling of 12 May 1989 in Case 320/87 *Kai Otuing/Klee and Weilbach*
OJ C 141, 7.6.1989

Ruling of 11 July 1989 in Case 246/86 *Belasco SA* v *Commission*
OJ C 199, 4.8.1989

Ruling of 13 July 1989 in Case 395/87 *Ministère public* v *Tournier*
OJ C 207, 12.8.1989

Ruling of 13 July 1989 in Joined Cases 110/88, 241/88 and 242/88 *Lucazean* v *SACEM*
OJ C 210, 16.8.1989

Ruling of 21 September 1989 in Cases 46/87 and 227/88 *Hoechst AG* v *Commission*
OJ C 266, 18.10.1989

Ruling of 17 October 1989 in Joined Cases 97, 98, and 99/87 *Dow Chemical, J. Bericau Alcudia and EMP* v *Commission*
OJ C 285, 11.11.1989

Ruling of 17 October 1989 in Case 85/87 *Dow Benelux NV* v *Commission*
OJ C 288, 16.11.1989

Ruling of 18 October 1989 in Case 374/87 *Cdf Chimie* v *Commission*
OJ C 288, 16.11.1989

II — Competition policy and government assistance to enterprises

1. Final negative decisions adopted by the Commission following the Article 93(2) EEC procedure

Federal Republic of Germany

Decision 90/223/EEC of 20 April 1989 concerning an aid project planned by the German Government in favour of a shipbuilding contract for which there is competition between yards in different Member States

OJ L 118, 9.5.1990, p. 39
Bull. EC 4-1989, point 2.1.79

Decision of 17 December 1989 on the compatibility of the award of State aid having a regional purpose by the *Land* of North Rhine-Westphalia to the firm Strepp GmbH and Co. KG Papierfabrik for an investment project in the labour market region of Düren with the common market

Bull. EC 12-1989, point 2.1.101

Belgium

Decision of 20 December 1989 concerning aid granted by the Belgian Government to undertakings in the pharmaceutical industry in the form of programme contracts

Bull. EC 12-1989, point 2.1.99

Spain

Decision of 20 December 1989 concerning aids in Spain which the central and several autonomous governments have granted to Magefesa, producer of domestic articles of stainless steel and small electric appliances

Bull. EC 12-1989, point 2.1.98

France

Decision 89/456/EEC of 8 March 1989 on the French Government's aid proposal in favour of Caulliez Frères, cotton yarn producer located in Prouvy, France

OJ L 223, 2.8.1989
Bull. EC 3-1989, point 2.1.71

Decision 90/70/EEC of 28 June 1989 concerning aid provided by France to certain primary processing steel undertakings

OJ L 47, 23.2.1990. p. 28
Bull. EC 6-1989, point 2.1.91

Decision of 20 December 1989 concerning aids granted by the French Government for the disposal of the assets of MFL (Machines Françaises Lourdes), producer of heavy-duty machine tools

Bull. EC 12-1989, point 2.1.100

Greece

Decision 89/441/EEC of 21 December 1988 — Ratification on 21 March 1989 — on aid granted by the Greek Government to the film industry for the production of Greek films

OJ L 208, 20.7.1989, p. 38

Decision 89/659/EEC of 3 May 1989 relating to Ministerial Decision No E/3789/128 of the Greek Government establishing a special single tax on undertakings

OJ L 394, 30.12.1989, p. 1
Bull. EC 5-1989, point 2.1.85

Italy

Decision 90/215/EEC of 3 May 1989 on aid granted by the Italian Government to the newsprint industry

OJ L 114, 5.5.1990, p. 25
Bull. EC 5-1989, point 2.1.100

Decision 90/224/EEC of 24 May 1989 on aid granted by the Italian Government to Aluminia and Comsal, two State-owned undertakings in the aluminium industry

OJ L 118, 9.5.1990, p. 42
Bull. EC 5-1989, point 2.1.99

Decision 89/661/EEC of 31 May 1989 concerning aid provided by the Italian Government to Alfa-Romeo, an undertaking in the motor vehicle sector

OJ L 394, 30.12.1989, p. 9
Bull. EC 5-1989, point 2.1.97

Federal Republic of Germany/Netherlands

Decision of 21 June 1989 concerning respective aids planned by the Government of Germany and the Government of the Netherlands under the Sixth Council Directive of 26 January 1987 on aid to shipbuilding for the building of a fishing vessel for the Community fleet

Bull. EC 6-1989, point 2.1.88

2.A. Conditional Decision adopted by the Commission following the Article 93(2) EEC procedure

Spain

Decision 89/633/EEC of 3 May 1989 concerning aid provided by the Spanish Government to Enasa, an undertaking producing commercial vehicles under the brand name 'Pegaso'	OJ L 367, 16.12.1989, p. 62 Bull. EC 5-1989, point 2.1.96

2.B. Review of Conditional Decision adopted by the Commission following the Article 93(2) EEC procedure

France

Decision of 15 November 1989 verifying that the decision of 29 March 1988 concerning aid provided by the French Government to the Renault Group has not been correctly executed and that the authorization of the aids amounting to FF 20 billion is null and void	Bull. EC 11-1989, point 2.1.77

3. Decision relating to Article 95 of the ECSC Treaty

Italy

Decision 90/89/ECSC of 13 December 1989, amending Decision 89/218/ECSC concerning aid that the Italian Government proposes to grant to the public steel sector

OJ L 61, 10.3.1990, p. 19

4. Judgments delivered by the Court of Justice

Judgment (2.2.1989) in Case 94/87 *Commission* v *Federal Republic of Germany*   OJ C 66, 16.3.1989, p. 4

Judgment (17.3.1989) in Case 303/88R *Italian Republic* v *Commission*   OJ C 107, 27.4.1989, p. 6.

5. Aid cases in which the Commission raised no objection

Federal Republic of Germany

25.1.1989	Extension of aid programme to assist restructuring of shipbuilding in the coastal *Länder*
25.1.1989	Extension of aid programme to assist the diversification of shipyards at Hamburg
27.1.1989	Business start-up aid provided by the *Land* of Hesse
27.1.1989	Award of aid to Sandstedt GmbH & Co KG under the 'Special programme for Bremen' within the framework of the Joint Federal Government/*Länder* programme for improving regional economic structures
8.2.1989	Shipbuilding — aid to HDW-Nobiskrug
22.2.1989	Shipbuilding — aid to Howaldstwerke Deutsche Werft
22.2.1989	Aid for R&D by small and medium-sized enterprises in Rheinland-Pfalz
22.2.1989	Shipbuilding — aid to Oldenburg Brand Werft
2.3.1989	Amendment of law on the promotion of the Berlin economy
8.3.1989	Aid to promote investment in environmental protection in the *Land* of Hesse
8.3.1989	Aid for the restructuring of the civil aircraft and aviation sector
8.3.1989	Programme of aid by Hamburg for R&D on artificial intelligence
8.3.1989	Aid for R&D on digital radio telecommunications
13.3.1989	Aid provided by the *Land* of Hesse for environmental protection and treatment of waste
21.3.1989	Shipbuilding — aid to Howaldtswerke Deutsche-Werft
21.3.1989	R&D aid for Eureka project EU-95 'TVHD'
30.3.1989	Compensation mechanism for 1988 — 'Drittes Verstromungsgesetz'
13.4.1989	Three awards of aid to Daimler-Benz, Securitas and J. A. Krause under the 'Special programme for Bremen' within the framework of the Joint Federal Government/*Länder* programme for improving regional economic structures
20.4.1989	Second programme to assist energy research and technology
25.4.1989	Amendment of vocational training aid scheme in Saarland
26.4.1989	Prolongation of structural programme for agricultural regions in the *Land* of Baden-Württemberg
26.4.1989	Aid scheme to promote innovation and technology in small and medium-sized businesses in the *Land* of Hesse
3.5.1989	Shipbuilding — aid to Neue Jadewerft
12.5.1989	Grant awarded by the *Land* of Bremen for investment in undertakings under the 'Special programme for Bremen' within the framework of the Joint Federal Government/*Länder* programme for improving regional structures
31.5.1989	Aid to shipbuilding — development aid for Algeria
7.6.1989	Aid for R&D on traffic and transport (part)

14.6.1989	Shipbuilding — two awards of development aid for Mauritius and Thailand
20.6.1989	Aid for the reduction and recycling of waste — North Rhine-Westphalia
21.6.1989	Aid to small and medium-sized businesses for the transfer of know-how in the region of Hamburg
29.6.1989	Guidelines on the award of regional aid in Lower Saxony
10.7.1989	Aid for innovatory environmental technology projects in the *Land* of Hesse
12.7.1989	Shipbuilding — aid to Sürken Werft
12.7.1989	R&D aid for the Eureka project EU-03 'Phototronics'
26.7.1989	Guidance for SMEs on environmental technology in Berlin
26.7.1989	Financial assistance for guidance under the national programme in the Community interest in Lower Saxony
27.7.1989	Award of aid to ERNO-Raumfahrttechnik under the 'Special programme for Bremen' within the framework of the Joint Federal Government/*Länder* programme for improving regional economic structures
27.7.1989	R&D aid for chemical process technology
9.8.1989	Draft 3rd Effluent Discharges Act
10.8.1989	Acquisitions in or refinancing of existing acquisitions in the technology sector (BJTU)
11.8.1989	Aid to publishers in Hamburg
25.8.1989	Aid to the film industry
20.9.1989	Aid to small hydroelectric plants
20.9.1989	Aid to shipbuilding — development aid for Indonesia
2.10.1989	Village renovation programme in the *Land* of Schleswig-Holstein
3.10.1989	HLT regional programme — Hesse
4.10.1989	Village renovation programme in Lower Saxony
4.10.1989	Shipbuilding — aid to Kötterwerft
17.10.1989	Award of aid to Krause Maschinenfabrik under the 'Special programme for Bremen' within the framework of the Joint Federal Government/*Länder* programme for improving regional economic structures
18.10.1989	R&D aid for the 'Work and technology' programme
31.10.1989	Aid for SMEs — Saarland
31.10.1989	Shipbuilding — aid to Arminius Werft
10.11.1989	Programme for medium-sized firms in rural regions of Baden-Württemberg
13.11.1989	ERP 1990 (European Recovery Programme) and aid for SMEs for the rational use of energy and utilization of renewable energy sources under the programme
13.11.1989	18th General Plan under the Joint Federal Government/*Länder* programme for improving regional economic structures
15.11.1989	Prolongation and extension of the North Rhine-Westphalia R&D programme for raw materials for metals manufacture to a development programme for products and raw materials applicable to the iron and steel industry

29.11.1989	Extension of shipbuilding aid programme
8.12.1989	Interest subsidies on operating credits awarded to SMEs — Schleswig-Holstein
8.12.1989	Measures to facilitate the creation of new enterprises — Schleswig-Holstein
8.12.1989	Investment aid scheme for employment — Schleswig-Holstein
12.12.1989	Guidance for enterprises — Schleswig-Holstein
15.12.1989	Measures to promote market analysis and technical studies — Schleswig-Holstein
15.12.1989	Award of aid to Messerschmidt, Boelkow, Blohm GmbH under the 'Special programme for Bremen' within the framework of the Joint Federal Government/*Länder* programme for improving regional economic structures
17.12.1989	Shipbuilding — aid to Deutsche Industrie Werke
18.12.1989	Aid for advisory activities for SMEs — North Rhine-Westphalia
20.12.1989	Environmental protection programmes — Baden-Württemberg
20.12.1989	Aid for data-processing techniques 'Mikrosystemtechnik'
20.12.1989	Shipbuilding — aid to HDW — Flensburger Schiffbau Gesellschaft

Belgium

22.2.1989	Industrial Renewal Fund — fourth phase
19.7.1989	Extension of time-limit for approval of new businesses in employment areas
31.10.1989	Recuitment aid — Law of 30.12.1988
17.12.1989	1989 refinancing of programme 'Participation in European R&D technology programmes'

Denmark

2.2.1989	Aid for the promotion and development of small industries and craft businesses
21.3.1989	Two shipbuilding aid schemes

Spain

18.1.1989	Aid for youth employment in Aragon
18.1.1989	Aid for young people and the long-term unemployed in the Canary Islands
18.1.1989	Aid for undertakings in Castilla-La Mancha
1.2.1989	Financing of research and technological innovation and acquisition of scientific infrastructures in the Comunidad in Madrid
8.3.1989	Employment aid in the region of Valencia
8.3.1989	Aid for R&D to assist the Eureka EU-18 project (mobile robot)
21.3.1989	Aid for rational use of energy — IDAE
13.4.1989	Measures to assist employment in cooperatives in the Canary Islands

26.4.1989	Investment aid for small and medium-sized enteræprises in the Comunidad Antónoma de Galicia
26.4.1989	Aid to MTM and ATEINSA, Spanish manufacturers of railway equipment
26.5.1989	Plan to create alternative employment in the Bay of Cadiz
31.5.1989	Measures to repair damage caused by flooding in the regions of Comunidad Valenciana and Murcia
14.6.1989	Draft decree on the regulation of investment promotion measures in Castilla-León
14.6.1989	Subsidies awarded to undertakings for environmental measures in the Basque country
15.6.1989	Regional aid in the Vall d'Uxo region
23.6.1989	Investment aid scheme in the Basque country
6.7.1989	Aid for publications in the Valencian language
12.7.1989	Promotion of technological innovation in the industrial sector — Basque country
27.7.198	Five aid awards for investments in General Quimica, Explosivos Rio Tinto and Krafft in the chemicals sector, Helados y Congelados in the foods sector and Ibermatica in the data-processing sector
27.7.1989	Increase in regional aid cellings in the Basque country
28.7.1989	Programme of industrial promotion and reconversion (SPRI) in the Basque country
28.7.1989	Aid scheme for industrial restructuring in the Basque country
7.8.1989	Investment aid for Vidrala SA in the hollow glassware industry
18.10.1989	Aid to promote tourism in the Basque country
18.10.1989	Aid for a mining area of Huelva
25.10.1989	Aid to publishing in the Basque country
31.10.1989	Aid scheme for the film industry
23.11.1989	Measures to assist SMEs in the tourism sector — Castilla-La Mancha
29.11.1989	Aid scheme for water facilities under the operational (ERDF) programme for Almeria-Levante
14.12.1989	Investment aid for the tyre manufacturer Safe SA
20.10.1989	Aid for SMEs under an ERDF programme for the Basque country

France

8.2.1989	Award to Exxon of regional planning grant in exceptional PAT area
22.2.1989	Pulp, paper and paperboard industry levy scheme
17.4.1989	Regional planning grant for Plastic Omnium in exceptional PAT area
3.5.1989	Regional planning grant for Kimberley-Clark in exceptional PAT area
31.5.1989	Financing of reindustrialization in mining areas (Sofirem, Finorpa, Fonds d'industrialisation des bassins miniers)
31.5.1989	Regional guidance aid funds (FRAC)

31.5.1989	Regional centres for innovation and technology transfer (CRITT)
7.6.1989	Aid for engineering and metals processing industries financed by a parafiscal charge
14.6.1989	Creation of a conversion company in the CGM group
14.6.1989	Aid to shipbuilding
21.6.1989	Four awards of research and development aid to Eureka projects EU-102 (Eprom), EU-16 (ES 2), EU-5 (ultramicrofiltering membranes) and EU-3 (phototronics)
28.6.1989	Environmental aid — AQA programme for aid quality (part)
5.7.1989	National agency for the promotion of research (Anvar)
5.7.1989	Aids for industry and services under the IMP — Phase 2
10.7.1989	Award of regional planning grant to France CERAM in an exceptional PAT area
12.7.1989	Aid for the restructuring of the ship-repair sector in Marseilles and Lorient
19.7.1989	Plan to set up an industrial development fund
27.7.1989	Award of regional planning grant to Raflatac in exceptional PAT area
13.9.1989	Research and technology fund (FRT) — refinancing for 1989
19.9.1989	Aid to the Torsyl company
20.9.1989	Six awards of research and development aid to Eureka projects EU-95 HDTV (Thomson, RTIC, Oceanic, CCETT, Radiotechnique, Angénieux), EU-55 Carminat (Régienov Renault), EU-43 esf (Cap Sogeti Innovation, Sema Metra, Matra, Inria), EU-20 East (Société française de génie logiciel), EU-18 Advanced mobile robots (Matra Espace, Framatome, Technicatome), EU-13 Carmat 2000 (PSA Gie, Etudes et Projets).
4.10.1989	Research and development aid to the project Eureka EU-45 Prometheus (Matra, PSA, Renault-Régienov)
11.10.1989	Aid to Pechiney for the construction of an electrolysis plant at Dunkirk
18.10.1989	Research and development aid to Eureka project EU-19 Formentor (Cap Sesa innovation, Aérospatiale)
31.10.1989	Industrial innovation fund
15.11.1989	Social aid for the closure of certain steel plants at Usinor-Sacilor
15.11.1989	Aid to shipbuilding — development aid for Morocco and Bangladesh
29.11.1989	Equipment grant and employment grant in the French overseas departments
17.12.1989	Specific aids under the adapted special programme 'grand Sud-Ouest'
17.12.1989	Aid to the Festa company

Greece

8.2.1989	Aid grants for venture capital companies acquiring holdings in companies investing in high technology
14.2.1989	Extension of IMP investment programmes
18.4.1989	Classification of the region (nomos) of Ilia in zone D of Law 1262/82

18.4.1989	Classification of the province of Langadas (nomos of Thessalonique) in zone C of law 1262/82
19.9.1989	Investment aids to Athens Paper Mills and Thessaly Paper Mills

Ireland

19.4.1989	Alteration of corporation tax to cover service industry companies at Shannon Airport

Italy

31.1.1989	Measures to assist the commercial sector in Molise
1.2.1989	Refinancing of special fund for applied research
1.2.1989	Proposed amendment of Law 46/1982 — Fund for applied scientific and technological research
22.2.1989	Aid to promote tourism under Law No 29 — Region of Piedmont
8.3.1989	Aid to promote tourism — ski-runs in Trento
5.4.1989	Budget estimate for 1989 and 1989-91 — Sicily — DDL 582A
5.4.1989	Three awards of research and development aid for Eureka projects EU-45 Prometheus (Centro Ricerche Fiat, Telettra, Vegila Borietti), EU-87 Eurofor (Massarenti SpA) and EU-102 Eprom (SGS-Thomson, Microelectronics SpA)
26.4.1989	Law No 22/87 — Applied Research Fund — participation in Eureka projects
24.5.1989	Two awards of research and development aid for Eureka projects EU-29 new ceramic and metallic materials for automobiles (Centro ricerche Fiat, Teksid SpA), and EU-104 mass production from animal cell cultures (Sorin Biomedica SpA)
14.6.1989	Aid to mining areas (part)
27.7.1989	Research and development aid to Eureka project EU-84 (Industrie Zanussi SpA)
27.7.1989	Measures to assist cooperation, commerce, small firms and fisheries (part)
13.9.1989	Three awards of research and development aid to Eureka projects EU-212 Famos Aria (Mesarteam SpA), EU-160 Membranes and product separation by fermentation (Farmitalia Carlo Erba SrC), EU-85 Flabex (Datamat — Ingeneria dei Sistemi SpA)
13.9.1989	Aid to Ferrari SpA for its research and development plan
4.10.1989	Research and development aid for the Eureka EU-203 project — Famos CIM, Pilot assembly plants (Bassani Ticino SpA)
11.10.1989	Research and development aid for the Eureka EU-137 project — Eurofar (Agusta SpA)
31.10.1989	Measures to assist tourism (Emilia-Romagna)
29.11.1989	Refinancing of research contracts for projects finalized by the National Research Council
1.12.1989	Regional laws extending the integrated Mediterranean programme — Emilia-Romagna
18.12.1989	Amendment to the regional laws concerning small businesses — Emilia-Romagna
20.12.1989	Research and development aid for the Eureka EU-255 project — serological determination of syphilis (Diesse Srl)

Luxembourg

27.7.1989	Aid for research and development programmes implemented by steel undertakings

Netherlands

1.2.1989	Promotion of technology in undertakings — modification and refinancing of PBTS programme for 1988
8.3.1989	Two aid awards for manure processing
4.4.1989	Susidy for the retail trade in small centres
5.4.1989	Regulation on credit guarantees for SMEs in 1988
25.4.1989	Amendment of energy-saving aid schemes and the development of altenative energy sources
3.5.1989	Shipbuilding — amendment of regulation on promotion of 1988 exports and withdrawal of 1987 rules on interest relief
16.5.1989	Aid to trade associations to cover the cost of advice on data-processing
21.6.1989	Promotion of business-related research by associations (1988)
12.7.1989	Aid for the processing of manure
27.7.1989	Research and development aid — refinancing of BTIP 1989 programme
27.7.1989	Aid for the long-term unemployed — amendment of the Vermeend/Moor Law
4.10.1989	Promotion of technology in undertakings (1989)
6.10.1989	Measures for the technological stimulation of international projects
18.10.1989	'Contractors' programme
6.11.1989	'Quality and logistics' programme
15.11.1989	Draft law on the reduction of wage costs relating to the minimum wage
15.11.1989	Measures to promote innovation
15.11.1989	Aid for the purchase of quieter lorries

Portugal

10.1.1989	Award of aid under Law 283-A/86 to the following companies: Macroluz (electrical equipment), Artur Ralmundo Brito & Couto (paper), Forjarte (tools)
1.2.1989	Pedip — programme No 2 — vocational training
22.2.1989	Pedip — programme Nos 5 and 6 — productivity, quality and industrial design
21.3.1989	Investment aid for Ford Lusitana SA

21.3.1989	Pedip — programme No 1 — basic and technological infrastructures
26.4.1989	Aid to shipbuilding
24.5.1989	Creation of duty-free zone in the island of Santa Maria (Azores)
31.5.1989	Scheme to promote the rational use of energy (Setúbal)
21.6.1989	Aid awarded to Portuguese shipowners under Order 7/89 of 28.2.1989
23.6.1989	Amendment of aid project for youth employment and the long-term unemployed
28.7.1989	Assistance under Law 283-A/86 for FACEAL (ceramics)
19.9.1990	Assistance under Law 283-A/86 for Techimede (pharmaceuticals)
20.9.1989	Aid for Ford Motor Co. (car radio equipment)
26.9.1989	Five awards of assistance under Law 283-A/86 to the following companies: Flavitur (paper), João de Barros Rodrigues & Filhos (tyres), Cires SA (synthetic resins), Novopan SA (wood processing), Sofarimex Lda (pharmaceuticals)
18.10.1989	Aid scheme for shipbuilding
18.10.1989	Shipbuilding — aid for Lisenave and Ain
31.10.1989	Pedip — revised programme No 2 — vocational training
31.10.1989	Extension of aid scheme for tin and wolfram mines
6.11.1989	Pedip — aid to specific sectors
15.11.1989	Amendment of programme of aid for job creation

United Kingdom

1.2.1989	Eureka project
6.3.1989	Establishing of new enterprise zone in Sunderland
21.3.1989	Aid to Short Brothers plc — Northern Ireland
21.3.1989	Research and development aid for the Eureka project EU-95 TVHD. (Rank Cintel, BBC, IBA, Quantel, Philips UK)
5.4.1989	Aid for the privatization of British Rail Engineering Ltd (BREL)
20.4.1989	Aid to Crossbows Optical Ltd, Northern Ireland
3.5.1989	Assistance for exceptional projects of research and development
8.5.1989	Expansion and modification of the Smart programme
8.5.1989	Programme of research and development on energy
21.6.1989	Research and development aid for Eureka project EU-191 — Advanced underwater robots (Ferranti, Ukala, Harwell, British Maritime Institute, Marconi Underwater, Transfert Technology, Lambridge Consultant)
18.7.1989	Cornwall enterprise fund

19.7.1989	Proposal to grant aid to Short Brothers plc (Northern Ireland)
26.7.1989	Scheme to assist industry — Cannock Chase District Council
26.7.1989	Two schemes to assist small firms — South Staffordshire
26.7.1989	Scheme to assist small firms — Middlesbrough Borough Council
27.7.1989	Aid to shipbuilding — sale of Harland & Wolff Shipyard
8.8.1989	Loans to small businesses in Cornwall
13.9.1989	Measures to assist Cabot-Carbon and Dow Corning in the chemicals sector
6.10.1989	Aid scheme 'Business growth training scheme'
18.10.1989	Shipbuilding aid — regional aid plan and research and development aid
14.12.1989	Refinancing of aid for R&D

6. Aid cases in which the Commission decided to open the Article 93(2) EEC procedure

Federal Republic of Germany

8.2.1989	Investment grant awarded by the *Land* of North Rhine-Westphalia to Strepp Papierfabrik
8.3.1989	Shipbuilding aid — development aid for Israel
26.4.1989	Award of aid by the city of Hamburg for manufacturing industries
7.6.1989	Aid for research and development in the traffic and transport sector (part)
14.6.1989	Shipbuilding aid — Bremer Werftverbund
14.6.1989	Two awards of aid to technological research and development programmes
19.7.1989	Shipbuilding aid — development aid for Chili
27.7.1989	Community framework for aids to the motor vehicle industry
2.8.1989	Nine regions under the Joint Federal Government/*Länder* programme for improving regional economic structures
17.12.1989	Aid to shipbuilding in the form of loans and guarantees awarded to Schiffswerft Germershelm

Belgium

18.10.1989	Aid to SA Smith Kline Biological — pharmaceuticals sector
25.10.1989	Shipbuilding — aid to Boelwerf for the construction of an LPG vessel

Spain

5.7.1989	Aid scheme for shipbuilding
27.7.1989	Community framework for aids to the motor vehicle industry

France

28.6.1989	Environmental aid — AQA programme on air quality (part)

Greece

8.3.1989	Assistance to Fimisco by the business restructuring body
21.3.1989	Aid to the film industry — decision to pursue the Article 93(2) EEC procedure — second phase

5.4.1989	Aid to a cement manufacturing firm (Halkis)
13.4.1989	Application of regional aid Law 1262/82 and its amendments to shipbuilding

Italy

3.5.1989	Shipbuilding aid scheme
14.6.1989	Aid for the mining sector (part)
5.7.1989	Regional Law 2/88 of the Fruili-Venezia-Giulla region and national Law 26/86
7.8.1989	Fiscal measures to assist industrial restructuring — Decree Law No 174 of 15.5.1989
4.10.1989	Aid for the installation of a forging press in Foggia
18.10.1989	Measures under Law 120/87 to assist certain areas affected by natural catastrophes in 1980
15.11.1989	Refinancing of research contracts of the National R&D Council concerning alternative energy sources (ENEA)
15.11.1989	Extension of procedure opened on 7.8.1989 to new draft Law No 4230
29.11.1989	Assistance for industrial development — Law of the region of Sicily

Netherlands

30.1.1989	Tax incentives for the purchase of 'clean' cars
28.6.1989	Aid for regional programmes
27.7.1989	Revision of agreements on aid for Volvo Car BV

Portugal

12.7.1989	Aid for the chemicals firm Quimigal

7. Aid cases in which the Commission decided to close the Article 93(2) EEC procedure

Federal Republic of Germany

8.2.1989	Shipbuilding aid for construction of a cargo ship for a German shipowner
27.7.1989	Shipbuilding aid — development aid for Israel
29.11.1989	Shipbuilding aid — withdrawal of notification of proposed aid
29.11.1989	Nine regions under the Joint Federal Government/*Länder* programme for improving regional economic structures

Belgium

8.2.1989	Shipbuilding aid schemes

Denmark

24.5.1989	Aid to the film industry

Spain

21.3.1989	Aid to the steel undertaking Patricio Echeverria SA
3.5.1989	Aid project for 1987-91 for the manufacturer of lorries and buses Enasa through the intermediary of the public holding company INI (part)

France

24.5.1989	Aid to the film industry
28.6.1989	Seven aid awards to the following enterprises: Velexy and GTS Industries in the metallurgy sector; Trefilunion in the wire sector; CFEM in the metal construction and offshore petroleum sectors; C3F and Chavanne-Ketin in the foundry sector and Metalinor in the scrap-iron sector (part)
5.7.1989	Aid to the foundry products — special levy
15.11.1989	Aid awards to Usines et Fonderies Arthur Martin (electrical appliances)
17.12.1989	Regional development premiums (PAT) awarded to 24 firms outside assisted areas
20.12.1989	Aid award to CDF-Chimie (Orkem) (two procedures)

Greece

20.12.1989   Aid to Elbaumin under Law No 1386/83 (non-ferrous metals)

Italy

1.2.1989   Refinancing of Law 111/85 on aid to shipbuilding in the period 1984-85

13.4.1989   Laws No 1213 of 4.11.1965 and No 163 of 30.4.1985 on aid to the film industry

Netherlands

8.3.1989   Tax incentives for purchases of 'clean' cars

United Kingdom

18.10.1989   Aid to shipbuilding — regional aid plan and aid for R&D (part)

8. Aid case in which the procedure provided for in Article 93(1) of the EEC Treaty was initiated to examine existing aid schemes

France

29.11.1989   Tax benefits of employment areas

III — Competition policy and government assistance in the agricultural sector

1. Aid cases in which the Commission raised no objection

Federal Republic of Germany

11.1.1989	Aid for the cessation of agricultural activities
28.9.1989	Aid for extensification of production in the form of aid for conversion to 'biological' products
24.11.1989	Existing measures concerning the regulation of the market structure (aid for the creation and operation of producer organizations)
24.11.1989	Modification of existing aid to investments in agricultural holdings for the protection of the environment
11.12.1989	Improvement of agricultural structures and coastal protection (measures in addition to the Joint Federal Government/*Länder* programme)
11.12.1989	Renewal of measures to improve agricultural structures and coastal protection for 1989-92 (measures forming part of the Joint Federal Government/*Länder* programme)

Schleswig-Holstein

11.1.1989	Measures for the conversion of arable land into pastureland to prevent the pollution of underground water
4.7.1989	Aid to promote ecological farm products
24.7.1989	Aid to promote the distribution and marketing of agricultural products and foodstuffs
1.8.1989	Aid to machinery syndicates to encourage the shared use of agricultural machinery
24.11.1989	Aid for forestry development
18.12.1989	Aid for extensification of production to protect the environment — programme to protect areas close to water

Rhineland Palatinate

11.1.1989	Improvement of meadowland to protect the environment and use of wet valley-bottom grassland in the southern Palatinate
20.1.1989	Programme to encourage environmentally friendly farming
2.8.1989	Measures to encourage farmers to invest in pollution reduction
11.12.1989	Aid for the rental of additional warehouses for wine and aid for the distillation of wine (because the Council approved this aid, the Commission did not adopt a position)

Bavaria

20.1.1989	Measures in favour of pulse producer organizations (start-up aid)
16.2.1989	Aid for the expansion of a dairy at Fischach-Aretsried
5.6.1989	Aid to purchase refrigeration plant for dairy farms

Hesse

14.2.1989	Measures to preserve the countryside between rivers (conservation of wetlands)
14.2.1989	Conversion of fields into meadowland
7.3.1989	Advertising aid to promote the marketing of agricultural products
11.4.1989	Structural policy measures not covered by the Joint Federal Government/*Länder* programme applied in 1989 by the *Länder*

Baden-Württemberg

30.1.1989	Aid for agricultural training
28.2.1989	Construction of housing for farmers
1.11.1989	Aids to advertising and quality control to develop the sale of quality-label products

North Rhine-Westphalia

19.1.1989	Measures to restructure the 'Niederhein EG' dairy
17.4.1989	Investment premium for foodstuffs for a manufacturer of meat products located at Kempen-Tönisberg
27.7.1989	Nature conservancy measures under the programme for highland areas

Lower Saxony

24.7.1989	Aid to combat atrophic rhinitis, Aujeszky's disease and paratuberculosis

Belgium

3.2.1989	Individual award under the Economic Expansion Law of 17.7.1959 to SA Van den Broecke, an undertaking in the potato-treatment sector
27.6.1989	Wallonia: Award of premiums for registering colts and fillies in the Stud Book
20.11.1989	Aid for the promotion of potatoes, hops, seeds and plants, financed in particular through compulsory levies on field-scale crops

Denmark

11.1.1989	Draft Law on improvement of agricultural structures (aid for afforestation)
11.1.1989	Amendment to existing scheme for the promotion of ecological agricultural products
17.3.1989	Training aid for farmers
20.3.1989	Aid for the improvement of forests
5.4.1989	Aid for the development of new agricultural products
6.4.1989	1989 budget for the 'pro mille' fund (financed by parafiscal charges levied per unit of area for certain activities (advertising, research training, etc.) in various agricultural sectors)
24.5.1989	Aid for veterinary fees (DK/183)
29.6.1989	Statement of expenditure in 1987 on the following 10 farming funds: 'pro mille', sheep, horses, rabbits, poultry, potatoes, beef/veal, seeds, milk, plant improvement
25.7.1989	1989 budget for the following nine farming funds: milk, sheep, horses, rabbits, poultry, potatoes, beef/veal, seeds, plant improvement

Spain

2.2.1989	Anti-acridian measures
13.3.1989	Royal Decree No 808/1987 'Aid for young farmers'
13.3.1989	Rules implementing the Decree and specifying the conditions for the award of aid to young farmers
21.11.1989	Royal Decree No 1030/87 of 31 July 1987 on the compensatory allowance in hill-farming regions
21.11.1989	Royal Decree No 995/87 of 24 July 1987 on joint farm-improvement investments in less-favoured regions
11.12.1989	Measures to promote the restructuring of wine-growing areas pursuant to Regulation (EEC) No 2741/89 (OJ L 264, 12.9.1989)

Aragon

2.5.1989	Draft Regional Decree on measures to improve the processing, marketing and promotion of agricultural products

Galicia

9.6.1989	Draft Decree No 100/1988 of 5.5.1988 and Draft Decree of 13.5.1988 of the 'Junta de Galicia' on financial aid for agricultural products (investment aid for processing and marketing, aid to make good the damage caused by natural disasters)
19.6.1989	Draft Ministerial Decree of 13.3.1989 on aid to improve the marketing and processing of agricultural products

Basque country

16.8.1989	Measures to assist producers' groups
1.9.1989	Investment aid for the primary sector and its downstream industries

Asturias

27.9.1989	Measures to assist afforestation

Rioja

7.12.1989	Draft Regional Decree on measures to improve the efficiency of agricultural structures, family holdings, young farmers and small agrifoodstuffs industries

France

11.1.1989	Measures to assist agriculture proposed by the Special Agricultural Conference on 25.2.1988 — Aid to improve the quality of pigs in upland areas (quality control, advisory services, investments)
17.3.1989	Measures to assist agriculture proposed at the Special Agricultural Conference on 25.2.1988:

    (i) creation of an agricultural debt-reduction fund;

    (ii) interest relief in the wine-growing sector;

    (iii) interest relief in the milk sector;

    (iv) aid for pigmeat producers in difficulty.

22.5.1989	Aid for farmers in difficulty; the aid is to finance farm analysis and to monitor the execution of a recovery plan for the farms concerned
23.5.1989	Measures to help agriculture proposed at the Special Agricultural Conference on 25.2.1988: (i) reduction of social security contributions in the dairy sector; (ii) reduction of social security contributions in the beef/veal sector. Both measures must be considered in the light of Regulation (EEC) No 768/89 establishing a transitional aid scheme for farm incomes.
30.6.1989	Proposed amendments to the existing scheme of the Fats Institute (ITERG)
11.10.1989	Measures to help agriculture proposed at the Congress of the National Federation of Farmers' Unions (FNSEA)
26.10.1989	Aid for the re-establishment of forests destroyed by the storms of October 1987
27.10.1989	Aid for investments in livestock shelters (pigmeat)
8.11.1989	Aid proposal concerning the restructuring of vineyards
20.11.1989	Aids for the sheepmeat and goatmeat sector in the form of an advance on Community aid for 1989; as the Council decided to authorize the measure pursuant to Article 93(2)(3) of the Treaty, the Commission did not adopt a position
7.12.1989	Measures to assist farmers affected by the drought in 1989

Greece

28.2.1989	Aid to poultry and arable farmers as a result of natural disasters
1.3.1989	Aid for stock farmers
1.3.1989	Programme of research, demonstration and other activities concerning crop production
7.3.1989	Approval of an aid programme for the reorganization of livestock production
4.4.1989	Tobacco levies for the National Tobaccco Office to finance its administrative expenditure
19.7.1989	Aid to farmers with holdings (both crop and livestock farms) damaged by fire in summer 1988
27.9.1989	1988 programme and research aid for livestock production
21.12.1989	Programme of demonstration, research, and other activities in the area of crop production in 1989

Ireland

9.6.1989	Farm investment aid

Italy

19.7.1989	Aid for three agricultural cooperatives in Valtellina damaged by floods in summer 1987
19.7.1989	Aid scheme to cover the cost of research by scientific bodies into health controls for hams
27.9.1989	Aid to promote Marsala wine, blood oranges, foodstuffs of animal origin, Parma ham

Sicily

22.3.1989	Draft Law on compensation for additional energy costs incurred by agricultural holdings and other forms of compensation for damage caused by natural disasters
30.6.1989	1988 estimate (Articles 10 to 14). Measures concerning agriculture and forests
14.7.1989	Measures to improve herds with tuberculosis and brucellosis
21.11.1989	Draft Law on regional aid for organizations for the protection of intensive farming

Lazio

18.5.1989	Aid for farmers with holdings damaged by floods (Viterbo) in October 1987
22.5.1989	Draft Law on measures to promote quality regional products (participation in fairs, food education, information on outlets)
19.7.1989	Measures on the gathering of truffles and other fungi not involving any financial aid
19.7.1989	Extraordinary aid following the storm damage of September and October 1987

| 19.7.1989 | Measures to improve bee-keeping (investment aid, disease control, advertising, advisory services, etc.) |

Liguria

1.8.1989	Draft Law on measures to safeguard farming in the Cinqueterra region in order to preserve the characteristic landscape of the region
4.7.1989	Draft Law on measures to safeguard environmentally sensitive areas — investment aid for the protection of the countryside and compliance with environmental standards
14.7.1989	Aid for the purchase of cold stores for farms

Abruzzi

| 11.11.1989 | Measures for the development of agriculture and afforestation in the period 1989/90 |

Netherlands

6.3.1989	Aid to agricultural innovation projects
27.4.1989	Aid to the pig sector for the development of the Community carcase classification system
19.10.1989	Natural gas rate for horticulture for 1989-94, as regards the part not containing aid elements. The part of the tariff which may comprise an aid element is to be decided on at a later date. The Dutch authorities have meanwhile agreed to suspend application of the latter part

United Kingdom and Isle of Man

19.1.1989	Individual award of aid for broiler units
28.2.1989	Measures to assist the British Egg Industry Council
28.2.1989	Feasibility study and marketing aids to encourage agricultural diversification
23.6.1989	'Potatoes: 1989 crop support arrangements'
27.7.1989	Countryside premium scheme — Set-aside land: a scheme to reduce cultivated area, pursuant to Regulation (EEC) No 1094/88
20.9.1989	Aid for a development area in Sunderland, Tyne and Wear, concerning investment in poultry farming
8.11.1989	Research and development aid in the oils sector
8.11.1989	Aid for an enterprise producing poultry-based prepared dishes
11.12.1989	Aid to O'Kane Poultry Ltd to repair without increasing production capacity, units damaged by fire which are used for the processing of poultrymeat
11.12.1989	Aid for the Beef quality scheme

Northern Ireland

30.1.1989   Aid for research in the sheep sector

30.1.1989   Aid for the expansion of a dairy

Isle of Man

19.1.1989   Indefinite extension and modification of Farm improvement scheme 1988

6.10.1989   Hill cow subsidy scheme — Amendment of aid in less-favoured areas for farmers with cows and heifers which have calved in the year in question and are not dairy cows, since the common organizations of the market are not applicable in these regions

2. Aid cases in which the procedure provided for in Article 93(2) of the EEC Treaty was initiated

Belgium

2.6.1989   Application of the Economic Expansion Law of 17 July 1959 to Brunehaut-Weez; investment aid in the sugar sector to promote the manufacture of nibs sugar and fondant sugar used in the food industry

28.9.1989   Aid for the promotion of products in the pigmeat, beef/veal, sheepmeat, goatmeat and horsemeat sector, owing to the method of financing in the form of compulsory levies also imposed on imports from other Member States at the slaughter stage and aid in the form of refunds of compulsory levies in the pigmeat sector in the event of export

28.9.1989   Aid from the Fund for animal health and production owing to the method of financing in the form of compulsory levies also imposed on imported products at the slaughter stage

30.11.1989   Aid to promote poultry and small livestock products, such aid also being financed by taxes on products imported from other Member States at the slaughter stage and on imports of compound feedingstuffs

Spain

Galicia

11.7.1989   Aid for certain olive oil manufacturers awarded in connection with the debts of the latter

28.7.1989   Two awards of aid (Mantequerías Arias and Lácteos de Galicia); application of Law No 50/85 and its implementing decrees; investment aids to improve the cheese and pasteurized milk production structures

Navarre

28.9.1989   Aid to irrigation, the levels exceeding that normally allowed (35%) by the Commission for this type of investment

Murcia

30.11.1989   Draft Regional Decree on compensatory allowances in certain areas, such areas not being included in the list of less-favoured areas of Directive 75/268/EEC

France

9.8.1989   Aid for fresh and dried cultivated mushrooms and for preserved mushrooms, such aid being financed by parafiscal charges also levied on products from other Member States. The Commission considered that this method of financing had a more protective effect than the aid itself

Italy

19.1.1989   Abruzzi: Assistance for cooperatives and agricultural holdings (aid level too high in relation to eligible expenditure in the form of financial debts connected with investment loans; aid for capital increases of cooperatives not connected with investments

6.12.1989   Measures in favour of cheese made from sheeps' milk (storage aid)

Luxembourg

14.7.1989   Winegrowers solidarity fund — aid to combat late frosts and harmful organisms; the procedure was opened in respect of the aid in question, the advertising campaigns and the payment of insurance premiums

Netherlands

23.5.1989   Amendment to the 'Regeling Stimulering Exportactiviteiten 1988'; this regulation provides for export subsidies for plant and animal reproductive stock

3. Aid cases in which the procedure provided for in Article 93(2) of the EEC Treaty was closed

Denmark

2.8.1989   Aids and parafiscal charges in the poultry sector, the parafiscal charge on imported products having been abolished

France

13.3.1989   Aids for the storage of hemp seed; in view of the extent of intra-Community trade in this product, the aid is not liable to affect such trade

17.4.1989   Aid for beef/veal producers specializing in fattening; the aid satisfies the Commission criteria (in particular aid to cover debts in the form of loans to finance investments)

Italy

14.7.1989   Aid proposal in the beef and pigmeat sector; the proposal was amended so that the conditions of award were compatible with the common market

14.7.1989   Multiannual Act on aid to agriculture; the measures objected to were either abolished or amended in accordance with Commission requests

Sicily

22.3.1989   Grant for the cooperative 'Mugnal e Pastal della Valle dei Platani', following the bankruptcy of the enterprise

23.5.1989   Grants in the cooperation, trade and small business sectors, the proposed measures objected to having been removed

Trento

17.4.1989   Amendments to provincial laws on agriculture, the Italian authorities having complied with the requests of the Commission

Abruzzi

11.7.1989   Measures to assist cooperatives and agricultural holdings, the aid in question having been amended as requested by the Commission

4. Aid cases in which the Commission adopted negative opinions under Article 92(3)(a) of the EEC Treaty

Belgium

5.6.1989   Aid to the fund to promote the pigmeat, beef/veal, sheepmeat, goatmeat and horsemeat sectors

France

8.11.1989   Aid additional to the Community ewe and she-goat premium for 1987

21.11.1989   Aid in the form of tax rebates for stock farmers growing cereals

Italy

20.6.1989   Aid for the storage and marketing of olive oil

Netherlands

7.11.1989   Aid financed from parafiscal charges for Produktschap van Landbouwzaatzeden (growers seed association)

7.11.1989   Aids financed from parafiscal charges for Produktschap voor Veevoeder (animal feeding-stuffs association)

5. Council Decisions under Article 93(2) of the EEC Treaty

Decision of 3.5.1989 on the award by certain Member States of aid for the short-term private storage of table wine and must

Decision of 25.9.1989 on the granting of national aid in the form of an advance on the premium for ewes and she-goats in France

Decision of 25.10.1989 on the granting of certain aids to the wine sector in the Federal Republic of Germany

IV — List of studies published in 1989 and to be published

Documents

Title	Research institute	Expert(s)
The evaluation of the employment enterprise zone	Segal, Quince, Wicksteed, Cambridge	B. Hodgson
The effect of different State-aid measures on intra-Community competition exemplified by the case of the automotive industry	Motor Industry Research Ltd Norwich	K. Bhaskar
The effect of conglomerate mergers on competition	London Business School London	J. Cubbin P.A. Geroski
Évolution de la situation concurrentielle consécutive aux joint ventures: cas de l'industrie petrochimique communautaire	Nomisma Bologna	G. Pecci
Takeover bids from the point of view of competition policy	Georg August Universität Göttingen	U. Immenga
The effect of subsidies for exports to third countries on intra-Community competition	Université catholique de Louvain Louvain	T. Peeters F. Abraham
Predatory behaviour in the aviation sector	University of Liverpool	J. S. Dodgson Y. Katsoulacos R.W.S. Pryke

European Communities — Commission

Nineteenth Report on Competition Policy

Luxembourg: Office for Official Publications of the European Communities

1990 — 305 pp. — 16.2 x 22.9 cm

ES, DA, DE, GR, EN, FR, IT, NL, PT

ISBN 92-826-1629-0

Catalogue number: CB-58-90-546-EN-C

Price (excluding VAT) in Luxembourg: ECU 20

The Report on Competition Policy is published annually by the Commission of the European Communities in response to the request of the European Parliament made by a Resolution of 7 June 1971. This Report, which is published in conjunction with the General Report on the Activities of the Communities, is designed to give a general view of the competition policy followed during the past year. Part One covers general competition policy. Part Two deals with competition policy towards enterprises. Part Three is concerned with competition policy and government assistance to enterprises and Part Four with the development of concentration, competition and competitiveness.